CONTIENT DE LA SACCHARINE
BROUWERIJ CAILLIAU VEURNE
GIGI GIGI GEROUVILLE GIGI GIGI
GRANDES BRASSERIES DE HOUGAERDE
BRASSEUR MOUSCRON
DE NEVE SCHEPDAAL
BRASSEUR LEUZE
FOOZ-BRUNOT BRASSEUR NISMES
EDULCOREE ARTIFICIELLEMENT
LAURENT & STEVENART BRASSEUR DINANT
BIERSTEKERY PALLAS R. VAN BOUWEL
EUGÈNE NAWAY
EESSEN
CERVIO AUBEL
BOCHOLT
BRASSERIE DE L'ABBAYE FOREST
CORTEMARCK
NEERYSCHE
VANUXEM FRES PLOEGSTEERT
AGACHE TEMPLEUVE
AALST
BRASSERIE JOUVENEAU BOUSSU
BIE ADANT LEVAL
BRASSERIE CLERINX KERCKOM
CAULIER BRUXELLES
HENRI MAES BRUGGE
BRASSEUR LESSIVE
CERCKEL TEL 32.901 DIEST
RIVA
BIE BISET-CUVELIER PIPAIX
BROUWERY LEYN SELZAETE
LOUIS PAUWELS BOURG-LEOPOLD
TONDREAU MONS
AARSCHOT
ROBERG IEPER
LOUIS ROSSEELS ZELE
BROUWERY MARTINAS MERCHTEM
Liège
BRY DESWAEF OOSTENDE
ULTRA GENT
XL
BAVIK'S BIER
BRASSERIE DE LA COMETE GERARD à OCQUIER
BROUWERIJ GOETHALS Meulebeke
DINANT
BRASSERIE LAHAYE FRES

Belgium by Beer
Beer by Belgium

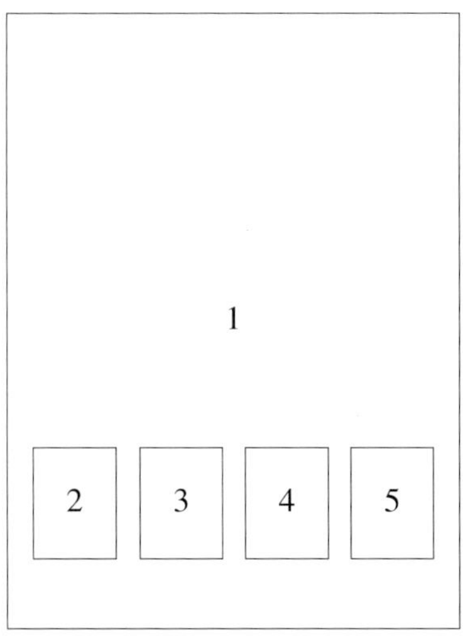

Cover pictures:
1 Brewing hall at Rochefort Abbey
2 Planned enamel plaque, oil painting for Brewery Meiresonne. Ghent, around 1960
3 Poster for Brewery Jack-op, Werchter, around 1950
4 Part of a publicity poster, praising the virtues of *faro* and *lambic*
5 The brewer Bourgois of Tournai in his new brewing hall, around 1920

The authors would like to thank the breweries who have answered their requests for documentation, and thereby assisted them in their research:
B. de l'Abbaye des Rocs (Montignies-sur-Rocs), B. Belle-Vue (Brussels), B. Bosteels (Buggenhout), B. de Brunehaut (Brunehaut), C.B.B. (Confédération des Brasseries de Belgique), B. de Chimay (Chimay), B. Corsendonk (Oud-Turnhout), B. Dubuisson Frères (Pipaix), B. De Gouden Boom (Bruges), B. de Hoegaarden (Hoegaarden), B. De Koninck (Antwerp), B. des Frères Trappistes (Rochefort), B. Friart (Le Rœulx), B. Haacht (Boortmeerbeek), B. Het Anker (Mechelen), Interbrew (Brussels), B. Leroy (Boezinge), B. Louwaege (Kortemark), B. Martens (Bocholt), B. Moortgat (Breendonk), B. d'Orval (Villers-devant-Orval), B. Palm (Londerzeel), Groupe Riva (Dentergem), B. Saint-Guibert (Mont-Saint-Guibert), B. de Silly (Silly), B. Sterkens (Hoogstraten Meer), B. De Troch (Ternat-Wambeek), B. Van Eecke (Watou), B. à Vapeur (Pipaix) and
Aubergier Septime, Barella Julienne, Prof. Baetslé Gilbert, Bernard Marie-Laurence, Bogaert Hubert, Prof. Bonenfant P., Boon Frank, Choquet Jean-Michel, Coisman Roger, Claasen Ab, Corduant Jean, Damiens Étienne (†), Dangis Tony, De Clerck Étienne, Decruyenaere Laurent, De Greef Betty, De Kindt Dany, Denooze Toon, Prof. Derdelinckx Guy, Derudder Gilles, Detournay José, Février Albert, Fischer Gustave, Fontaine de Ghélin Edgar, Gocar Marcel (†), Hannicq Georges, Homburg Brigitte (†), Illochroma (Bruxelles), Laneau Rosemary, Lorang Claude, Maenhout Erik, Manessier Daniel, Meura (Tournai), New Belgium Brewing Company (Fort Collins, Etats-Unis), Niset Guy, Peene B., Pelthier Pierre, Petrisot Gilbert, Pirotte Raymond, Planchet Jean-Yves, Quitton Marc, Rijke Pamela, Royal Museum (Canterbury, Angleterre), Samain Edgard, Tioch René, Vaes Jean-Paul, Van der Haeghen Didier, Vandersijpe Willy, Vanneste Paul, Van Roy Willy, Verdonck Guy, Waegeneer Jean-Pierre, Waterlomat (Bruxelles), Welter Edouard et Wets Alain, retired brewers, Belgian brewing museums, agents, café owners and suppliers also have their rightful place here in recognition of the documents, archives, and artefacts which they so willingly provided.
After twenty years spent in compilation, this work is edited. We endeavoured to obtain the necessary authorisations. Unfortunately it was not possible for us to obtain any information on different beneficial owners. Our hope is that this edition will result in our discovering their names or those of their heirs, to whom visual rights are already reserved, on our account.

The authors especially thank **Gustaaf Du Four**, a brewer and the son of a brewer, for his help on technical matters and with the translation into Dutch. His entire life has been dedicated to brewing, to special beers, and white beer in particular. His career was crowned in 1992 by the silver trophy of the *Objectieve Bierproevers* (Objective Beer Tasters) for the most deserving brewer.

The Chapter "The time to regroup" is to the credit of *Charles Fontaine*.

ISBN 2-87953-047-4

Design and production : Lucien HILGER, Luxembourg
Photographic documentation : Charles et Edgar FONTAINE DE GHÉLIN, Romedenne
Photos : Jean-Claude VANDENBRANDEN et Studio ATP, Bruxelles
photo-setting : DE SETZER, Luxembourg
Photogravure : GAM, Luxembourg
English translation : Robert West, UK
Printing : Victor BUCK, Luxembourg
Book-binding : SCHEEDERS van KERCHOVE, Saint-Nicolas

Belgium by Beer
Beer by Belgium

Annie Perrier-Robert and Charles Fontaine

SCHORTGEN
GRAND-DUCHY OF LUXEMBOURG

This Flemish painting, by J. Koeke (1885) adds to the interest of the old-time beer drinker, by including one of the first pieces of brewery "advertising".

FOREWORD

Belgium itself possesses five of the six existing Trappist abbeys, producers of noble beers, of age-old renown. It is true that this country became famous for its beer and that its history was coloured by it. For example, the world motocross champion, Roger de Coster, was a grandson of brewers in Neerijse. Likewise, the City of Bruges had as its bishop, until 1984, Monseigneur De Smedt, whose father held the reins of the De Smedt Brewery in Opwijk.

Tradition is extremely ancient here. This soil has known breweries and maltings since the Roman era. The Middle Ages saw the development of monastic brewing. Two splendid survivors from among these medieval abbey breweries, Villers-la-Ville (1215) and Floreffe (1250), bear witness to this vital period for what today is our "beer culture". Thus, in his manual on the manufacture of malt and of beer, the celebrated German author Julius Thausing wrote, "Belgium was part of the great cultural empire of the Burgundians in the 14th and 15th centuries. The industrial and brewing nucleus formed by the provinces of Brabant, Flanders, Artois, Hainaut, and the Lorraine, is the point of origin of the great development of the brewing industry in Northern Europe at the end of the Middle Ages and during the Renaissance. Its influence was felt as far away as the Scandinavian countries and the Baltic regions of Germany."

It is no wonder that, in the 16th century, the Spanish soldiers of the Duke of Alva were somewhat taken aback in observing that babies' bottles contained beer. Neither is it any wonder that, in the 18th century, Joseph Gérard, Secretary of the Academy founded by Empress Maria Theresia of Austria, saw the white beer from Hoegaarden on the tables of the Brussels taverns. And finally it comes as no surprise that a statistical census carried out by the French regime at the time of the Revolution indicated that a quarter of all cereals were at that time utilised in the manufacture of beer.

It was the growth of laws governing beer, and emanating from the Dutch, which generated the Belgian Revolution of 1830. What is more, the first government contained members of the Rodenbach family, of whom we know the brewery, situated in Roeselare. Coming from across the Channel, the Industrial Revolution resulted in a strong English influence on technical evolution - of men as of machines - at raw material level (notably hops and sugar), and in respect of the press concerning this sector. This influence also affected actual taste. Is not present day Belgium the continental nation which drinks the most Scotch and Pale Ale?

Endowed with a rich history and deep-rooted traditions, Belgium has become, in the 20th century, the cradle of Europe. And, happy consequence of fate, the parliament of this new entity has its seat in Brussels, on the site of the former Léopold Brewery. Its brewing future is encouraging as much for the reputation of its beers well beyond its borders, and for the exports which result from this, as for the significance of the associated industries (malt, machines, labels, glassworks, bottlers, etc.). May this volume contribute to the placing of this country, and the great diversity of its beers - which are its originality and its fame - at the very heart of the brewing world! May it also, dear beer-lover, arouse your interest and touch your heart, whether you are an enlightened fan or simply curious about this universal beverage!

Charles FONTAINE

CONTENTS

Built in the 15th century, the *Gruuthus* in Brugge, is testimony to the wealth of grist merchants in the Middle Ages.

BEER THROUGH HISTORY

Certain dates give history a rhythm, define its great periods, and mark its social and economic evolution. But history will not be confined in a chronological yoke. If Belgium, as a state, was only born in 1830, the territory which it covers is rich even in pre-history, and it is impossible to place this past in the shade, because yesterday and today constitute a whole. To recount the appearance and the evolution of beer in Belgium is to discover its origins in this part of Europe, then to relate its fortunes and its misfortunes through the centuries, up until it truly became "Belgian", and at last to cross the official frontier of time, to follow it step by step until today

THE "FIRST DAYS" OF BEER

For a long time it was believed that the Egyptians were the first to manufacture beer. Did not Herodotus attribute its invention to Osiris, the civilising God of Egypt? This theory was, to say the least, simplistic. For beer was probably born in prehistoric times, with the gathering of wild grasses, and then it became established as a result of the first cereal farming. It was enough for man to ferment the grain adding water to it in order to bring about its basic formula...

The "barley wine" of the Ancients

However that may be, successive discoveries have shown that the Middle East knew this beverage. It is true that in Mesopotamia the water was not very hygienic and wine was reserved for the rich: it was considered at one and the same time as a healthy drink and as a basic food, indispensable in a rather frugal diet. The first recipes to reach us date back to the 3rd millenium BC. There already existed various types of beer, black, red, white, and so on. Cuneiform texts, engraved on Sumerian clay, bear witness that, among the victuals at banquets, beer was omnipresent. The importance of the banquet was assessed according to the "amount of beer consumed". Generally made from barley, but sometimes also from wheat, or from a mixture of the two, it was called *shikarou*. It was contained in earthenware jars, and drinkers sucked it up through long straws.

Like the Mesopotamian peoples, the Egyptians very early showed a love for "barley wine", which was their national drink. The principle of manufacture was the same: barley, germinated or not, was ground, given a little water, and then submitted to a light cooking. The loaves of barley which were obtained were crumbled and moistened. They were left to ferment for several days. The paste was then kneaded, before being drained in baskets placed above the jars. Thus beer was obtained. Its name varied according to its mode of preparation, its flavour, and its colour: it came to be softened with honey, and perfumed with spices. Among more frequent names, we have *zythos* (or *zythium*) and *curmi* - for a softer beer.

The name *zythos* goes back to the Greeks; it became *zythum* with the Romans. But neither the one nor the other accords the same favour to the beer as the Egyptians to whom it had been made known. Certainly some Greek writers, such as Aeschylus, Sophocles, and

In 54 BC, Ambiorix, Chief of the Eburons, destroyed the Roman garrison at *Atuatuca* (Tongeren, the oldest town in Belgium). This was the last rising against the Roman occupiers.

Theophrastus, mention wine made of germinated barley. But this was not very much appreciated. Its only interest was in the therapeutic values attributed to it. And its beneficial properties were subject to much debate. The Galien school claimed that a beverage born of "corruption" (by this was meant "fermentation") could only generate noxious effects. This lack of consideration given to beer resulted in an absence of information on the method used for its manufacture. Without doubt it was not very much different to that which we have previously mentioned.

It was, all the same, under the influence of the Romans that beer was introduced in the Iberian peninsula, and then in Gaul. The Germans adopted it in the 1st century AD; they made it with barley, with wheat, or with malted oats, and flavoured it with honey, ginger, or even with mushrooms or various barks. In his treatise on the customs of the Germans, Tacitus speaks of a wine made from soaked grain; barley and wheat are mentioned. And he places the accent on the tendency towards intoxication which characterises the people. Analogous disapproval is to be read under the pen of Pliny the Elder. "The nations of the West make themselves drunk with mouldy grain." However, beer won ground. The Germans broadcast its use to the countries of the North, who made it their exclusive beverage after the 3rd century AD.

Popular cervisia...

Unlike the Mesopotamian civilisations and the Egyptians, who had genuine breweries at their disposal, Gaul made the creation of beer a family practice. Thus it was in Great Britain as well. Rare factors nevertheless permit the assertion that there were some organised breweries, which brewed "on contract" and delivered the beer immediately after fermentation. In the province of Namur, the ruins of Gallo-Roman villas from the 3rd and 4th centuries - at Ronchinne, Anthée and Mettet - contain the remains of brewery workshops. The villa at Ronchinne (between 250 and 380 AD), of which plans were drawn up in 1894, held both a brewery and a malt kiln. Other evidence of this activity includes the 3rd century bas-relief preserved in Arlon, on which one can see *cervisiarii* ("ale producers") at work.

At this time, one did not speak of *beer*, but of *cervesia* ("ale" or "cervisia"). This term, which Pliny the Elder is the first to quote, alludes to *Cereris vitis* ("vine of Cérès") and also makes reference to the legend according to which Cérès, goddess of the harvest and of cereals, had discovered the drink and had given the benefit of it to the people whose land did not lend itself to the culture of the vine.

This beermat, issued around 1950 by the Saint-Denis Brewery, in the province of Namur, recalls the virtues of the old ale. The brewery no longer exists.

Ale was thus appreciated by the people of Gaul. The popularity which it has come to know through recent centuries is attributable to the fear of maladies which might be occasioned by the consumption of water, it not usually being fit to drink. By its manner of manufacture, ale appeared as a beverage without risk. For this reason, it became a part of the daily diet, continuing to be what it was at its very origin, a veritable "liquid bread". The cereal used was wheat, more often used than barley, and the favourite spice was cumin. Honey was sometimes added. The preparation strongly resembled that of the

A souvenir of times gone by, advertising playing cards produced in the Thirties by the Brasserie De Bocq at Purnode, in the province of Namur, which continues to produce La Gauloise, in three versions (blond, amber, and brown). R. Desmecht collection.

Ancients. Nevertheless brewing progressed. The Gauls take credit for having invented the tun and the wooden cask. The first was kept for fermentation and for maturation; the second for conservation and transportation. And, of course, the patron of coopers was Sucellus, patron saint of cervisia.

Until the 9th century, the manufacture of ale did not evolve. It remained empirical. Brewing was generally done at home, according to a recipe handed down orally, from generation to generation. Production was intended for the family circle, but this did not prevent any possible surplus being sold to neighbours.

A turning point in the evolution of the brewery

During the reign of Charlemagne, the habit of drinking ale became widespread and left the realms of "home" manufacture. The interest shown by the Emperor contributed a great deal to this. Every small imperial farm brewed ale. What is more, the famous De Villis chapter ("The Domains") is of extreme importance on this subject. Among the instructions given to stewards of imperial domains, it prescribed that they should take care to have good makers of drinks. This ordnance is interesting in two respects. On the one hand, for the first time a sovereign tackled the question of ale, and with this, the foundations were in a way laid for the sort of state monopoly to which brewing would be subject during the entire Middle Ages. On the other hand, and also for the first time, manufacture was considered as a matter for experts.

Through the course of the centuries which followed, brewing became organised. Home production ceased. Each village had its public brewery, where the local inhabitants could go to brew on appointed days, in return for a fee paid to the lord of the manor. For their part, the monasteries, which had settled in these regions, undertook brewing for the requirements of their communities. The technique was scarcely modified. Emphasis was placed on cooking, to avoid any danger of illnesses, and on the addition of aromatic herbs, to improve the beverage. As in Gallo-Roman times, the brewery was often annexed to the mill, for their activities were closely linked, and, what is more, they were the two sources of dues for the lord. The method of payment was variable, be it by means of ale for the brewery and with grain (in *bracis*, "malt") for the mill, or in money for the one or the other. Payment in ale corresponded to a due described as "of feudal service", which was in force for brewers until the end of the Ancien Regime.

The secret of the Abbeys

One of the great characteristics of medieval society rests in the influence exercised by religion. In the 6th and 7th centuries, a real religious structure arose, with the division of the lands into four dioceses - of which, it should be made clear, the limits were beyond the borders of Belgium today. The diocese of Tongres was subject to the authority of the Archbishopric of Köln, those of Thérouanne, Arras-Cambrai, and Tournai-Noyan were attached to the Archbishopric of Rheims. In parallel, numerous monasteries were established, here and there, which came to contribute to the economic and intellectual growth of the surrounding regions. This influence increased from the 13th century, when the Church had acquired enough power to offer protection rather than having to seek it for itself. "Its authority was then confirmed, feudality was no longer so tyrannical, thanks in part to its efforts. The Church no longer had to battle as it were for itself and for the oppressed. Its deeds, still as powerful as before, were more gentle; but to be less conspicuous, it was no less strong and constant." (Philippe De Bruyne.)

The country was then thronging with numerous rich abbeys, and it is to these that agriculture owes its prosperity. Often confronted with uncultivated and arid land, which had been given to them, the religious folk succeeded, by dint of hard work and resolve, to render them productive. For they had to provide for the needs of their community. Affligem, Tongerlo, Leffe, Grimbergen, Orval, and so on. So many abbeys still bear witness today to those medieval times, all producing famous beers! This is not surprising. Beer was a part of everyday monastic life. Was it not for a long time the only "nourishment" authorised during fasting?

Within the abbey, a stone building was kept for brewing. More often it was a little away from the monastery buildings, like the bakery, the forge, and the malt house, because the danger of fire was great at this time. But it was necessary for the brewery to be near to a supply of water. This explains why it was often near the water mill. On the other hand, the brewing residues *(draff)* were saved to feed the livestock, so it was frequently near the stables.

The brewery was generally run by the *principal* (or *cellarius*), responsible for food and drink. The beers produced were rather heavy, rendering them nutritionally "useful" during periods of fasting. A daily ration (on average 2 litres) was allocated to each monk; the beer

One of the main leaders of the First Crusade, Godfrey of Bouillon (1061-1100), inspired this label from the Dachy Brewery, which ceased its activities after the Second World War. Today the Moortgat Brewery perpetuates the memory of the famous Crusader with its amber beer, *Godefroy* (5.8 % vol. alcohol).

was served to him in a pitcher and, during a meal, he drank it from a silver goblet or from a pewter mug. the lay staff of the abbey were also entitled to a beer ration - in the order of two pots, or 2.6 litres per day. In fact this constituted a part of their wages. It was the same for workers who came to carry out work inside the abbey precinct. As for passing visitors (pilgrims and so forth) and permanent guests (persons, aged and alone, who granted part of their estate to an abbey in return for living there), they likewise consumed the beer made by the abbey.

From the end of the Middle Ages the contribution made by these religious establishments appears to have been vital, in perfecting methods of brewing and the quantities of ingredients used.

The reign of gruit

The flavour of ale was then very different from that which we know among beers today. This did not stem from the cereal of which it was composed, because from ancient times nothing changed. It seems that wheat and barley were used a great deal, although in the 12th century Abbess Hildegard of Bingen described beer as a drink made of oats. But various cereals were certainly used: barley, oats, spelt, and according to 13th century documents, *siliginum*, which was probably rye. It is to be noted, however, that at the end of the 13th century, in the provinces of Liège and Namur, brewers paid their dues in spelt, which leads one to believe that beer was indeed made with this cereal.

The difference in taste was due to another ingredient, added to malt, namely *gruit* or *gruyt*. From the year 999, there is mention of gruit in a diploma which the German Emperor Otton III delivered to the Bishop of Utrecht. In the following century, in 1060, a document emanating from the Bishop of Metz, and concerning the Abbey of Saint Trond, indicates that the Bishop supplies *grutum* to the abbey in order to improve the quality of the beverage. Gruit or grutum, a rare word, has aroused such controversy both as to its etymology and as to its meaning. Some see it as a proper cereal, others as milled grain, others yet as malt. Thanks to the study of the accounts of Dutch towns, A Schulte succeeded, in 1908, in clarifying it definition and its composition.

The gruit was a mixture of five or six plants, dried, and then reduced to flour. The plants were carefully selected, principally marsh plants, such as Brabant myrtle (or *gagel*), marsh ledum, and wild rosemary. To these herbs was added bay and a little pine resin. But for what purpose was this mixture introduced in the manufacture

FROM WINE TO BEER

Although it did not have true vineyard areas, the Netherlands consumed a great deal of wine. Like other drinks, this wine, sometimes local (Hoegaarden wine and Huy wine, for example), but more often imported from abroad (France in particular) was hit by seigniorial and communal taxes. In the 13th century and at the beginning of the 14th, imposts on wine still provided a very significant part of the revenues of a city. It is in this context that beer came to be relevant, since it ceased to be produced at home and gave rise to a real trade. Through the development of "excise" on it one can see the progress of its implementation. Thus one observes that during the first half of the 14th century, it gradually replaced wine in Antwerp. In Leuven, the process took place around 1345, and in Brussels, it was later, in 1350. It was not until the beginning of the 16th century that one saw this in Hasselt and Namur.

One of the causes of this shifting of the profitability of excises (indirect taxes) from wine to beer, is without doubt the excessive taxes applied to wine, which resulted in a fall in its consumption. This was all the more to the advantage of beer since, thanks to the lower price of grain, this drink was accessible. That is without taking into account the agreeable flavour, on which the hops conferred an undoubted charm!

of ale? It has been advanced that the gruit acted as a fermenting agent. The Latin name *fermentum*, which one frequently encounters in medieval texts, has also been given to it. This interpretation is not very convincing, to the extent that it was added before the brewing process. It wort therefore be agreed that, beyond the fact that it perhaps aided conservation, gruit acted to improve the quality of the beverage, to flavour it and to give it a piquant taste. Besides, it was sometimes called *pigmentum*. In support of this hypothesis, there is a document dated 1068, in which the Bishop of Liège authorises the brewers of Huy to obtain *pigmentum* (here it was a matter of wild rosemary) where they could, because the waters of the place were not suitable for its growth.

Of course, gruit was first used above all in areas where one could pick these plants, notably on the North Sea coast and in Brabant. But its preparation required a certain savoir-faire and the appropriate equipment. The craftsman gruit-preparer soon had his raison d'être. Each had his secret blend; it even came to the point where he combined a little malt flour to the gruit to avoid the "recipe" being discovered.

It was therefore necessary to buy the gruit from the gruit-preparer; and as the lands belonged to the lord it was the latter who organised its sale. He fixed its price and determined the quantity in which it was to be used - one used some 2 kilograms of gruit per hectolitre. The revenues from the *grutum* were considerable! In Bruges, for example, the lords of the *gruuthuse* were the most powerful in the town. They were entitled to have fifteen men-at-arms in their service. And, paradoxically, they had a fee paid to the town for imported beers which were not made with their gruit. 10th and 12th century texts contain numerous mentions of the "gruit duty" *(jus grutæ)*: this is especially the case for the cities of Liège

The collection of gruit in the Middle Ages. Reproduction of an original housed in the Cathedral of Tournai, this stained-glass window adorns the entry hall of the firm of Meura.

and Tournai. Taking account of this appreciable source of wealth and power, the gruit monopoly was paramount. However the abbeys avoided this duty; the lord was not interested in overwhelming them with fees, because they could be useful to him.

The greatest innovation of the Middle Ages

What would beer be without hops? Today it is a vital ingredient *(see page 95)*. And its contribution would have been inestimable in the medieval era. It seems, however, that its use in brewing was attempted well before this period, perhaps even by the Ancients. Originally from Babylon, then cultivated in the West by the Slavic races, this plant was for a long time used as food - as early as the 1st century BC the geographer Strabon mentioned the "asparagus" of hops - or as a remedy by virtue of the medicinal qualities attributed to it.

It was in the abbeys, it seems, that the hop was first truly adopted in brewing. The monks knew it well, having cultivated it for a long period of time. As proof: in the 8th century, the King of France, Pepin the Short, had given to the Abbey of St. Denis some lands where hops were being grown. Otherwise one finds traces of hops in the revenues of various abbey estates. However that may be, its official appearance in the manufacture of beer dates back to the 12th century. In fact Hildegard of Bingen denied it a beneficial effect on health, but recognised its other virtues. "Its bitterness," she wrote, "nevertheless combats certain harmful fermentations in drinks to which it is added, and allows the latter to be preserved for a long time."

In allowing longer preservation of the beverage, the hop aids its transport and gives a greater spread to its trade. But outside this significant advantage, it is also of interest not least of all for giving the beer more lightness and conferring upon it a better taste. These are some of the reasons for its success; a success which came at a period when the economy was rediscovering a certain dynamism and when the trade associations were beginning to become organised *(see guilds, p 28)*.

The brewing process then experienced a decisive "Revolution". It took place progressively, since gruit was well established and the lords did not show themselves to be particularly favourable towards the intrusion which would see them lose the benefits of their gruit duty. At first, hopped beer appeared in the Hanseatic towns of North Germany, during the second half of the 13th century. Then, at the beginning of the 14th century, it gained favour in Holland, where the cultivation of hops was established by the 1370's. It was necessary to wait until the end of the 14th century before hopped beer made its entry into the Belgian "region". Beer was imported before it was manufactured according to the new process. And it was only in the 15th century that gruit was finally supplanted by hops. The "memory" of gruit lived on, nevertheless, through the different aromatics and spices which compose Belgian beers, and vary from region to region.

Forced to adapt to the circumstances, the lords first applied a tax to the imported hopped beer. Then, as soon as it began to be made there, a fee was introduced at the mash-tub. Gruit duty no longer existing, excise duty was born. With the disappearance of cervisia there commenced the history of beer (flavoured with hops).

Poster of the Mater York Brewery, for the beer *Van Artevelde*. This beer, brewed today by the Huyghe Brewery, in Melle, owes its name to an illustrious figure in Ghent history.
Was he a merchant draper or rather a brewer? Doubt still remains as to the true occupation of Jacob Van Artevelde (Ghent 1290-1345). According to the Belgian historian Henri Pirenne, he was a hotel tenant. It is true that, at that time, each establishment brewed for its own consumption. This explains the confusion, especially as, having married the daughter of a brewer, it is quite possible that he worked alongside his father-in-law.
Becoming Captain-General of Ghent (1337), Van Artevelde was the instigator of the rising against the Count of Flanders, Louis de Nevers, who, at the beginning of the Hundred Years War, had suspended trade with England. He entered into an alliance with the King of England, Edward III, whose sovereignty was recognised by the Flemish. Accused of treason, he was assassinated by the people.

A STRANGE RIGHT OF "SIGNAGE"

The inability of brewers in the Middle Ages to explain the phenomena which controlled the manufacture of beer, made still more mysterious the accidents which were likely to occur during the process. And numerous were those who saw in them a manifestation of occult forces, even of evil spirits. There existed several methods to avoid such "diabolical" intervention: either the use of signs reputed to be beneficial - such as the sign of Solomon or the six-pointed star - or the recourse to certain rituals - like adding of pinch of salt to the boiling wort or reciting ritual phrases at the commencement of each operation - or even the blessing, by the priest, of the beer made in his parish.

The latter preventative measure, in Hainaut, gave rise to abuse on the part of the parish ministry. In fact, following the other sacramentals, the right of "signage", during the course of which the priest, dressed in his stole, blessed the mash-tub, was not free as it was supposed to be. The "rights of the stole" *(jura stolœ)* were established, which would end by becoming obligatory. The customary offering was transformed, in effect, into a real tax, of which the amount was determined by the priest himself. For example, in StamBrugge and in Harchies, it amounted to four lots (or pots) per mash-tub.

The practice started many cases between priests and brewers, for non payment of the so-called salary. And in general the Church won. However that may be, this parish fee, levied on the manufacture of beer, persisted until the end of the Ancien Regime. As for the blessing of the mash-tubs which justified it, that was soon replaced by a simple placing of altar candles, taken among those that the parishioners placed in the church.

SOME SIGNIFICANT DATES

• **51 BC:** at the end of the Gallic War, all the Belgian tribes were placed under the rule of Rome. In the context of the *pax romana*, a Belgo-Roman civilisation developed.

• **5th - 6th centuries:** Belgian territory formed part of the Frankish kingdom. It was thus subjugated to two successive dynasties, the Merovingians and the Carolingians.

• **843:** the division of the Carolingian empire into three kingdoms redrew the map of Western Europe. *Francia Occidentalis*, which went back to Charles the Bald, rejoined the countries situated to the West of the Scheldt, the Meuse, the Saône, and the Rhône. Flanders thus formed a part of it. *Francia Orientalis*, attributed to Louis the German, covered the regions of the right bank of the Rhine. As for *Francia Media*, which Lothair inherited, it corresponded to the area between these two kingdoms, the North Sea, and Italy.

• **879:** Lotharingia, that is to say the North of *Francia Media*, comprising Lorraine and the lands of the future Netherlands, was tied again to *Francia Orientalis*. The valley of the Scheldt henceforth formed the border between the Kingdom of France and the German Empire.

• **10th - 13th centuries:** taking advantage of the struggles of Carolingian succession, and the invasions of the 9th century, certain noble dynasties created principalities, which joined together minor lords and which, in acquiring autonomous power, remained under the suzerainty of the King of France. Flanders was one.

The same process took place on the German side, where feudal principalities were formed: the Duchy of Brabant, the Duchy of Limbourg (joined to Brabant in 1288), the Earldom of Hainaut, the Earldom of Looz, the Earldom of Namur, the Duchy of Luxembourg, and the ecclesiastical Principality of Liège.

• **1366:** the Principality of Liège annexed the Earldom of Looz.

• **1369:** Philip the Bold, Duke of Burgundy, married Marguerite, daughter of Louis of Mâle, Count of Flanders, and inherited Flanders on his death (1384). The seigneuries of Mechelen and Antwerp also passed to him.

• **1421 - 1451:** Philip the Good extended the suzerainty of the Duchy of Burgundy to the Earldoms of Namur and Hainaut, to the Duchies of Brabant, Limbourg, and Luxembourg.

• **1466:** Charles the Fearless, who gradually interfered more and more in the affairs of the episcopal Principality of Liège, ended, in 1456, by imposing his nephew, Louis of Bourbon, as Bishop of Liège. In 1465, on the instigation of the King of France, Louis XI, the party of the Vrays Liégeois pronounced the dismissal of Louis of Bourbon, and revolted against the Duke of Burgundy. He won and, by the Treaty of Saint Trond, made Liège a real Burgundian Protectorate. The city of Dinant rose then. The rising was mercilessly put down. The sacking of Dinant is a disastrous reminder.

This panel advertising a brewery in Dinant, today disappeared, recalls the sacking of the town by Charles the Fearless, in 1466. R. Desmecht collection.

• **1477:** Marie of Burgundy, only daughter of Charles the Fearless and Isabelle of Bourbon, married the Archduke of Austria, Maximilian, who became German Emperor from 1493 to 1519. The Belgian "regions" thus passed into the sovereignty of the Habsburgs. On the death of Marie of Burgundy (1482), Maximilian I became Regent. This he remained until 1494, the year when Philip the Beautiful, his son, took power.

• **1496:** Philip the Beautiful, married Jeanne, heiress of Castile and of Aragon.

In tribute to Marie of Burgundy, the Verhaeghe Brewery, in Vichte, produced an old brown *Duchess de Bourgogne* (6.2 % vol. alcohol).

AT THE BORDERS OF LEGEND AND HISTORY

Above, the Lefebvre Brewery honoured King Gambrinus with its label for the *Quenast* (5 % vol. alcohol).
Top, letterhead of the Brasserie du Centre.

Undeniable "Patron" of brewers, Gambrinus belongs to the imagery of beer, and is inseparable from its tradition, a mythical personage whose origin remains a mystery! Yet one might recognise Jean Primus in him. Born in Brussels around 1252, this son of Duke Henry III and Princess Alix of Burgundy, came at a very early age to reign over Brabant, which was then a powerful principality in the Netherlands. In fact, on the death of his father, in 1261, the Duchess, his mother, was first of all a Regent. Then, faced with the incapacity of his elder brother, Henry, as Governor, it was he who took power, in 1268, under the name of Jean I. The following year, he married Marguerite of France, daughter of the King Saint Louis, who died in 1271, without having born him any children. He went on to marry a second time, two years later, Marguerite, daughter of the Count of Flanders, Gwijde van Dampierre. Of this marriage was born a son, in 1275, the future Jean II.

Of a cultivated spirit, an ardent epicurean, and endowed with a character which harmoniously combined audacity with wisdom, Jean I was extremely popular in his lifetime. His warrior qualities were certainly well known. He had a great many opportunities to prove them. The most famous was the Battle of Worringen, in 1288, which he won brilliantly, and which allowed him to conquer the Duchy of Limburg. But he stood out above all else for his innate political sense and for his fierce desire to develop the economy of his state.

It was in 1292 that, preoccupied with putting an end to the disorder and to the inherent abuse in the practices of his time, the Duke of Brabant enacted his celebrated *Land keuren*. This Code of Laws laid the foundations for a more coherent social order, and for more centralised power. Among this long list of penalties and fines adapted to different "crimes", there figured a measure relating to beer. Penalties and fines were fixed for "those who willingly adulterate wine, ale, or any other beverage, as a felony" and for "those who strike a pot."

The Duchy was flourishing when Jean I was mortally wounded, in 1294, on the occasion of a tournament in Lorraine. His body was burned on the spot, and his remains were interred, according to his wishes, in the choir of the church at the Franciscan monastery built in Brussels in 1238. However, the monastery buildings were destroyed during the bombardment of Brussels by the French army at the end of the 17th century. No thought was given to recovering the remains of the Duke of Brabant until, in 1988, works being carried out in the capital, near the Bourse, brought to light the ruins of the monastery. Today, a museum, *Bruxella 1238*, houses these ruins, which were the last resting place of Jean I.

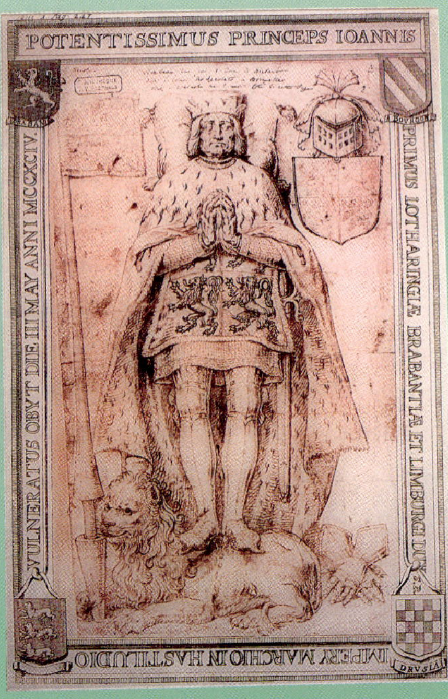

Drawing of the cenotaph of Gambrinus, which was in the church of the Monastery of the Récollets, in Brussels.

THE SALE OF BEER IN BRUSSELS, IN THE MIDDLE OF THE 15TH CENTURY

"A brewer could only have one sales place, on penalty of 20 escalins fine, and his drawer could only establish a tavern at a distance of sixteen houses at least.

"The brewer had to deliver to him a cask or half cask, and the beer sent could not be returned, but had to be sold completely. The price at which the brewer delivered his beer to the drawer had to be determined in advance, as well as the amount of the cask duty *(voerlief)* left by the brewer with the drawer. If the brewer granted a larger bonus without the unanimous consent of the four treasurers of the city, he lost the trade for three months, and incurred a fine of 20 escalins. In order to promote the export of beer, it was established that one would only pay in the future 3 pieces of Brabant coin per cask instead of 6.

"If the brewer made a beer so weak and bad that the drawer had claims against him before the treasurers, these could summons the brewer to appear, and if they found the complaint proved, they could authorise the publican to take beer from a brewer who did not have a drawer. As for the brewer guilty of having made a beer so detestable, and which deprived him of his drawer, he had to remain without same until the following 1st October, and the agreement concluded between him and the drawer was annulled."

(G Des Marez. *Organisation of work in Brussels in the 15th century*. 1904)

Even the gilded bronze clocks of the last century are set right to Gambrinus. Collection of the Ch'ti Brewery.

ARNOLD THE PATRON SAINT OF BREWERS

A single patron saint common to all brewers does not exist, but several, according to the specific region and country. As in the North of France, the most venerated in Belgium is Saint Arnold (1040-1087), canonised in 1120, and celebrated on 15th August. Originally from Tiegem, in Flanders, he became Abbot of Saint Médard, at Soissons, before becoming Bishop of that town. He thereafter founded a monastery at Oudenburg, in the diocese of Bruges.

The plague and cholera being common at that time in the region of Soissons, the saintly man recommended to his flock that they consume beer instead of water: in fact made with boiled water, beer was then much more hygienic than plain water. Those who drank beer were thus saved, as if by a miracle.

Saint Arnold had as a trait a "stuickmand" *(see page 112)*. He is represented in bishop's dress and holding a crook.

A gold commemorative medal was struck on the occasion of the 900th anniversary of the founding of the Abbey of Oudenburg by Saint Arnold, in 1084.

The Abbot of the Benedictine Abbey of Steenbrugge, established in Bruges, received, in 1934, the right to lay claim to the Saint Pierre Abbey of Oudenburg, closed during the French Revolution. *Abbaye de Steenbrugge* beer is brewed by the De Gouden Boom Brewery, in Bruges.

THE PREMONSTRATENSIAN ABBEYS AND THEIR BEERS

Created by Saint Norbert in 1120, in Prémontré, in the Aisne (France), the Premonstratensian Order obeyed the rules of Saint Augustine. Like the Cistercians, the regular canons of Prémontré (also called "Norbertines") did not hesitate to work with their hands in the fields or on the farms, both to provide for the needs of the community and to help their fellow men.

Nestling on the right bank of the River Meuse, to the North of Dinant, the **Notre Dame Abbey of Leffe** owes its creation to the Count of Namur, Henry the Blind, who, in 1152, presented the two churches which existed here to the Premonstratensian Abbey of Floreffe in order that it found a priory. And in 1200 this priory took the status of abbey, also becoming independent of Floreffe. Its first abbot, Wéric, was conferred with the high honour of archdeacon by the Prince and Bishop of Liège. During the 13th century, the abbey's estate grew and became organised. Thus in 1240, the father-abbot of Leffe bought from a certain Gossuin, church clerk in Dinant, several assets, including a brewery, situated at Saint Médart, on the other bank of the River Meuse. But the abbey went on to have a tumultuous history, marked by the warlike conflicts which ravaged the region, as well as by the devastating flood of the Meuse, in 1460. Then there was the terrible disaster of 1466. When the Burgundian armies marched on Dinant, Charles the Fearless established his headquarters in the abbey, of which he had the archives burnt, pillaged the brewery, and then razed the buildings to the ground. The canons were exiled.

Following this, the abbey, whose title deeds had been destroyed, went to great effort to "defend" its estates. It even had to sell some of them in order to cope with the successive cases. The brewery was "ceded" to a lay person, charged to "manage" it under the supervision of the father-abbot, who remained owner of the manufacturing process. At the middle of the 17th century, the abbey rented the brewery for 30 florins and collected 250 florins from it in taxes. The brewing activity was solely to cover the needs of the religious community. But it happened that the beer, having acquired a certain reputation, overstepped the walls of the monastery, and that the father-abbot offered some casks to his parishioners for festivities and important events.

Under the authority of the abbot, Perpète Renson (1704-1743), the abbey underwent considerable growth. A new abbey church was built. The brewery was enlarged and renovated. All this was ruined by the French Revolutionary troops, in 1794. Declared national property in 1796, the abbey was sold in successive lots and sank into oblivion....until, in 1903, the Premonstratensians of Saint Michel de Frigolet, hounded from their French monastery by the Combes Law, acquired the buildings of the former abbey and restored them to their religious vocation. The Great War hampered their endeavours, and they eventually left the place in 1928. In the following year the Premonstratensian order from the abbey at Tongerlo (Brabant), which was itself in part destroyed by fire, settled in the abbey at Leffe. And since then, this community, Dutch speaking, has endeavoured to restore the original estate of the abbey.

The financial difficulties suffered by the monastery had repercussions on the brewery. In 1954, the father-abbot, Nye, concluded an agreement with a brewer from Overijse, Albert Lootvœt, in such a way that the latter would continue the brewing tradition of the abbey. And he did this until 1978, the year when the brewery was taken over by Stella Artois and closed down. Since then, Leffe has been produced by the Saint Guibert Brewery, in Mont Saint Guibert. Its manufacture was transferred to Leuven at the end of 1995.

The fate of the **Abbey of Grimbergen**, in Brabant, was no less stormy. Founded in 1128 by Saint Norbert, on the initiative of the Lords of Grimbergen, it suffered the violence of the long conflict which, over the course of the first half of the 12th century was waged by the lords against their suzerain, the Duke of Brabant. Then reconstructed, it underwent an era of prosperity until the religious wars during which it was again destroyed (1566). The damage could not be repaired until after 1629. The existing buildings were restored, new buildings were constructed, and a brewery was reinstalled. It is not

surprising that the abbey should then be given a phoenix as its emblem!

The abbey then had its brewer, who earned 60 florins in 1762, equivalent to the salary of a first farm hand. It seems that the brewer then fulfilled the parallel function of porter. Like the other abbeys, Grimbergen had, since the Middle Ages, possessed its own hop fields - its *hoplochting* ("hop garden" in the Brabant dialect). The beer was made from wheat, barley, and hops.

The brewery was completely modernised during the 1770's. But the abbey hardly profited. Having, like its colleagues, become national property in the era of the Revolution, it was dismantled and put up for sale in 1798. Its new Brussels owners, the de la Palliere brothers, one of whom had also bought the monastery of Affligem, demolished it almost entirely. Religious life was only re-established there in 1834, with the arrival of a new congregation.

From then on, the canons had to be supplied with beer from outside brewers. Around 1840, beer was made by Messrs Janssens and Peeters, following the directions of the monks. This situation continued until 1958, the year when the Premonstratensians of Grimbergen decided to launch *Grimbergen*, in collaboration with the Maes Brewery. It has been made since 1982 in Jumet, at the Brasserie de l'Union, which belongs to the Alken-Maes Group.

The **Abbey of Tongerlo** owes its foundation, in the years 1130-1133, to the conversion of a lord, Giselbert, who renounced a large part of his goods for the benefit of this new monastic establishment. It had as its first father superior a Premonstratensian from the Saint Michel Abbey in Antwerp. During the course of the 12th century, successive donations (rural and church exploitations) contributed to rapid growth in the abbey estates and its spread over the Campine region. In 1298 its properties ranged over more than sixty localities. It is no surprise that Tongerlo Abbey played an important role in the government of the Duchy of Brabant. This prosperity, however, had some set-backs, for example by the diocesan restructuring of the Spanish Netherlands (1559), and in the following century by the taking of Hertogenbosch by the Calvinist troops, who forced the community to take refuge in Mechelen (1637-1640). Finally there was the coup de grâce delivered by the Revolution. The one hundred and thirty canons dispersed in 1796.

The monastery buildings were the object of successive embellishments over the course of the centuries. Half of the Renaissance edifices were razed by successive owners, after the Revolution. Restored to the community, from 1840, the abbey was ravaged by a fire in 1929. However, these avatars did not prevent the rediscovery of an intense monastic life.

It seems that the abbey had possessed, from its origins, a most particular brewery. Its lands furnished wheat and barley for the brewing. As for the beer called Tongerlo, it was made by the Marine Brewery, in Brussels, until its take-over by Artois, in 1979. Production was then interrupted. Today, once more, it is produced for the Haacht Brewery in Boortmeerbeek.

Founded before 1138, by the abbey of Floreffe, the development of the **Abbey de Postel** was favoured by its favourable geographical position, at the

crossing point of the Antwerp-Cologne and the Leuven-Hertogenbosch roads. It only obtained its independence from the mother abbey in 1613, thanks to the support of Archduke Albert and Archduchess Isabelle. It was in this era that, between other new constructions, it acquired a brewery. Like all the others, the abbey became national property in 1797 and lived through a long period of oblivion until the return of the monks in 1847.

In 1854 a genever distillery was installed in the abbey, but it only existed for a short while, because its activity was stopped in 1866. Concerned to find financing for the restoration of the abbey, the monks spoke to the Campina Brewery, in Dessel, with a view to the manufacture of *Postel* beer. When the brewery was taken over by Maes in 1986, this beer was in competition with Grimbergen *(see above)* and its brewing was entrusted to the De Smedt Brewery, in Opwijk.

The **Abbey du Park**, in Heverlee, was founded in 1129, on the initiative of the Duke of Brabant, Godfrey I. Its history remains obscure. The community had to leave during the Revolution, in 1797, and in 1834, ten of the monks, who were still alive, settled there once more.

Abbaye du Park beer was being produced by the Breda Brewery, in Leuven, when it was taken over by Artois, in 1976. Brewing was ceased until 1995, the year when the l'Union Brewery, in Jumet, took over production.

OTHER ABBEYS... BENEDICTINES... OTHER BEERS...

• Founded in 1074 and inhabited by Benedictines from 1083, the **Abbey of Affligem** benefited, from the very beginning, from the support of the Duke of Brabant. When it was closed, in 1796, its monks were exiled to Dendermonde. It could only be re-occupied by a religious order in 1869. The brewery which it housed from that time only "lived" until the First World War.

Beer carrying the name of this abbey is made by the De Smedt Brewery, in Opwijk.

• The **Abbey of Saint Pierre de Steenbrugge** was founded in Bruges in 1879, by monks coming from Dendermonde. Under the authority of the Abbot Modest van Assche, it obtained the right, in 1934, to lay claim to the Abbey of Saint Pierre d'Oudenburg, founded by Saint Arnold, patron saint of brewers, and closed during the French Revolution.

Beer carrying the name of this abbey is made by the De Gouden Boom Brewery, in Bruges.

• The **Abbey of Maredsous** was founded in 1872 with the aid of the Tournai industrialist Henri Philippe Desclée* . In response to financial requirements, the monks undertook to produce hops and to manufacture beer. This was first of all brewed by the Faleau Brewery, in Châtelineau, according to the recipe supplied by Father Attout, himself the son of a brewer. Its success was considerable.

Since the closure of the Faleau Brewery (1961), the beer has been made by the Moortgat Brewery in Breendonck.

• The **Abbey of Ter Duinen** (The Dunes) of Koksijde, founded in 1107, adopted Cistercian rule in 1122. The monks left in 1627 to settle in Bruges.

Saint-Idesbald beer, which prolongs its memory, is made by the Huyghe Brewery in Melle.

* He installed, in Roubaix (France), the very first coal gas factory, and developed this source of energy in Belgium

IN MEMORY OF THE PREMONSTRATENSIAN ABBEYS WHICH DISAPPEARED

• The beer *Abbaye de Dielegem*, brewed by the Huyghe Brewery in Melle, alludes to the **Notre Dame Abbey of Dielegem**. Founded in 1095, in Jette, by the Augustinians, this monastery joined the Premonstratensian Order in 1140. The French Revolution brought about its closure, in 1797, and it was later doomed to demolition, with the exception of a quarter of the abbey, which was transformed into a cultural centre.

• The beer *Bonne-Espérance*, produced by the Lefebvre Brewery in Quenast, recalls the **Notre Dame Abbey of Bonne-Espérance**. Created by Premonstratensian canons in 1125, in Ramignies, this abbey was transferred a little later to Sart-Richevin, before being established finally in Bonne-Espérance, in 1130. It also had to be closed in 1796, as a result of the Revolutionary torments. It was not until 1829 that its restoration was undertaken. A brewery operated there from 1905 until 1914. The building, which belongs to the Bishop of Tournai, is today occupied by a small seminary and by an educational establishment.

• Similarly, it is the Lefebvre Brewery in Quenast which brews the beers of *Floreffe*. Situated near Namur, the **Notre Dame Abbey of Floreffe** was in fact the first Premonstratensian abbey established in Belgium (1121). It founded the abbeys of Beaurepart, Heylissem, Leffe, and Postel. Closed by the Revolution in 1797, it then became the property of the Bishop of Namur, housing its small seminary there since 1817.

From its inception, the abbey of Floreffe had its brewery. The building in which it was installed, constitutes one of the oldest remains of monastic breweries following the brewery of the abbey of Villers-la-Ville. At the present time, it is the setting for a tavern where one may consume the *Floreffe* beers.

• Finally, the beer *Saint-Feuillien* recalls the **Saint Feuillien Abbey of Rœulx**, founded in 1125 by the Premonstratensian canons, on the initiative of the Bishop of Cambrai. Closed in 1796, on account of the Revolution, the monastery was razed in 1858.

Saint-Feuillien, distributed by the Friart Brewery in Rœulx, is brewed by the Friart Brewery (1.5 litre bottles) and by the Du Bocq Brewery in Purnode, for the Friart Brewery (25cl and 75cl bottles).

The Friart Brewery, situated in Rœulx, took for its Christmas beer, the picture by Pieter Breughel the Elder portraying *The Census in Bethlehem* (Royal Museum of Fine Arts, Brussels).

IN MEDIEVAL TERMS...

Until the beginning of the 13th century, deeds and other documents were written exclusively in Latin. Then Latin gradually disappeared, and when the Latin word *cervesia* (or *cerevisia*) faded before the common tongue, it was replaced by the word *cervoise* in the area of Romance language and by the word *bier* (or *biere*, or even *bire*) in the Germanic language, the latter word deriving from the old Saxon *bere* ("cereal"). Without doubt the word bière, used from the 15th century in the French language to distinguish drinks with hops from cervisia or ale, is taken from the Germanic term.

• **Bracena.** From the 13th century, this word replaced the word *camba*, to indicate the brewery. One also finds *braxina*, *brasyna*, and *braxatorium*. When the common tongue took it, the Roman area adopted *bressine*, or *brassine*, exclusively used from the 14th century.

• **Bracier.** Derived from brais *, this word signifies "brasser" (to brew). It is the origin of this word, and of "brasserie" (brewery).

• **Brais.** Derived from the Latin *brace* ("spelt"), this word indicated "barley brewed to make beer".

• **Brassator.** The word succeeded *brasciator* (derived from *braxina*) and gave *brasseur* (brewer)

• **Bruwers Huse.** This expression, mentioned for the first time in 1288 indicated, like *panhus* *, the brewery in old Dutch. From it is derived the word *brouwerij* (brewery).

• **Camba.** Derived from the Celtic, this term was the first to indicate the on-site brewery. It was used from the 9th to the 12th century. It then gradually gave way to the word *bracena* *. In the *camba*, one brewed, but one could also sell the bottles.

Gallicised, it gave the word *cambe*. From the 12th century it was made a duty upon villagers to use the cambe, that is to say the lord's brewery.

• **Cambarius.** This term, derived from *camba* *, indicated the brewer. One encounters it in the 9th century. It became *cambier* in the Romance tongue.

• **Cambagium**, **cambage**, or **gambage** (by deformation). The term literally signifies a "duty on the brewery". This duty, which was applied to the manufacture of beer, was paid to the local lord. For example, in the manor of Ecussines-Lalaing, in the 15th century, the fee consisted of a levy of one pot on every cask broached. Two thirds of the cambage was destined to the lord, and the rest went to the community.

• **Foragium**, **forage**, or **afforage**. This tax on the sale of beer was levied on the broaching of the cask.

• **Grutarius** ("**gruitier**"). This person was charged with making the *grutum* ("gruit", "Gruyt", or "grute"), and selling it - that is to say of levying the tax on the breweries. It was often an inherited charge. Thus the abbey of Saint Trond had its own *grutarius*. One finds the same type of office in numerous locations, sometimes under a different name. For example, in Leuven, it was the office of the *maere*, and in Tournai, the office of the *mairia*; these two terms are part of the terminology of gruit.

In Flanders, one finds the variants *gruutheer*, *grutere*, and *gruitere*.

• **Gruuthus.** This was the place where the gruit was sold.

• **Halster.** This measure was utilised, in Flanders, to indicate the quantity that one could brew - the quantity above which the brewer could be fined for, and for which he risked the destruction of his equipment. Thus, in 1288, the quantity so authorised was 9 halsters (6 of oats and 3 of barley), that is to say 482.85 litres; it was increased in 1337 to 12 halsters (8 of oats and 4 of barley), that is to say 643.80 litres.

• **Panhus.** This indicated the brewery in old Dutch. The origin of the term (from "pan" and "huis" ("the house of the tank") showed that the equipment used for brewing consisted of several tanks. One knows nothing about these, except that they were made of metal. It is probable in any case that often a single tank served for all the processes; mashing, boiling, and fermenting.

• **Pot or lot.** This measure, used for liquids, varied from locality to locality. For example in Hainaut, in StamBrugge, Quevaucamps, and Harchies, it was 1.85 litres.

• **Rewards.** In Namur this name was given to the "beer inspectors", sworn inspectors in the service of the lord, who visited breweries testing the beers before they were sold and collecting duties. This trade also existed in other cities.

• **Signage.** *See p 14.*

ORGANISATION AND GROWTH

The 16th century, for the lands of Belgium as it is today, was marked with the seal of greatness and of decline. In the reign of Charles V, the strong demographic growth was accompanied by a no less rapid increase in economic prosperity. The community independence from which most towns benefited contributed a great deal to this prosperity. The most remarkable example was, without doubt, Antwerp, which by its exceptional position at a maritime and terrestrial cross-roads, took the rank of commercial capital of Europe. It eclipsed Bruges, which until then had played the role, but saw its vitality dull after the end of the 15th century, with the silting over of the Zwin, and the decay of the cloth industry.

The Netherlands were therefore flourishing, when from the 1560's there succeeded, without respite, social revolt, religious upheaval and war. In the torment, the Southern provinces, Flanders and Brabant, lost the benefits which had been bestowed upon them in the first half of the Renaissance. Conversely, the United Provinces (the Northern Netherlands) then built their fortune. Amsterdam took over from Antwerp, which saw itself divested of its commercial importance, the mouths of the Scheldt being blocked by the Dutch. When, in the 17th century, the authority of the King of Spain was re-established in the Southern provinces, their situation was disastrous.

Label of the Van Den Bossche Brewery, in Sint Leuvens - Esse. Lamoral, Count of Egmond and Prince of Gavere, born in La Hamaide (Hainaut) in 1522, was one of the great captains of the Renaissance. He made a name for himself in numerous battles, and was promoted Captain-General of Flanders and Councillor of State. His hostility towards Cardinal Antoine de Granvelle, and his role in the crisis which shook the Netherlands, led him to the scaffold. Arrested in 1567, on the order of the Duke of Alba, he was beheaded the following year, on the Grand Place in Brussels.

Such was the climate in which the brewery industry began to organise itself and to participate actively in the local economy. Its growth was favoured in areas where the cloth industry had been prominent, because it was necessary to face up to its ruin and to align the working population towards a new activity, brewing. It was thus in Hasselt, Leuven, Diest, and Hœgaarden.

The taste for beer

The Middle Ages had known several sorts of ale, and had then adopted beer which was hopped. At their origin, all the beers were of spontaneous fermentation; the phenomenon of fermentation had not been explained. It was only from the 15th century that the brewer began to add yeast to the wort or the fermented residue deriving from a preliminary brew. It was a matter of yeasts active at high temperature.

The beer was usually of a good gravity, which might be assessed at least 7 to 8° Balling and on average 13 to 15° Balling. Why should it not be a food supplement? It seems that, in certain regions, this role still had some importance at the Renaissance, and even in later eras. In fact one can read, at the beginning of the 16th century, in the encyclopaedia of plants by Jacques Théodore Tabernæmontanus, "The beer in Flanders is a good beer. Above all the double beer, such as is brewed in Ghent and Bruges, surpasses all the beers of the Netherlands. It satisfies and nourishes to perfection. It gives rich blood and a good complexion, at the same time beautiful and gleaming with life, to the point that a simple glance shows who are the people who have been drinking since their youth." The double beer of Fanders, which is referred to here, flaunted a gravity of 19° Balling !

But it was not always thus. If the strong beers were truly so, the beer of common consumption did not achieve the alcohol content of a pils of today. For example, during the first half of the 17th century, between 30 and 50 per cent of the beer consumed in Antwerp was small beer. And this proportion even reached 55 per cent in

Mechelen. Because beer was the normal beverage, wine was very costly, and water rarely drinkable. This defective quality in water was, besides, a problem for the brewers, and the creation of a waterworks in Antwerp is a perfect illustration of this *(see page 101)*.

Beer was therefore for regular and considerable consumption. In times of peace, as in times of war. And, in 1568, the soldiers who were stationed in the Antwerp garrison were entitled to some two litres of beer each day. Despite the ravages to which it was subjected during the last quarter of the 16th century, the city counted, in 1584, at least 376 public drinks outlets. Around 1620 the annual average *per capita* consumption rose to more than 400 litres; during the last decade of the 17th century, it had fallen to a little more than 260 litres, which was quite considerable. And it was just the same in a good many other towns. Another example is Mechelen. The annual average *per capita* consumption of beer was approximately 400 litres at the very beginning of the 17th century, and some 250 litres at the middle of the same century.

The taste for the drink even went to excess. Many tales from voyages in the 17th century bear witness. Confirmation of it is likewise provided by the war memoires of the Spanish Captain Don Alonzo Vasquez (1617), who recalls the importance of beer to the Netherlands, and the tendency often to drink more of it than was reasonable. "In these countries, the beer is drunk like wine (...) Beer, which is brewed on a base of wheat, has a colour as clear as linen and it froths when one pours it into the jug. One talks of it in casks. This beer intoxicates as rapidly as wine, contrary to beer of barley, which is healthier but dear and less sensuous. (...) Less costly beer, such as is brewed on a base of bran (in fact on the brewer's grain or draff already used), this beer is very weak. (...)

"It is affirmed that English beer is the best, but there are also good Netherlands beers brewed in Antwerp and Leuven. In the Liège region certain beers are brewed which are more full-flavoured and more perfumed by virtue of the addition of hops and certain aromatic herbs. It is this which renders this type of beer more flavoursome and more sensuous. (...)"

Each region already had its specialities, which could only be consumed within a certain radius outside the place of their production. In Brussels, for example, one could drink the white beer *(wæghbært)*, red beer *(rœtbier)*, black beer *(swartbier)*, or *cuijte* (or *coitje*, or even *queute*), which was light beer made without hops. In the 16th century, the latter gained in quality and in gravity *(dobbel-cuijte)*.

But if brewers were not favourably disposed towards large trade in beers, foreign beers, were on the other hand imported and this was profitable. These imports were in part through foreign merchants established in the ports. In the 16th century one could drink, in Brussels, beers from the Baltic, Ireland, and Hamburg. In the middle of the 17th century, in Antwerp, among the beers sold in the greatest quantity were those of Antwerp, of Mechelen, Diest, and Leuven, but also beers from Gouda, Danzig, Brunswick, Hamburg, and England.

The imposition of regulations

In becoming specialists, the art of the brewer acquired a truly professional structure, which translated into the establishment of guilds *(see page 28)*. These guilds governed the trade and its practices. For example in 1606 the charter of the Namur guild of brewers forbade the use of ingredients other than grain and hops, as well as delivering for consumption beer which had not been cellared for at least eight days.

At the same time brewing was subject to regulation by the strictest edicts of the sovereign and to the observance of which the commune paid great head, in agreement with the guilds. These regulations, linked to the sale price of the beer (which had to remain accessible), varied, quite clearly, according to the town, and were often amended according to the price of grain. The slightest infraction was subject to fine. So, in Namur, an edict of 1587 fixed at one and same time the maximum number of sacks of grain which were to be used for a mash-tub of 10 tonnes and the maximum sale price of the beer. The turbulences of history having brought about tough periods of famine, the manufacture of beer had to adapt itself to these difficult times. Its quality suffered, but its price remained reasonable. Care was taken that beer did not fail the population. This was the case in Namur, in the winter of 1709. The brewers were authorised to make good beer at four sous a pot, and "mediocre" at two sous a pot, "on condition that it be of a goodness proportionate to the price and not to put in any wheat."

Besides the price, everything was stringently regulated. For example in Charleroi, an edict by Charles II at the beginning of the 17th century fixed the capacity of the cask at 110 pots, each of 2.86 litres. The casks were gauged and marked, as were the measures for selling the beer, since the sale was also taken into account. "We forbid anyone to draw or deliver the said beers, and any other, other than in a full pot of pure beer, and without considering the head or cream, and also to use ingredients or other inventions, such as putting the pot in hot water or otherwise to give the beer a head, on penalty of three florins fine for each pot or half pot which shall otherwise be delivered."

If it was forbidden to brew on Sundays, it was likewise forbidden to serve drinks during church services *(see "Beer Places" page 173 etc.)*. Any fine was applied both to the person who sold the drinks and to his client.

Increasing taxes

As in the Middle Ages, beer continued to feed the coffers of the commune. The dues became ever more onerous. In Liège for example, during the first half of the 16th century, the excise duty on mash-tubs brought in an average 25,000 florins. In Antwerp, the taxes on beers represented, at the end of the 16th century, more than 60 per cent of the receipts of the town. In Namur, in the 17th century, the taxes on the tun of beer were numerous: town tax, "chambiage" duty, hop and "thibus" duty, "ferté" duty, and "banvin" duty. Inevitably, such taxation often brought about a fall in the quality of the beer. In fact, because it made it profitable for them to sell at the price fixed by the town, certain brewers made economies on the ingredients, especially the hops, and made the beers rather weak, and without much bouquet. But this charging of taxes sometimes had the effect of inciting the brewers to group together in order to fight more strongly. This phenomenon was to be observed in Antwerp. The old town, with thirty brewers at first, counted no more than five in 1602, and then two in 1642, who covered the market in the city and the region.

Brewers could not escape taxation. Controls were very strict. Taxes being levied when the beer left the cellar, transport of the product was not free. This was to prevent any fraud. Thus in Bruges, the manufacturers were very dependent upon the guild of beer carriers. *(see page 30)*.

From producer to private individual

It was tradition that the bourgeois could brew and have brewed for their own consumption. In certain towns (Antwerp and Mechelen, for example), private individuals went for this to special communal breweries. In other cities, the brewers made the beer for private people under certain conditions. So in Namur, at the end of the 17th century, those who brewed for the bourgeois had to purchase what was called a "small trade" and pay a fee for entry into the brotherhood. They were only permitted to do this, while the brewers in the "large trade" could brew both to sell and for individuals.

It is interesting to note that a number of private individuals continued to brew themselves. A statement from the brewery in Bruges, drawn up in 1673 shows that there were large brewers and small brewers, and a mass of "amateur brewers". In 1685, 425 cauldrons *(huisbrouwten)* were counted, shared among the bourgeois of the city. This figure went to 621 in 1718, the breweries in convents being included. A cauldron served to make from four to eight casks of beer.

Private individuals suffered taxation on their beer, like professional brewers, but to a lesser degree. A means of avoiding certain taxes consisted of storing the beer at the brewery and going there to shop for one's requirements as one went along, rather than buying it by the pitcher at the drinks outlet. During the 17th century more than a third of the beer produced seems to have been diverted from sale in the drinks outlets.

SOME SIGNIFICANT DATES

• **1516-1555:** The son of Philip the Beautiful and Jeanne the Mad, born in Ghent in 1500 and brought up in the Netherlands, Charles V, Emperor of Germany, King of Spain, and King of Sicily, reigned over the Netherlands (then composed of 17 provinces). He installed the central government in Brussels and entrusted it to a Governor General. This was first of all his aunt, Marguerite of Austria (1519-1530), and then his sister, Marie of Hungary (1530-1555).

In 1526, by the Treaty of Madrid, Charles V did away with the link of vassalage which connected Flanders to the Kingdom of France - Flanders had become a domain of the Habsburgs in 1477.

In 1549, he unified the seventeen provinces, by the Pragmatic Sanction of Brussels.

• **1556:** Charles V having abdicated, power passed into the hands of his son, Philip II. From 1559 he had the Netherlands governed by his half-sister Marguerite of Parma. She was regent until 1567, and had as éminence grise, until 1564, the Cardinal Antoine de Granvelle, Archbishop of Mechelen.

• **1566-1648:** The Spanish monarchy was faced with an Eighty Years War with the Netherlands, when its suzerainty and its religious intransigence (the Inquisition) were violently contested. In the 1570's, a split took place. The Northern Netherlands (Zeeland and Holland, among others), formed the United Provinces, and gave themselves as sovereign the Prince of Orange, William the Silent. The Governor of the Netherlands, Alexander Farnèse (1578-1592), son of Marguerite of Parma, re-established Spanish domination on the Southern provinces, which correspond somewhat to the Belgium of today.

In 1648, by the Treaty of Münster, Spain recognised the independence of the United Provinces.

• **1598:** Philip II ceded the sovereignty of the Netherlands to the infant Isabelle and her husband Archduke Albert of Austria.

• **1633:** When the infant died, without heir, the Netherlands returned to Spain, and lived to the rhythm of the conflicts which took place, notably with France, throughout the 17th century.

Above: the brown beer *Charles Quint* (7 % vol. alcohol) is produced by the Haacht brewery in Boortmeerbeek.

Below: this advertising panel for the La Binchoise Brerwery carries the coat of arms of Marie of Hungary, sister of Charles V.

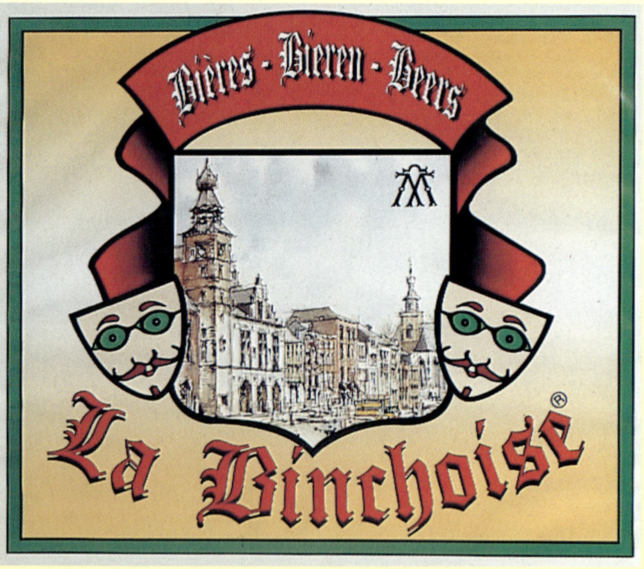

"And in order that the beers always be of a good and regular composition, we order that they be made of good grains and hops, without being able to blend any other ingredients, herbs and other illicit substances, often poisonous and damaging to the human body, exciting to drink and leading to drunkenness, from whence come quarrels, blasphemies, and other misfortunes, forbidding even brewers from acquiring them, on pain of 60 florins for each fine and besides that confiscation of the beer which might be found composed of such forbidden ingredients, one third of all applicable to our profit, another to that of the officer, and the third to be divided between the said master and the informer."

(Charter of the Namur Guild of Brewers, 1688)

FROM BEER TO GENEVER

Before becoming a centre for genever, the capital of the Belgian Limburg, Hasselt, had a strong brewing vocation. In fact, this agricultural city, which benefited from a most favourable geographical location at the heart of the Earldom of Loon, at the borders of the Hesbaye and of the Campine, produced beer in not insignificant quantities. As proof of this, in 1515 the excise duties on beer represented a little more than 60 per cent of the receipts of the town, and went on to reach almost 70 per cent in 1622. The decline of the cloth industry in the 16th century, contributed to the growth in brewing activity, upon which the municipal authorities looked with jealousy, as much for the revenues it would obtain as for fear of satisfying the needs of the community for quality beer at a suitable price.

The majority of breweries were, quite clearly, established near waterways, in the proximity of the Démer and along the Halbeek. In 1664, 54 brewers could be numbered, while Hasselt counted no more than 4,000 inhabitants. It was above all a matter of small enterprises, and, to survive, certain of them had to organise a co-operative, in order to the utilise the same equipment in turn. Total production was approximately 9,870 amen* in the middle of the 16th century. A century later, it had increased to some 8,200 amen, a sufficient quantity to cover the local demand. From 1625, 30 per cent of this beer was directed towards other cities in Limbourg, and even as far as Diest and Maastricht. On the other hand, the town imported a little "foreign" beer: Jupenbier, originating in Haarlem and Danzig, as well as the beer from Hœgaarden. From 1674 only the latter was authorised to be imported.

But Hasselt also produced eau de vie and it was not rare for a brewer also to distil genever. At the beginning of the 19th century eau de vie overtook beer and the industrial era revived the economy of the town on new foundations.

* a mash-tun of beer contained an imposed number of measures [or "amen", ± 138 litres].

OLD-FASHIONED BEER

"The Flemish use for their beers a sort of barley, named winter barley. After having germinated it in water, then drying and milling it, they add an eighth part of short oats, milled without being germinated, and boil the lot for twenty four hours. They then barrel the liquid in half hogsheads where it ferments by means of a certain amount of yeast. Fifteen days later, the beer is fit to be drunk. As for its strength, this depends on the quantity of barley which is put in."

(Recipe transcribed by the Intendant of Flanders in 1698.)

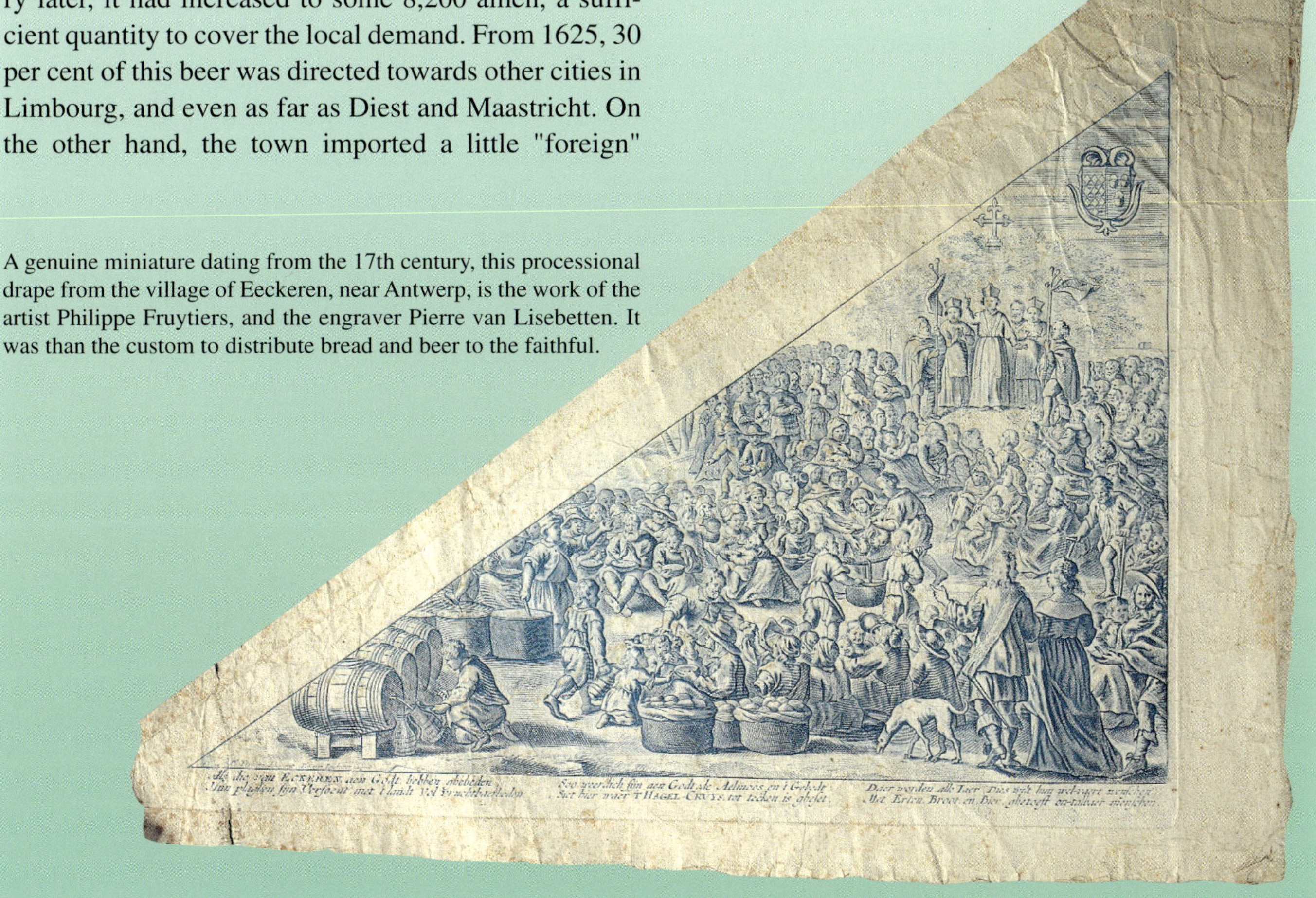

A genuine miniature dating from the 17th century, this processional drape from the village of Eeckeren, near Antwerp, is the work of the artist Philippe Fruytiers, and the engraver Pierre van Lisebetten. It was than the custom to distribute bread and beer to the faithful.

AT THE TIME OF THE GUILTS

Relative peace having returned and the time of the Crusades at an end, Europe turned towards commerce and industry. Communes began to shake off the yoke of feudal power. A communal system was gradually put in place, as privileges were accorded to cities by their sovereigns. Leuven, Brussels, Antwerp, and so on. The principal towns were granted charters. A burgomaster, a mayor, or even a bailiff, represented the sovereign. Behind him, a certain number of deputy mayors were in charge of justice and the finances of the locality. This communal development had to have beneficial effects on the economy of the country and on its well-being, to the extent that the population no longer had to dread seeing the fruits of its labours "recovered" by a sometimes tyrannical lord. Furthermore, various trade organisations were established, and played a role in the life of the city. Thus were born the *guilds*, each of them having its own regulations and being placed under the authority of jurors (later called *doyens*), elected by the assembly of members and having extensive powers.

Powerful guilds

Among these professional communities, that of the brewers was, from the very beginning, one of the most important, whatever the city to which it belonged. The guild of brewers in Bruges was one of the first to obtain its privileges, at the end of the 13th century, benefiting from the interest taken in it by the Count of Flanders, Gwijde van Dampierre. It flourished, and played an important role among the nine members of the city council. The guild of brewers in Namur, where twenty five trade bodies could be counted, obtained its charter in 1376, to be renewed or amended later in 1606, 1688, and 1724. The brewers of Liège determined the statutes of their trade in 1381. But the first general regulation only dates from 1518. The jurisdiction of the Liège guild extended to all those concerned with beer, be they manufacturer or tavern keeper.

On this pewter plate from 1758, originally from Mechelen and offered on the occasion of a baptism, are engraved the symbols of the Guild of Brewers. R. Dangis collecton.

Until the beginning of the 15th century, the brewers of Brussels were part of the group of food and drinks merchants. In was not until 1421 that the trades organised themselves officially in Nine Nations, each of them placed under the protection of a Saint. The Nation of St. Jacques gathered together the bakers and confectioners, the millers, the coopers, the cabinet makers, the tilers, the wine merchants and... the brewers. The trade of brewers *(brauwere)* had as its arms: "Gules, holding a silver fork with golden handle, and a gold handled sinople placed in saltire." Governed by four jurors and a council of elders *(oudermannen)*, the guild saw its importance increase with time, above all in the 17th century - from 67 in 1620, the number of master brewers passed 80 in 1658, then 94 in 1678. Its power was such that it never hesitated to oppose decisions which it judged to be contrary to its interests, including orders emanating from Charles V, demands for subsidies such as those by Philip II in 1556, or interferences by the commanders of the garrison. And most of the time it won its case.

At the end of the 18th century, like other trade bodies, the brewers' guilds suffered from sharp attacks. Besides the fact that their power and their wealth was disturbing, the rigour of their regulations was paralysing. And at a time of openness to the outside, their concern about preserving their monopoly became an obstacle to commerce. But this would have had no effect on their situation, if the French Revolution had not occurred. On 17th March 1791, the Constituent Assembly declared the suppression of guilds. The decision was rendered applicable to Belgium by a decree on 14th Brumaire IV. In 1796, in Brussels, the archives and

Formerly each city possessed its Brewers' Hall.
Right: the Brewers' Hall in Lier, in the province of Antwerp.
Far right: the Brewers Hall in Ieper, in West Flanders.

the furniture of the various trade organisations were dispersed through a sale in the Grand Place...

Organisation and authority

To be admitted into the brotherhood, it was necessary to have undergone an apprenticeship with a master. Even the son of a brewer was required to do this. The duration of the apprenticeship varied according to the town. In Bruges it was two years, in Namur, at first, only one. It went up to two years in 1724. At the end of this period, in the absence of being able to complete a "master piece" as was the custom with other trades, the apprentice generally had to pass a sort of practical examination, which probably consisted of making a mash in front of the masters. He could then set up as a master or work as a journeyman for a member of the guild. Admission into the community was, of course, subject to an entry fee, of which the amount varied according to the locality.

The guild was all-powerful. It had the twin aims of protecting the interests of the trade and of maintaining a spirit of brotherhood within the profession. It regulated work, its duration and its organisation. So, in Brussels, the brewing bell, installed in the tower of the old Church of St. Géry, at the heart of the Grand Ile, chimed, throughout the day, the times of work and rest. The guild had its relief fund for the sick and infirm. But its role sometimes exceeded the context of the trade to participate in communal "politics". It even happened that it was brought to take arms, if the situation required it. This was the case in 1422, when the Nation of St. Jacques, to which the Brussels brewers belonged, was charged by the city with defending the Porte de Coudenberg (later the "Porte de Namur" - "Namur Gateway").

This support of municipal life was, to everyone's good fortune, generally more peaceful, and consisted simply of taking part in public celebrations. The guild of brewers always occupied a place of honour on such occasions, notably in the processions where it paraded. Each guild was preceded by torches, displayed its banner, decorated with the emblems of the trade, and sometimes carried the statue of its patron saint. A composition by the Flemish painter and engraver Anthonis Sallaert (Brussels, 1590-1658) is an interesting testimony to this custom, since it portrayed a procession of trade bodies on the Grand Place in Brussels in 1620.

Each guild therefore had its protecting saint, which it venerated either in a chapel belonging to it, or in a church in the town where an altar was dedicated. Masses were regularly celebrated there. In Namur, for example, the brewers acquired their own chapel in the 16th century, which had been erected in the 13th century in honour of Saint Hilaire and situated in the rue des Vis or des Vifs, later called the rue des Brasseurs. This religious fervour on the part of the guilds likewise manifested itself in gifts to the Church.

An original guild: the beer carriers of Bruges

A picturesque spectacle is that of the "beer carriers" *(Biervoerders)* of olden days, carrying, in pairs, a cask fixed to long poles resting on their shoulders! Nearer to the present day, a sight no less surprising is that of these porters pulling their carts by hand through the streets of Bruges and so delivering the beer at home! They could still be seen at the beginning of the 20th century, before the lorry took over such deliveries. But, with progress, there disappeared one of the oldest traditions of the city, and, with that tradition, an entire guild faded. It had been one of the rare ones to survive the Revolution, and over the centuries had jealously held on to its monopoly.

It was in 1477 that the municipal authority forbade brewery boys from transporting beer within the boundaries of Bruges, and for that purpose created the "office" of beer carrier. At its origins, whoever wished to carry on this trade had to hire his charge, for a period of six years. Later, it was necessary to buy it, and it was very expensive. The beneficial owner of the office could not carry out the work himself. In fact, some did not reside in Bruges, and sublet their right to a person who carried on the trade in their place. However that may be, the number of beer carriers was at first 38, remaining above 30 for a long time. In the 1910's it was no more than 23, this still being considerable in an era when motorised transport became a formidable competitor.

Each new member of the guild was constrained to face certain obligations, at the very least onerous. In 1650 he had to pay the doyen 2 pounds and 2 escalins, to offer to the guild 1 tun of beer to celebrate his entry into the trade, organising a feast in the section where he would make his debut. The city gave him a uniform. This consisted of a paletot *(journeye)* of red cloth, on which two small casks were embroidered, one on the back, and one on the front. At the end of the Middle Ages, there was more than one single cask. Then later the colour changed and the paletot became green.

The beer carriers were placed under the authority of a doyen *(koning)*, elected for one year and assisted by five deputies. Each of these had responsibility for a district of Bruges, the city being divided into five sec-

The *biervoeders*, photographed here at the Floor Brewery, in Bruges.

tions, and the guild split into five teams. One should note in passing that this dividing of Bruges into five parts was not modified from 1650, and remained the same until the 20th century. Every month, a drawing of lots indicated to which district each team was appointed. Each day, work completed, the porters met together in their local, *T'huyscken op de Markt*, and submitted to the *pagador* ("paymaster" in old Spanish) the receipts for their journey. At the end of the month, at a general meeting, the distribution of profits took place. All the carriers received an identical sum, even those who had been forced to interrupt their work during the month on account of illness.

The work of the carriers was double. On the one hand they had the task of cellaring the beer, including foreign beers or beers brewed in the city. The private breweries (that is to say the private manufacturers of beer for their own personal consumption), just like the large breweries, had to use them. On the other hand, the carriers had the exclusive right to transport beer within the city. To serve their clientele, the brewers of Bruges were constrained to turn to their services. Similarly, the brewers from surrounding areas, who delivered beer to Bruges, stopped at the gates to the city and gave their loads to the carriers.

Throughout its existence, this guild of beer carriers was much appreciated by the Bruges brewers, as much for their efficiency as for their total neutrality in respect of the different beers that they were appointed to transport. For them beer was only a merchandise like any other, and they were wise enough to remain outside the rivalries which prevailed between their clients.

REFLECTION OF THE PAST, WITNESS OF THE PRESENT

The present day Confederation of Belgian Brewers *(see page 82)* is established, as was the former Brussels Guild of Brewers, in a magnificent building on the Grand Place in Brussels. The place is marked by history.

At the end of the 13th century, a house was already located on this site, first of all called *De Hille* ("The Hill"), then later *L'enfer* ("The Hell"). It belonged to the Masters of the Table of the Poor of St. Nicolas, when in 1483 the tanners acquired it. While at that time the majority of houses on the Grand Place were of wood, this one was constructed in stone, with a beautiful triangular pediment with high and narrow crenelations. It was renamed *L'Arbre* ("The Tree") and finally, in the following century, *Den Gulden Boom* ("The Tree of Gold"). The tanners transferred it, in the middle of the 16th century, to the tapestry-makers, of both high and low warp.

For their part, from the end of the 16th century the brewers occupied the house called *Galice*, likewise situated on the Grand Place. They only purchased the house known as "The Tree of Gold" at the beginning of the 17th century, and they restored it in 1638. But it came to be destroyed in 1695 during the bombardment of Brussels by the French army under the command of Marshal Villeroy. Its reconstruction was entrusted to Guillaume De Bruyn, the city architect, commencing in 1698 and being completed in 1707. At the summit of its tall facade, marked with the seal of the baroque and of the Flemish decorative art, there initially stood an equestrian statue of Maximilian Emmanuel, Elector of Bavaria, by Marc De Vos le Vieux. This work, cut down by a hurricane, was replaced, in 1752, by an equestrian statue in copper of Charles of Lorraine, benefactor of the guild, created by the goldsmith and engraver André Simon. This new statue disappeared during the second invasion by the French, in 1794. A statue of the same Charles of Lorraine, created by the sculptor Jacquet, took its place on the building in 1854. It is still there today.

After the abolition of the guilds, the "Maisons des Brasseurs" passed into various hands. It even housed a café, in 1840. It was in 1951 that the brewers re-established their professional organisation there, restoring it to its former role. The old cellars were fitted out, from 1952, as a Brewery Museum *(C.B.B. - Museum)*. Here, is the brewing equipment used in the 18th century. The most modern techniques available for the manufacture of beer are displayed there. A summary of the "Belgian Beer Culture" in an historic context....

On the Grand Place in Brussels, in front of the Brewers' Hall, during the Belle Epoque.

THE BROTHERHOODS ("CONFRÉRIES") OF TODAY

For the profession:

• *Chevalerie du Fourquet des Brasseurs.*
Address : Maison des Brasseurs, Grand-Place
B-1000 Brussels.

• *Confrérie des Maîtres Brasseurs et Distillateurs de Wallonie.*
Contact : Jean Baudoux.
Address : 10, rue des Sorbiers B-5101 Erpent Namur

For the type of beer:

• *Confrérie de l'Ordre du Faro.*
Contact : André Libert.
Address : 38, avenue Bergmann Boîte 4.
B-1050 Brussels.

For one beer:

• *Confrérie des Chevaliers d'Aulne.*
Beer : *Abbaye d'Aulne.*
Contact : Mme Genny Meunier.
Address : 152, rue Bury B-6534 Gozée.

• *Confrérie Charles Quint du Val d'Heure.*
Beer : *Charles Quint.*
Contact : Serge Salmon.
Address : 76, rue de la Station B-5650 Walcourt.

• *Confrérie de la Double Enghien.*
Beer : *Double Enghien.*
Contact : Robert Wauters.
Address : 22, rue des Combattants
B-7850 Petit Enghien.

• *Confrérie de la Bière Godefroy.*
Beer : *Godefroy.*
Contact : Philippe Gourmet.
Address : 26, route du Christ B-6830 Bouillon.

• *Confrérie du Franc Thour Notre-Dame de Ciney.*
Beer : *Ciney.*
Contact : Raoul Fosseprez
Address : 3, avenue du Stade B-5590 Ciney.

• *Confrérie des Chaussons et de l'abbaye de la Moinette.*
Beer : *Moinette.*
Contact : Jacqueline Cambier.
Address : 11, rue de Frasnes B-7890 Ellezelles.

• *Jurade Princière de Chimay.*
Beer : *Chimay.*
Address : 4, Grand-Rue B-6460 Chimay.

• *Confrérie des Sossons d'Orvaulx à Orval.*
Beer : *Orval.*
Address : Pavillon du Tourisme, place Albert Ier
B-6820 Florenville.

• *Confrérie de la Gausalle de Rochefort.*
Beer : *Rochefort.*
Address : 9, rue de la Goletette B-5580 Rochefort.

• *Confrérie des Mougneus d'Vète Trêpe.*
Beer : *Saison 1900.*
Contact : Ninie Du Chenne.
Address : 34, rue de la Station B-1350 Orp Jauche.

• *Le Bon Métier des Brasseurs.*
Beer : *Jupiler.*
Contact : Ernest Chalseche.
Address : 7, avenue Mahiels B-4607 Feneus.

• *Ambassade du lapin à la bière.*
Beer : *Schwendi.*
Contact : Serge Leffineur.
Address : 15, place de Neuville B-5600 Neuville.

• *Confrérie de Roze Olifant.*
Beer : *Delirium Tremens.*
Contact : Albert Urbain.
Address : 124, Geraardsbergsteenweg B-9090 Melle.

• *Confrérie de la Marckloff.*
Beer : *Marchloff.*
Contact : Michel Trine.
Address : 115, rue du Comte d'Ursel B-6940 Durbuy.

The most famous citizen of Brussels, even the world, also wore the uniform of members of the Confrérie de l'ordre du Faro.
R. Laneau photo collection.

ON A STORMY PATH

Towards the end of the conflict generated by the Spanish Succession, which had extended the long series of wars seen in the 17th century, the Southern Netherlands found themselves once again plunged into an economic depression, and cut off from world commerce. The establishment, by the Treaty of Barrière (1715), of a customs tariff favouring the importation of products coming from Holland and England, the creation of new taxes; all of this was enough to cause further trouble. In 1717, the uprising of the Brussels trade organisations - and among them there were the brewers - was severely suppressed and lead to a reinforced hold on the Belgian provinces by the monarchic power. But even this did not prevent the principalities from preserving their particular traditional structures.

The accent was placed on the economy, especially during the second half of the 18th century. Agriculture and industry developed. Commerce was favoured. This return to a certain degree of prosperity entailed a rapid demographic growth. To the ends of this policy of recovery, the Empress Maria Theresia of Austria (1740-1789) showed some versatility in her government. In 1760, to remove the unfair competition which was represented by the seigniorial breweries, until then exempt from taxes, she ordered the destruction of all the seigniorial breweries on Frankish soil. Some brewers profited from this to win their independence as farmer-brewers. This was the case with Joseph Leroy, brewer for the seignior of Ghissegnies, in Western Hainaut. In 1769 he was able to create his own brewery, which survives today - the Dubuisson Brewery.

This growth was to be checked, however. The year 1789 arrived. While the Revolution exploded in Paris, contributing to the collapse of the Ancien Regime and to the abolition of feudal privileges, the measures taken by Joseph II of Austria against Belgian territory triggered the "Brabant Revolution". After the restoration of Austrian sovereignty, the Belgian provinces were contested between Austria and France, ending up under French domination. A hard period commenced, in the course of which they were to be stripped of their riches, and then to fall into disorganisation and misery. The terrible winter of 1795, and the shortages which followed it, fuelled the grave economic crisis of year III, bleeding the country dry.

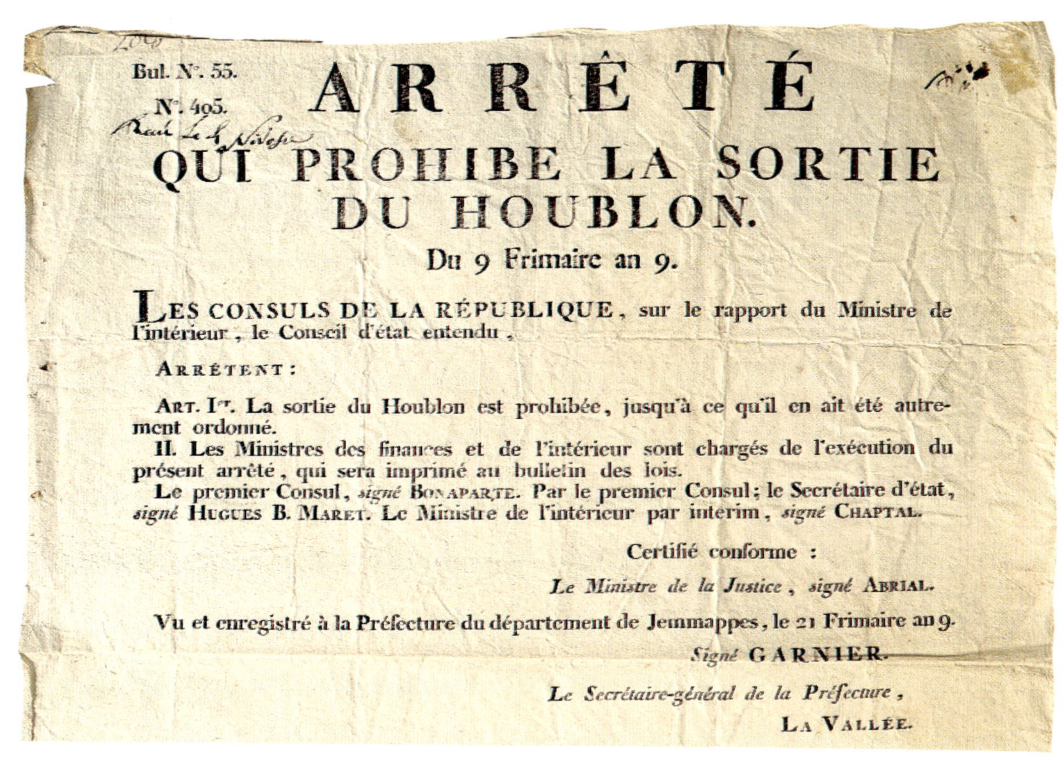

Bul. N°. 55.
N°. 405.

ARRÊTÉ
QUI PROHIBE LA SORTIE DU HOUBLON.

Du 9 Frimaire an 9.

LES CONSULS DE LA RÉPUBLIQUE, sur le rapport du Ministre de l'intérieur, le Conseil d'état entendu,

ARRÊTENT :

ART. Ier. La sortie du Houblon est prohibée, jusqu'à ce qu'il en ait été autrement ordonné.

II. Les Ministres des finances et de l'intérieur sont chargés de l'exécution du présent arrêté, qui sera imprimé au bulletin des lois.

Le premier Consul, *signé* BONAPARTE. Par le premier Consul; le Secrétaire d'état, *signé* HUGUES B. MARET. Le Ministre de l'intérieur par interim, *signé* CHAPTAL.

Certifié conforme :

Le Ministre de la Justice, signé ABRIAL.

Vu et enregistré à la Préfecture du département de Jemmappes, le 21 Frimaire an 9.

Signé GARNIER.

Le Secrétaire-général de la Préfecture,

LA VALLÉE.

For fear that the chaos of the Revolution should not affect the brewing industry, trade in raw materials was regulated, as here for hops, in 1800.

Although affected by these difficulties, the brewing sector does not seem to have suffered too much. A report in 1802, intended to inform the Paris government on the state of the economy in the Namur region in 1789, indicated "although beer is not exported outside the country, it is however consumed in considerable quantities, because beer is the principal, and it can also be said the only drink." And it added, after the Revolutionary troubles, "the brewery appears hardly to have suffered any change. It is in this branch of commerce, like all of those which tend to the first needs of life, that public events only have a minor influence." However they forget there that the ravages inherent in any war do not spare breweries, and that religious communities were forced to go into exile. In addition, the abbey brewers had to close their doors in 1797, ecclesiastical property being sold as nationally-owned property.

See Premonstratensian Abbeys page 18 etc.; Trappist Abbeys page 128 etc.

At the end of the 18th century, the more famous beers were the uytzet (see page 138), the white beer of Leuven, the beers of Diest, Hœgaarden, and Mechelen, as well as the faro of Brussels. Consumption of beer remained significant. The techniques of its manufacture had hardly evolved. The only notable progress was in 1760 when, thanks to Baverstock, the thermometer was introduced into brewing, and in 1784, when Richard invented his mercury saccharimeter.

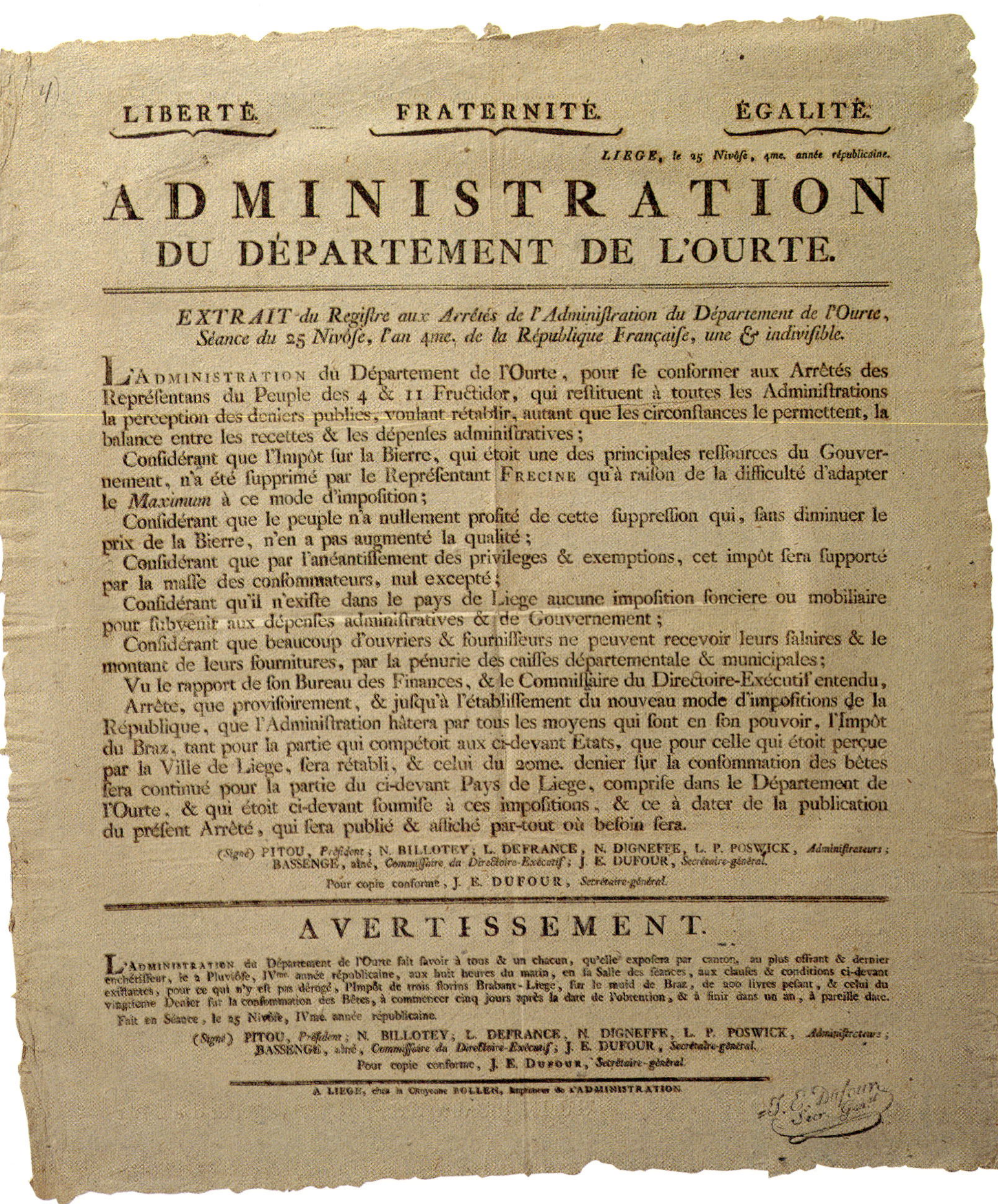

LIBERTÉ — FRATERNITÉ — ÉGALITÉ

LIEGE, le 25 Nivôse, 4me. année républicaine.

ADMINISTRATION
DU DÉPARTEMENT DE L'OURTE.

EXTRAIT du Registre aux Arrêtés de l'Administration du Département de l'Ourte, Séance du 25 Nivôse, l'an 4me. de la République Française, une & indivisible.

L'ADMINISTRATION du Département de l'Ourte, pour se conformer aux Arrêtés des Représentans du Peuple des 4 & 11 Fructidor, qui restituent à toutes les Administrations la perception des deniers publics, voulant rétablir, autant que les circonstances le permettent, la balance entre les recettes & les dépenses administratives;

Considérant que l'Impôt sur la Bierre, qui étoit une des principales ressources du Gouvernement, n'a été supprimé par le Représentant FRECINE qu'à raison de la difficulté d'adapter le *Maximum* à ce mode d'imposition;

Considérant que le peuple n'a nullement profité de cette suppression qui, sans diminuer le prix de la Bierre, n'en a pas augmenté la qualité;

Considérant que par l'anéantissement des privileges & exemptions, cet impôt sera supporté par la masse des consommateurs, nul excepté;

Considérant qu'il n'existe dans le pays de Liege aucune imposition fonciere ou mobiliaire pour subvenir aux dépenses administratives & de Gouvernement;

Considérant que beaucoup d'ouvriers & fournisseurs ne peuvent recevoir leurs salaires & le montant de leurs fournitures, par la pénurie des caisses départementale & municipales;

Vu le rapport de son Bureau des Finances, & le Commissaire du Directoire-Exécutif entendu,

Arrête, que provisoirement, & jusqu'à l'établissement du nouveau mode d'impositions de la République, que l'Administration hâtera par tous les moyens qui sont en son pouvoir, l'Impôt du Braz, tant pour la partie qui compétoit aux ci-devant Etats, que pour celle qui étoit perçue par la Ville de Liege, sera rétabli, & celui du 20me. denier sur la consommation des bêtes sera continué pour la partie du ci-devant Pays de Liege, comprise dans le Département de l'Ourte, & qui étoit ci-devant soumise à ces impositions, & ce à dater de la publication du présent Arrêté, qui sera publié & affiché par-tout où besoin sera.

(*Signé*) PITOU, *Président*; N. BILLOTEY; L. DEFRANCE, N. DIGNEFFE, L. P. POSWICK, *Administrateurs*; BASSENGE, aîné, *Commissaire du Directoire-Exécutif*; J. E. DUFOUR, *Secrétaire-général*.

Pour copie conforme, J. E. DUFOUR, *Secrétaire-général*.

AVERTISSEMENT.

L'ADMINISTRATION du Département de l'Ourte fait savoir à tous & un chacun, qu'elle exposera par canton, au plus offrant & dernier enchérisseur, le 2 Pluviôse, IVme année républicaine, aux huit heures du matin, en sa Salle des séances, aux clauses & conditions ci-devant existantes, pour ce qui n'y est pas dérogé, l'Impôt de trois florins Brabant-Liege, sur le muid de Braz, de 200 livres pesant, & celui du vingtieme Denier sur la consommation des Bêtes, à commencer cinq jours après la date de l'obtention, & à finir dans un an, à pareille date.

Fait en Séance, le 25 Nivôse, IVme. année républicaine.

(*Signé*) PITOU, *Président*; N. BILLOTEY; L. DEFRANCE, N. DIGNEFFE, L. P. POSWICK, *Administrateurs*; BASSENGE, aîné, *Commissaire du Directoire-Exécutif*; J. E. DUFOUR, *Secrétaire-général*.

Pour copie conforme, J. E. DUFOUR, *Secrétaire-général*.

A LIEGE, chez la Citoyenne BOLLEN, Imprimeur de l'ADMINISTRATION.

J. E. Dufour Secr. Gal

After the French annexation of the Belgian provinces and the country of Liège, "in order to provide for administrative and Government expenses", a tax was levied on beer, in 1795.

THE BEERS OF LIÈGE IN THE 18TH CENTURY

The renown of the beers of Liège was considerable and to a great extent went beyond the frontiers of the province, since it was transported as far as India. In *Délices du Pays de Liège*, Français Saumery wrote, "It is useless to praise the excellence of the beer: it is known in all places in the world. A prodigious quantity of barrels have been transported to the Indies for several years. The brewers in Liège are innumerable: and it is not a surprise. The children learn to suck beer with their milk. And when there is no nurse, who is normally the mother, beer takes their place.

"The poor and the wealthy, domestics and masters, children and parents, everyone makes it an ordinary drink: almost all the natives of the country prefer beer to the more mellow Burgundy...Beer which is made there is better than any which might be made in Europe, even according to foreigners."

Dark and generally brewed with spelt, of moderate cost and excellent flavour, the beer of Liège was of an incomparable quality.

LA MONEUSE

Brewed by the Blaugies Brewery, in Hainaut, the beer *La Moneuse* owes its name to an 18th century personage, at the same time highly colourful and formidable, one Antoine-Joseph Moneuse, who became illustrious for his exploits at the head of a band of brigands, the "Chauffeurs du Nord" ("Heaters of the North"), so named because they "heated" the feet of their victims on an open fire to make them confess where their money was hidden.

Robbery profited from the disorder which characterised the post-Revolutionary period. Armed bands ruled with terror in the country. Born in Marly, near Valenciennes, in 1768, Antoine-Joseph Moneuse was the son of a miller. His career as a bandit seems to have been revealed very early. But it was only in 1788 that he left his village and trace was lost ... before his "high deeds" made people talk of him. Attacks on stagecoaches, assaults on the person, attacks on farms and inns, all of this was accompanied by pillage, torture and murder. Such a career naturally led him to the scaffold! And so died the captain of the Chauffeurs du Nord, in Douai, on 18th June 1798.

SOME SIGNIFICANT DATES

• **1700:** Charles II, King of Spain, born in 1665, died without issue. By his will his heir was a grandson of the King of France Louis XIV: Philip Duke of Anjou, who became King of Spain under the name of Philip V.

• **1701-1713:** The War of Spanish Succession blew up, in the course of which Spain and France were opposed to those countries which refused the domination of the Bourbons over the Netherlands, that is to say England, the German Empire, and the United Provinces. In 1713, the Treaty of Utrecht put an end to the war. Losing some territory, the Southern Netherlands became a fief of the Habsburgs of Austria. With the exception of the enclave which constituted the Principality of Liège, the Belgian provinces covered the territory which is theirs today.

• **1744-1780:** Charles of Lorraine, brother-in-law of Maria Theresia, was Governor General of the Netherlands. Under his influence, Brussels really took on the rank of capital.

• **1745-1748:** The land became one of the theatres of operation in the War of Austrian Succession, and was occupied by the French (1745-1748).

• **1787:** Joseph II substituted for the division into provinces, nine areas, subdivided into districts. This reorganisation, which did not take into account local peculiarities, provoked the Brabant Revolution of 1789.

• **1790:** The states in general, reunited to Brussels, proclaimed the independence of the *United States of Belgium.*

• **1795:** Following its victory at Fleurus (1794) the French Republic annexed the Belgian provinces and the country of Liège. Austria ratified this annexation by the Treaty of Campoformio (1797)

THE GOLDEN AGE OF THE BREWERY

Annexed to France, Belgium was divided into nine departments, a split which took account neither of the linguistic frontiers, nor the borders of the former principalities. It was henceforth subjugated to the Laws of the Republic, and French was promoted as the sole official language there. This "allegiance" was not without its opponents, inspired principally by conscription and, as we have seen, by the anti-clericalism of the Revolutionary government. But from 1799, with the arrival in power of Napoléon Bonaparte, the country saw its industry develop and its market broaden. It was not long, however, before the foreign policy adopted by the Empire hindered the economy. It was only with Dutch sovereignty (1815) that a recovery began, on the initiative of King William I, very much in favour of a growth in the economy.

"Before the rest of the Continent, the Belgian regions experienced the beginnings of the Industrial Revolution. Financed by the major families of industrial or commercial origin, it was characterised by an increasing concentration and by a generalisation of modern processes, borrowed from England and perfected on the spot." In a few words, Marie-Thérèse Birsch summarised perfectly the industrial phenomenon which the Belgian brewery witnessed at the beginning of the 19th century.

The defeat of Napoleon and his army at Waterloo placed Belgian territory under Dutch sovereignty. The beer *Napoléon 1er*, brewed by GéVé, recalls on its label the monument commemorating the battle. Today this beer is brewed by the De Smedt Brewery, in Opwijk.

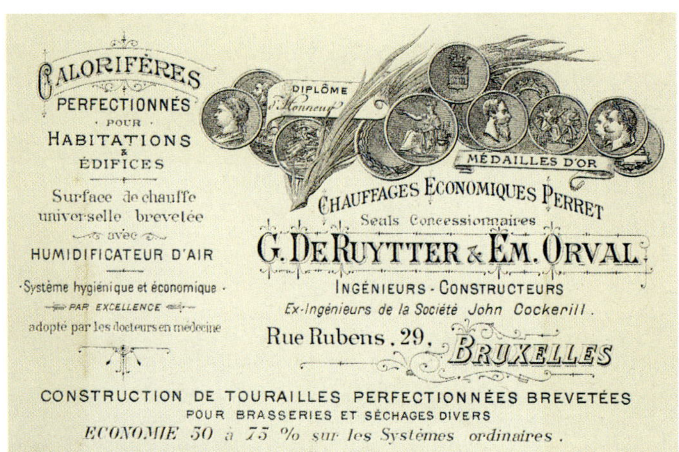

Belgian steel entered its industrial phase with John Cockerill. Engineers who had worked with him became builders of maltings.

In fact, the first country to know large breweries was England.

The Revolution in 1830 indeed created a breach in this impetus. The financial and economic crisis which followed the birth of the Belgian State caused enormous difficulties in the brewing world. Then there was a temporary improvement. And at the end of the 1830's it proved disastrous. The crisis took hold even more strongly. Industrial foundations would in fact only be assured after 1850, with the support of the banks and thanks to railways. It was likewise at this period that the extensive series of inventions began which would decide the physiognomy of modern Belgian brewing.

According to La Cambre, in 1856, the beer-drinking habit was very widespread in Belgium. Enormous quantities were made of this "very healthy, refreshing, and nutritive" beverage. The country, which counted some 4 million inhabitants, produced 900 million litres of it annually, which, having regard to exports, an insignificant amount, corresponded to an annual per capita consumption of more than 200 litres. But, as we will see, this expansion was accompanied by more or less latent "threats".

A tax system which slowed down progress

The Law of 1821, which introduced a new system of taxation, inevitably concerned the brewers. It establi-

On the Centenary of the Birth of Belgium, advertising took on a "Revolutionary" connotation...
L. Decruyenare collection.

The drawing by Cham (c. 1850) shows the arrival of the French at the Belgian customs.

shed, for beers, "a tax of 70 centièmes (cents) for each barrel (hectolitre) capacity of the tanks or other vessels serving to prepare the prime material in the brewing of beer". This regulation was amended by the Law of 2nd August 1822, which clarified the excise duty on beer manufactured in the kingdom. A duty was thus established according to the net capacity of the mash-tub.

This Law was restricting for manufacture, since the brewer could not, as they did in Germany, use two mash-tubs and one boiler, unless he was prepared to pay excise duty on such equipment. His concern was rather to limit the tax and often he put in amounts disproportionate to the size of the tank, which created innumerable technical problems. While in Germany, Austria, and Bohemia, the amount did not exceed 18 kilograms per hectolitre - the beer there gained in finesse - in Belgium, it reached 28 kilograms per hectolitre.

The 1822 Law thus provoked strong protest and criticism. It even incited brewers to participate in the Belgian Revolution against the Dutch regime which had introduced it. The first Belgian government, moreover, included three members of the Rodenbach family - they taxed coffee to compensate for the reduction in the tax on beer!

Nevertheless, in 1883, a campaign was undertaken by the brewers, in an attempt to modify it. This led to the Law of 20th August 1885. Tax was henceforth paid on the quantity of flour declared, at the rate of 0.10 Francs per kilogram. This was in a way a liberating Law for the brewery, especially as following the Law of 1822 it was impossible to produce bottom-fermented beers, since one could not obtain a dick-maische.

In this struggle to improve the fiscal regime, Benoni Bauters, Secretary of the Ghent Society of Brewers, and Minister Tack (of the Tack Brewery in Kortrijk), played a particularly active role. It was, in fact, thanks to their intervention that the administration finally adopted the scientific hydrometer, in 1889. But the Law of 1885 remained imperfect. And the brewers never ceased to complain about it. They nevertheless had the choice of working under the regime of the Law of 1822,

An illustrious figure of his time: P. Tack, a member of the Chamber of Representatives.

or that of 1885. In 1894, some 11 per cent of brewers continued to comply with the older Law.

The threat of the monopoly

Brewers were therefore very anxious about the future reserved for them. In particular a Limited Company for the Development of Breweries in Belgium was planned, and only waited for the agreement of the Government to finalise it. And in 1836 the Brussels brewers addressed a petition to the King that he not approve its memorandum and articles. "The freedom of industry is the capacity guaranteed to everyone to carry out all his industrial means without injuring the rights or means of others. It has as an adversary the monopoly, which tends to place in the hands of a small number of individuals, all the industrial means, in such a way that, more powerful than others, these individuals mercilessly crush all those who offend them [...]." The creation of a "Central Brewery", with thirty five million Francs at that time was an awesome prospect.

But the idea of the monopoly took its path. And two years later the brewers of Leuven addressed a letter to their colleagues in the rest of the country, informing them that a limited partnership was going to open a brewery and that it was necessary to fear the pretensions of its owners. "They openly announce that a monopoly is their aim, privilege their object, and that above all they propose to build, on the ruins of the old breweries, factories established according to a new system in Belgium." Beside this disturbing competition, they intended to oppose exemptions from the Law governing the excise on beer, which was being requested by this company, which had introduced a severe imbalance into the brewing industry.

Porcelain card dedicated to the Society of Belgian Brewers, in Leuven.
"It is not only the beer of Leuven which competitors claim to counterfeit, it is every type of beer which they want to imitate and to replace." The disquiet of Leuven brewers was great, the threat of monopoly hovered over their future.

The advent of bottom-fermentation

At the beginning of the 1880's, Belgian breweries exclusively produced top-fermented beers. They were, at the same time, very numerous and very different, but of an inconsistent quality. This lack of regularity favoured foreign, notably German, bottom-fermentation beers, which "invaded" the country, and which were achieving increased favour among consumers.

It was within such a context that, in 1886, the Great Kœkelberg Brewery, the first Belgian brewery specialising in bottom-fermentation, was created. "It was at first only a manner of fighting against a fashion which rendered us dependants of Bohemia and Germany, but as a result the young brewery captured the sympathies of the public, not by nationalist fervour, but by taste. And not only Belgian distinctions confirmed this success. Kœkelberg did not hesitate to go to Munich even to solicit the votes of the experts, in 1899 taking the Gold Medal and the Certificate of Honour which henceforth created for them all the obligations of great renown." Such was the motivation of the company as explained in *Le Soir*, on the occasion of the fortieth anniversary of the brewery, in 1927.

Its first products, a pale Bock beer and a dark beer of the Munich type, were launched in 1887, in the Café Continental, on the Place de Brouckère in Brussels. Success was immediate. But it was necessary to wait some years yet before the sale of fine beers was sufficient to guarantee the firm its position and, in the meantime, it had also to make a table beer, by the name of Petite Bavière.

Another celebrated brewery which undertook the manufacture of bottom-fermented beers was La Vignette, in Leuven.

The fight against fakes

With industrial growth, certain beer makers, avid for money, were tempted to have recourse to cure-alls, even unmentionable procedures. Others were also forced to do so, to maintain a competitive edge on these forgers. And these practices became more and more frequent. Among them was the use of liquorice, various foaming agents, and so on. "Any products which only find their name among charlatans," declared the President of the General Association of Brewers in 1895. Certain substances were used to improve the beer or to give it special properties: Indian berry to make the beer more intoxicating and more vigorous, molasses to colour the porter, quassia amara and wormwood to replace the hops, Guinea pepper or grains of Paradise to lift an insipid beer or one too weak. An excessive addition of lime served to remedy distortions. A contribution of sulphuric acid transformed a new beer into an old beer. And finally there was the use of salicylic acid, in contravention of the regulations.

The beer merchants themselves were customers of "scandalous fiddles", as La Cambre explained in 1856 in his famous treatise. He denounced the beer merchants of Brussels "who demanded excessively hopped beers to mix with weak beers, and to hide the fraud they added sugar or molasses, which allowed them to sell small beers as strong, and they thus obtained enormous profits, while the brewers often lost out."

It was not until the end of the century that the State took measures to prevent such abuses. There was the Law of 4th August 1890, relating to the falsification of alimentary commodities; the Royal Decree of 22nd June 1891, relating to the organisation of a service to inspect the manufacture and trading of alimentary commodities; the Royal Decree of 21st September 1894, specifying the attributions of inspectors. Following beers, sales equipment was henceforth the object of careful examination. All apparatus in prohibited metal or not carrying the name of its manufacturer resulted in a heavy fine. Finally, and significantly, the Royal Decree of 30th December 1896 prohibited the use of saccharine and

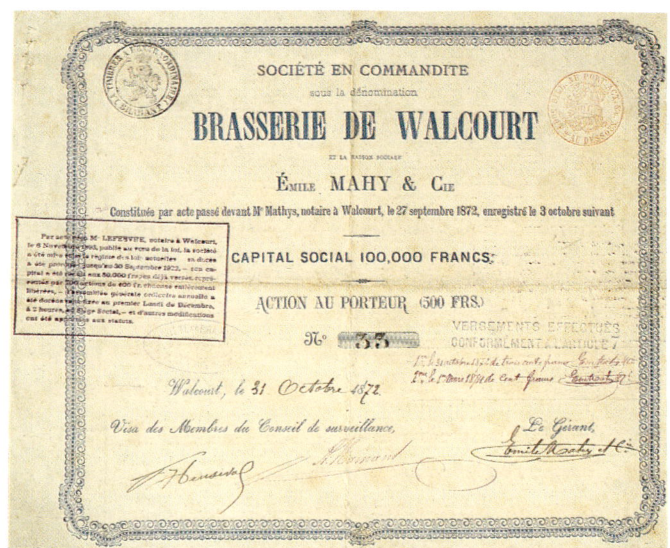

SOCIÉTÉ EN COMMANDITE

sous la dénomination

BRASSERIE DE WALCOURT

Émile MAHY & Cie

Constituée par acte passé devant Mr Mathys, notaire à Walcourt, le 27 septembre 1872, enregistré le 3 octobre suivant

CAPITAL SOCIAL 100,000 FRANCS.

ACTION AU PORTEUR (500 FRS.)

No 35

VERSEMENTS EFFECTUÉS CONFORMÉMENT A L'ARTICLE 7

Walcourt, le 31 Octobre 1872.

Visa des Membres du Conseil de surveillance,

Le Gérant,

Share Certificate of the Walcourt Brewery (1872).

other sweeteners in the preparation of beers. Henceforth only proper sugars were authorised (saccharose, lucose, invert sugars, etc.).

At the turn of the century

Despite these tribulations, the figures seemed promising: 2,535 breweries in 1869, 2,625 in 1886, 3,148 in 1898....; 11,383,000 hectolitres in 1893, 12,572,000 in 1896, 14,046,000 in 1899... Several factors caused the multiplication of enterprises: the increase in population, the improvement in its well-being, as well as the rapid technical and scientific progress to which beer would henceforward owe its biological stability and its better quality. All this combined with legislation which, after 1860, was favourably disposed to limited companies.

Furthermore, Belgium occupied an important place on the world brewery map. For 1897-98, German

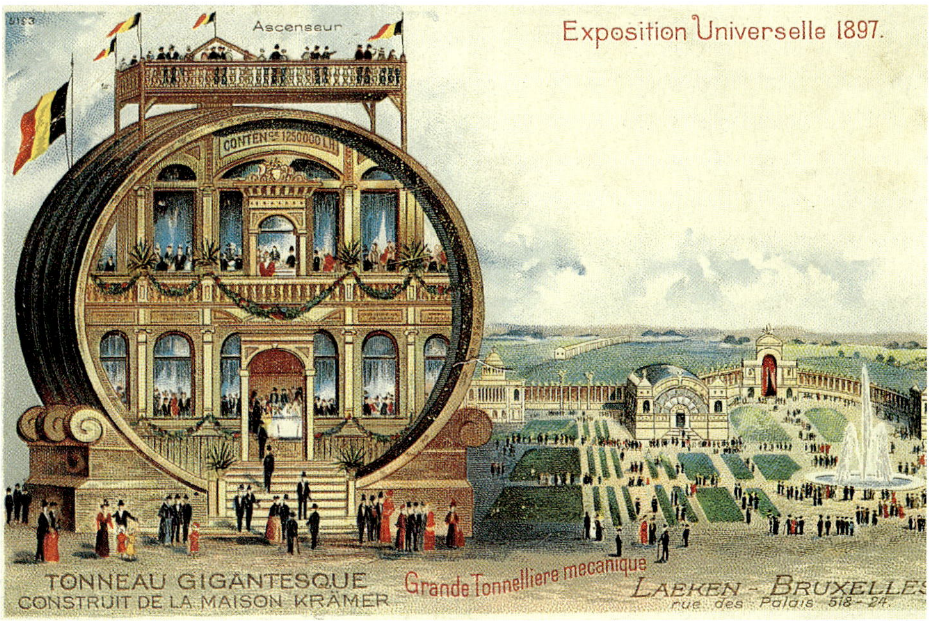

In the context of the Universal Exhibition of Brussels (1897), the stand of the Kramer cooperage in Laeken.

statistics attributed to it second place for consumption per inhabitant, with 169.2 litres, behind Bavaria (235.8 litres). The beers most consumed in the country were then the acid beers of Brussels, the beers of Leuven (white and Peeterman beers), the dark beers of Mechelen, the white beer of Hœgaarden, and the beer of Liège, made on a basis of barley, spelt, wheat, and oats. An important competition which took place in Amsterdam in 1895, had shown that the majority of these beers were ideally suited to export and that they could be enjoyed outside Belgium for their quality and their flavour. Brewers reckoned a great deal on exhibitions to promote their products. 1894 saw the Antwerp Universal Exhibition where breweries and maltings were well represented. The two industries were symbolised by an imposing monument, with a surface area of 120 square metres, representing, at its centre, a brewery worker holding a fork; cherubs and brewery implements were arranged around it. Three years later, the Brussels Universal Exhibition once again highlighted beer. The Brewery section was a great success. The interior designer Édouard Govaerts made its entrance portico, Henri Baes the murals, on the manufacture of beer, and the painter and stained-glass maker Contini the superb window showing the evolution of the brewery, by science, the press and the associations.

But all this, was it enough to guarantee the Belgian brewing industry a happy future? The shadows were many at the end of the 19th century. Firstly there were the co-operatives. According to some, their members were "tax evaders". It is true the brewers had good reasons for being disturbed by the importance taken by co-operative companies, which, more and more, encroached upon their domain: 311 co-operative companies in 1894, 1,128 in 1898... To combat their power, certain brewers were forced to acquire, by purchase or lease, real property housing the best cafés, because once in the places they succeeded in imposing their products on the inn-keepers guaranteeing their sale. Sometimes the strategy failed: it happened, in fact, that a co-operative proposed to the café-owner that he supply him with beer, at lower cost, and the café-owner moved.

On 20th March 1899, the General Association of Brewers presented a petition to the legislative chamber, to draw their attention to these companies, who from co-operatives of consumers, created to help workers, had become "veritable co-operatives of capitalists", because many were those which profited from their statutes. The object of this action was to obtain a revision of the Law of 18th May 1873 on co-operative companies.

Another reason for disquiet was the increase in imports of foreign, notably German beers. 135,000 hectolitres were imported in 1898, 140,000 in the following year! After the period of commercial treaties, which had begun in 1861, and had generated tax reductions and allowances, Belgium was turned, from 1879, towards a protectionist policy. The introduction of import duties and the increase of taxes had dealt a severe blow to the economy.

This poster created at the end of the 19th century for beer of the Munich type from the Kœkelberg Brewery represents the symbol of the city of Munich, the *Münchner Kindl*. R. Desmecht collection.

THE ROYAL FAMILY AND BEER

Even if one did not know the connections between Léopold I and beer, one could say that the Belgian Royal Family always maintained a good relationship with the brewing world. Léopold never refused to drink the occasional glass of beer. Albert I's preference was for Brussels beers (faro, lambic, gueuze). His wife, Bavarian by origin, did not enjoy Belgian beers so much. Today (Baudouin I having given the example), the Royal Family avoids being seen with glass in hand.

At the Trade Fair in Brussels in 1920, King Albert I congratulates the agent of Ind Coope Brewery for the introduction of Ind Coope beers in Belgium.

The Royal Family was used as an advertising emblem by the Léopold Brewery and by the great Atlas Brewery (Queen Astrid). A beer merchant represented Baudouin as the Duke of Brabant.

SOME SIGNIFICANT DATES

- **1798:** conscription was introduced by France.
- **1808:** the cultivation of sugar beet was introduced in Belgium. Refineries were set up.
- **1814:** the allied armies entered Belgium.
- **1815:** after the Battle of Waterloo and the defeat of the Napoleonic army, the Congress of Vienna ratified the incorporation of Belgium into the Kingdom of the Netherlands, under the sovereignty of William I. Luxembourg was made a Grand Duchy, and became a personal fief of King William I, within the framework of the German Confederation.
- **1821:** a Law dated 12th July, determined the foundations of a system of taxation in the Kingdom of the Netherlands from 1822.
- **1822:** King William I created the "Société Générale or General Company for the Development of National Industry".
- **1830:** on 25th August, insurrection occurred in Brussels. This patriotic Revolution lead to the independence of Belgium which, in January 1831 was declared perpetually neutral. The new State, which reunited the Belgian provinces (except Liège) according to their 1830 frontiers, was established as a constitutional monarchy.
- **1831:** on 21st July, Léopold of Saxe-Coburg-Gotha became King of the Belgians, under the name of Léopold I.
- **1850:** the Belgian National Bank was created. It replaced the Société Générale as "State Cashier", and received the right to issue banknotes.
- **1861:** a commercial treaty was signed with France, inaugurating a free trade policy.
- **1865:** on the death of his father, Léopold II came to the throne of Belgium.

Drawing done in 1931 by Raymond Van Doren. To the left, Léopold II; to the right Léopold I; in the centre the future Léopold III.

SOME STAGES IN THE HISTORY OF THE BREWERY

• **Around 1800:** the development of the steam engine brought its power to the brewery and served to heat the boilers.

• **1802:** the floor kiln was used for the first time in malting. It facilitated the drying of the malt.

• **1805:** Richardson's saccharimeter was used in brewing.

• **1831:** The Company of Brussels Brewers was founded, with the object of "promoting and protecting Brussels breweries".

• **1833:** Payen and Persoz managed to isolate the diastase of malt, by precipitation of alcohol.

• **1843:** the Guillaume tavern, on the rue du Musée in Brussels, served the first English beers.

• **1845:** J.C.Jacobsen brought back the yeast for bottom-fermented beer to Copenhagen, from the Seldmeyer Zum Spaten Brewery in Munich.

• **1848:** the cooking of beer with steam was practised for the first time in the Velten Brewery in Marseilles (France).

• **Around 1850:** the scientists Rohart and La Cambre began to study the chemical phenomena which accompanied the manufacture of beer.

• **1850:** Munich beer was served for the first time at Putt, in Ixelles, and the Café de Munich, on the rue d'Arenberg in Brussels.

• **1860:** Bertholet isolated invertase from the extract of beer yeast.

• **Around 1870:** the use of the steam engine became widespread.

• **1873:** the electric motor was invented. It was applied to brewing.

• **1876:** Louis Pasteur published his *"Studies on Beer"*, the result of his researches, in Lille, in 1854. They concerned fermentation. On 13th March 1873, the scientist filed his patent application to apply his processes to the manufacture of beer.

• **1880:** an International Congress of Brewers was held in Brussels.

• **1885:** Christian Hansen, from Denmark, introduced the use of pure yeast in brewing.

• **1886:** C. Hansen and Kuhla created the first apparatus for the propagation of yeast in the brewery.

• **1889:** the milling of grain, which until then had been traditionally done by means of the mill-wheel, henceforth used cylinders of iron or iron covered with porcelain.

• **1894:** a Royal Decree prohibited the addition of antiseptics to beer.

• **1895:** a Law established an import duty on malts and yeasts from abroad.

• **1897:** Buchner isolated the alcoholic diastase (the enzyme responsible for fermentation) of yeast.

• **1897:** the first co-operative brewery, Le Progrés, was created in Jolimont by the Belgian Workers' Party. Designed by the Van Hœgaarden brothers, engineer-constructors in Blanc-Misseron (Nord), this brewery housed the most sophisticated equipment. It very soon had a branch in Bracquegnies (same designers).

The success of this brewery was dazzling: 5,996 hl during the eight months of its first year, 17,313 hl in 1898, 20,073 hl in 1900, 35,701 hl in 1904, and 54,193 hl in 1909.

• **1899:** the General Association of Belgian Brewers *(see page 82)* authorised George Maw Johnson (see page 190) to insert at the head of the Le Petit Journal du Brasseur: "Agreed organ of the Association of Belgian Brewers, for the publication of its official communications".

Steam engine in the Slaghmuylder Brewery in Ninove, in the machine hall, today converted into a museum.

A FAMOUS BREWERY

The brewery *La Vignette* assumed its name from an old Benedictine convent which belonged to its founders. The enterprise, founded in 1831 by Renier Hambrouck in Leuven had, in order to face up to the economic difficulties of the time, to transform itself into a more powerful company, Les Brasseries Belges (1836). The famous engineer La Cambre had drawn up the plans of the plant and chose its brewery equipment. But crisis challenged the company. In 1844 it was taken over by Renier Hambrouck, François Coppens, and Martin Van der Haert, three of its founders, under the name of "Hambrouck, Van der Haert and Company". The company name was then changed with successive managements: "Van Kelecom and Company, limited partnership" (1871), "Lallemand and Company" (1875), "Eugène Bauchau and Company, partnership limited by shares" (1877), and "Michel and André Bauchau and Company, simple limited partnership" (1925).

It was in the "reign" of Eugène Bauchau that the business grew. The most modern techniques and equipment were used there, both for the mill and the brewery. But with the tragic events that befell Leuven in 1914, the company was to a great extent destroyed, some of the staff taken prisoner, and the equipment requisitioned. The reconstruction which followed the war was only completed in 1924. A drum maltings, erected by the Skoda Company of Pilsen, commenced operation that same year.

The brewery was taken over by Stella Artois before 1937.

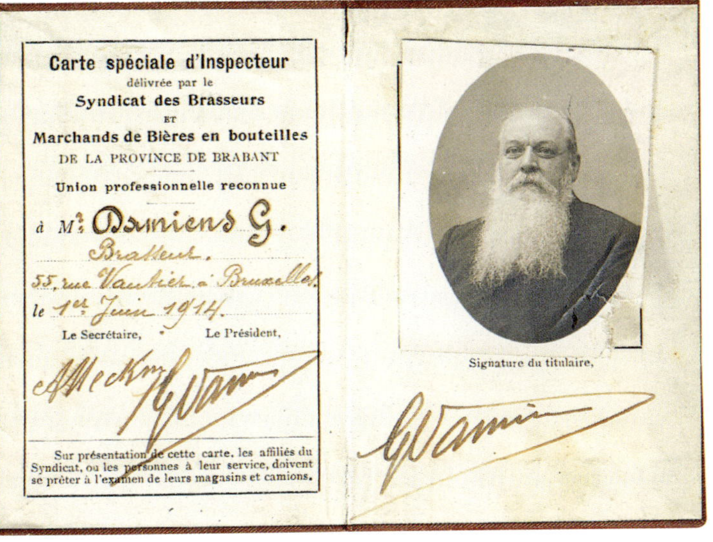

Carte spéciale d'Inspecteur
délivrée par le
Syndicat des Brasseurs
ET
Marchands de Bières en bouteilles
DE LA PROVINCE DE BRABANT

Union professionnelle reconnue

à Mr Damiens G.
Brasseur.
55, rue Vautier à Bruxelles
le 1er Juin 1914.

Le Secrétaire, Le Président,

Sur présentation de cette carte, les affiliés du Syndicat, ou les personnes à leur service, doivent se prêter à l'examen de leurs magasins et camions.

Signature du titulaire,

A GREAT BELGIAN BREWING FAMILY

Joseph-Henri Damiens, born in Brussels in 1805, took over the brewery of his father-in-law Antoine Keymolen, on his death in 1832: it was the Saint Hubert Brewery in Ixelles. Having in 1859 acquired a vast piece of land near the zoological gardens (Parc Léopold), he moved the brewery there and then named it the "Brasserie Léopold", in honour of the first Belgian sovereign. With his death in 1864, the business remained in the hands of the family until 1962.

Among the six children of Joseph-Henri Damiens and Jeanne-Antoinette Keymolen, Georges (1847-1932) also left his mark in the history of Belgian brewing. In his father's footsteps, he managed the family brewery with great talent, and was among the first to embark upon bottom-fermentation. Thanks to him, George Maw Johnson made his debut in Belgium *(see page 190)*. In fact the Brasserie Léopold housed his first laboratory. Beside his work as a brewer, George Damien stood out for his deeds in the service of corporate life.

It was his son, Edmond (1881-1939) who succeed him as Chairman of the Board of Directors of Brasserie Léopold. His role in defence of corporate discipline was no less. But he became famous above all for creating the Consortium, participating in the sorting out of breweries after the Great War, and contributing to the growth of quality bottom-fermented beers. Founder of the National Institute of Fermentation Industries of Brussels, he also took on numerous responsibilities within employers', workers', and company organisations.

His son, Pierre (1887-1952) retook the brewer's torch, himself followed by his son Georges (1911-1962). The latter indeed presided over The Léopold Brewery, but also the Nouvelle Brasserie de la Couronne ("New Crown Brewery") in Uccle, the Brasserie du Lac ("Lake Brewery") in Bruges and various other companies.

The pre-1900 economic crisis led breweries to finance cafés and café-owners to become owners of their bars. In return they required exclusive sales of their beers. Inspectors ensured compliance with the contract.

THE BREWERY IN CRISIS

This engraving, an extract from the *Globe Illustré*, dated 23rd January 1887, bears witness, through the Ghent weavers' strike, to the social malaise which dominated the era. Beer won its followers.

On the threshold of the 20th century, the situation in the Belgian brewery began to deteriorate. Circumstances were no better for other industries. Far from being a carefree era, as one tends to think, the Belle Époque saw protests and strikes. The considerable economic growth which the country had known, under the stimulus of a free trade policy, had not been accompanied by measures allowing the prevention of social problems inherent in an industrial acceleration of such a scale. Thus, while the master brewers benefited from the economic leap, the workers continued to experience enormous difficulties in their lives.

Furthermore, the brewing world suffered from several factors. First and not least was its division into more than 3,000 breweries, while some 1,000 would have been sufficient to cover the needs of the population. The record figure was achieved in 1907, with 3,387 breweries! The following year an article in *Le Petit Journal du Brasseur*, devoted to Walloon mining said, "after the formidable development of the industry which followed the War of 1870, the breweries here pushed on as if by magic and until recent years their number only increased. However the industry declined [...]. The means of production of all these breweries was beyond proportion to the needs of consumption and competition arose, dreadful, ridiculous, [...]."

It was inevitable that the same multiplicity led to fierce competition. This resulted in over-production. For example, the Brussels brewery of Wielmans-Ceuppens, which occupied second place in 1902, with 504,360 kg, rose to first position in 1905 with 2,264,800 kg, increasing to 2,759,000 kg in 1908. Thus an excess of production occurred without relation to consumption which anyway between 1905 and 1910 suffered a slight decline.

Influencing the sale price of beer, downwards, "the rush to increase production at all costs" rendered it difficult to achieve the profits relied on. Business accordingly became less profitable, as overheads did not cease to grow until 1914, especially under the effect of company laws and new insurance costs.

There was a need to respond to this competition, which was so disastrous for the breweries. And attempts were made in this direction. In 1909, the brewers of Brussels agreed to adopt a common policy of loyalty. They fixed the tariffs for malting and for finishing beer, regulated credit to clients, etc. However that may be, competition only benefited more major enterprises, notably in the regions of Antwerp and Brabant. Certain small breweries were forced to close.

At the end of the 19th century and the beginning of the 20th century, employers were accustomed to distribute tokens to their workers, permitting them to drink beers.

A remedy: central breweries?

It was in union that some thought they would find a solution to the crisis. The appeal made to the brewers, in 1901, by Louis Van den Hulle, Director of the Institut Supérieur de Brasserie in Ghent, is still well known. "Unite in an association, for it is only in that way that you will have the power to overcome. Group together. It is only in grouping that the remedy exists. Follow the social movement. It is the reign of large capital and common endeavour which is beginning, but individual efforts are nothing and just a waste of time. [...] If brewers had been content modestly and gradually to follow social evolution, in doing away with existing abuses, in reducing overheads, the brewing industry would still be flourishing at the present time and it always would be, since the needs are there, and consumption tends steadily to increase." And further on, "Get rid of your old breweries, make a central brewery which will serve all your clientele, change your method of sale, reduce your overheads, and above all do good trade, and I promise you complete success and an unassailable position. [...] The creation of different brewing associations will achieve victory over all the obstacles which might present themselves on your route, but unfortunately what paralyses at the moment is the lack of confidence which members have one among the others."

"The grouping together of the brewers of one region or one locality in one central brewery serving all the clientele of the associates will have the effect, on the one hand of "a notable reduction in the sale price of the beer, maintaining sufficient profit for the associates", and on the other hand, "an impeccable beer, always good, in summer and in winter, to the great advantage of the consumer."

This plan, which aroused lively reaction among small brewers, persisted throughout the first decade of the 20th century. Indeed the prosperity of the great English and American breweries went along with this, but would it be the same in Belgium and in France? "The absorption or disappearance of thousands of small and medium-sized family breweries, sometimes patriarchal, from Franco-Belgian lands, is it really to be desired? [...] From the social and political point of view, the disappearance of small industry will be an irreparable loss," affirmed G.M.Johnson, in December 1911. And on the eve of war, the question remained unanswered.

The keen interest in bottom-fermented beers

In 1900, another blow to the brewing industry was the campaign on the part of the French wine-growers to substitute wine for beer in daily consumption. Indeed, their target was the North of France, but the Belgian neighbour was affected, especially as, to achieve their ends, any means was acceptable: prices were slashed to render wine, until now a luxury product, available to all. Aggressive and even libellous talk was the order of the day. The image which they gave to beer was that of a drink which was weak, or adulterated, even poisonous. The affair of arsenic allegedly being added to beers which then exploded in Britain, supported their argument. And the "war" was to some extent won. Wine replaced beer at meals, and the latter took the rank of refreshment.

This advertising post card (c. 1900) of the Brussels firm G. Baron, importer of French wines, praises the merits of wine as opposed to beer.

Despite the difficulties, some breweries did not hesitate to take part in exhibitions abroad. And they met with success there. Thus the brewer Damiens was awarded a Diploma of Honour in Milan in 1906.

This change of role came to be favoured by the vogue for bottom-fermented beers. Relatively low import duties allowed foreign breweries, above all German, to establish their beers in Belgium. The Belgian brewers were disarmed. On 17th November 1905, the supplement to Le Petit Journal du Brasseur gave them the following advice: "Bottom-fermented beers gain ground every day. The small brewer should fight against this invasion, since his top-fermented beer, as good as it may be, no longer suffices for all tastes. Many a brewer feels constrained to sell bottom-fermented beer in the bar which is his property. He does not profit from it, and even this each day reduces the sale of his beer to it. The brewer who has an eye open to the future, who will march in front, should he remain impassive, his arms crossed, before this invasion into his domain of bottom-fermented beers, be they brewed in his country or should they come from abroad? No, he should take action, since the remedy is at his door. If the sales outlet, the science, and the capital, are lacking to him to build a bottom-fermentation brewery, he should procure it himself at a cost price allowing him to resell with profit.

"[...] It is only the first step which costs! And it should be said here. Reach an agreement with a famous brewery and, in your interest, give preference to a foreign brewery making a beer of a special type which answers all the requirements. Assure yourself of sales exclusivity for this beer in your country. Thus you will yourself be a supplier of bottom-fermented beer. If later its sale increases and you have created a sufficient clientele for this type of beer, you may try, with greater chance of success, to make bottom-fermented beer yourself. Thus you guarantee the future of your brewery for your descendants."

Certain breweries therefore embarked on bottom-fermentation, and this was effectively a success. One of the most significant examples was that of Hæcht, who with 325,180 kg occupied thirty fifth place in 1902, the year when it changed from top-fermentation to bottom-fermentation. It took 12th place in 1905, with 912,800 kg, the seventh place in 1908, with 1,220,700 kg. But these bottom-fermented beers, could they rival German and Austrian beers? The Grande Brasserie de Kœkelberg-lez-Bruxelles was at the heart of the contest, with its Bock, Pilsen, and Munich Hahnenbräu. The analysis of these beers, carried out by Henri van Lær and Albert Bergé, in 1903, showed that they presented "the characteristics of the best of similar products imported into Belgium." Besides that, they had the advantage "of being brewed on site, of not suffering from the transport to which foreign beers are subject, and by the economy of freight, import duties, and the costs of an intermediary, of costing much less."

Of course, the Munich brewers took offence at Munich-type beers being brewed in Belgium. They even took legal action against the Belgian brewers. And these were dismissed. "It hardly appears possible for us to remove from the public consumer the habit of asking for a "Munich" to indicate a drink of deep colour and to distinguish it from pale-coloured "Pilsen"," one read in *Le Brasseur Belge*, of 31st May 1912. The title "Munich beer" was no longer the monopoly of the brewers in Munich. It had lost the meaning of its provenance and had become a generic denomination.

A severe problem: gravity

To withstand the competition, national or foreign, and to be able to "reduce" the sale price of the beer, numerous were those who gradually reduced its gravity. In 1908, for example, the beers sold in more than a half of the bars in Wallonia did not attain 2°. The consumer did not always respond favourably, and a slump was noticeable in sales of this type of beer. Special beers continued to be favoured.

In order to check the tendency, it was necessary to impose a minimum gravity. Before then no country had taken this sort of measure. From 1906 to 1913 studies were undertaken which, at first, aroused strong opposition, then ended by gathering the brewers around a proposal which was as follows: to fix a minimum degree of gravity of 3.5° for beers delivered to cafés (the plan did not concern beers not sold in public), and to prevent any fraud, exercise strict controls in taking samples at the publican's premises.

For the same reason, regional experiments were made to raise the quality of beer. It was thus that in 1908 the Union of Brewers for the improvement of Liège beers was created. The aim of this association was to "regulate the gravity of beers for sale in bars, under a common marque to be determined, "the permissible gravities being 3.5°, 4°, and 4.5°, with a tolerance of 1/10 of a degree, with a check to be carried out each month on a number of samples to be fixed by a committee of the Union. Likewise, in 1910, the Union of Charleroi Brewers for the improvement of local beers launched an appeal to drinkers of beer, urging them to ask in cafés for beers from the Union of Brewers: "Why do you continue to drink foreign beers, sometimes harmful to health, or beers from this country with a laughable gravity, when the Union's plaque assures you in a formal manner of the gravity and the purity of our beers.

"Almost all the brewers in our region are part of the group and can supply beers of a gravity, guaranteed and controlled, which never falls below 3.5°."

Other causes of dissatisfaction

Elsewhere, the situation was hardly brighter. From their side, the maltsters organised themselves to face up to foreign imports. In 1902 they ran a campaign to obtain an increase in import duties on malt and a regulation of the use of maize and sugar in brewing. Their presence at the Liège Universal Exhibition (1905) allowed them to make known their major problem. "The malting industry has a great future before it [...]. Gradually competition will grow between brewers, they will have more and more need of their capital to augment their sales or to keep their clientele. Given the present tendencies of the industry, one can foresee the day when the average brewery will prefer to buy its malts from a maltster than to commit its capital to building maltings and to stock-piling

This enamelled plaque from 1908 was put up on café walls in Liège, when the gravity of beer was guaranteed.
R. Desmecht collection.

grain. There will be no more, to manufacture their malt themselves, than the very large brewers, with very considerable capital, and small brewers in the country, who have plenty of growers among their clients." (*Le Petit Journal du Brasseur*, 10th November 1905). A greater publicity campaign and the desire to make a malt superior to the average, permitted the hastening of this process. Unfortunately, there remained much to be done.

An equal concern to improve production seemed to be the solution to the hop growing question. Organised by the General Association of Belgian Brewers, the Expo-Bourse of hops, barley, and indigenous winter barley, which took place in Brussels in October 1906, showed that brewers had much to gain from an improvement in indigenous farming, and that growers were interested in increasing the quality of their products so that the brewers ceased to be beholden to foreigners.

Belgian hops were blamed for an abundance of seeds, due to "the non-observance of regulations by Belgian growers, above all those in the districts of Poperinge, as regards the ban on male plants. The pollen which the wind removes, as a fine dust, from male plants, fertilises the female plants - it is the flower of the female plant which forms the hops for the brewer - and thus produces an abundance of seeds, which considerably increase the weight and the volume of the harvest, but which diminish the finesse and the relative richness of the hops from a brewing point of view." (*Le Petit Journal du Brasseur*, 1899). Another reproach against Belgian production was the great proportion of stalks and leaves, due to careless harvesting. Therefore Belgian brewers preferred the hops from Saaz or Bavaria, more in compliance with the regulations.

The great exhibitions

Against a background of crisis, breweries nevertheless experienced some happier times, especially with the help of numerous exhibitions which marked the first years of the 20th century. Belgian beer appeared there, was enjoyed, and imposed its image on a European scale. This series of events was of course inaugurated by the Paris Universal Exhibition of 1900. All the Belgian brewers occupied a huge pavilion, of elegant appearance, fashioned in wood with an ornate pediment. The Flemish tavern which it housed attracted a veritable throng of beer fans.

In 1905 the Universal Exhibition, which was held in Liège, provided the setting for an International Competition of Beers and a National Competition for the improvement of Belgian beers (see page 88). One of the centres of interest in the brewery section was the stand of the community of Belgian maltsters, designed by a Bruges architect, M. Delacenserie, who is known notably for the railway station in Antwerp. This stand, with a height of 9.5 metres, held crystal bottles containing samples of malt. The following year there were two international exhibitions for food, brewing, wine, and liqueurs, one in Antwerp, in the gardens of the Cercle Royal Artistique, and the other in Namur, in the Kursaal, by the River Meuse. Among the exhibitors in Namur was the brewery and maltings des Carrières de Marbre, located in Bouge-lez-Namur and famous for its huge cellars and cold rooms which covered some four hectares. In 1907 a similar exhibition was held again in Antwerp, and was the occasion for an International Competition of Beers.

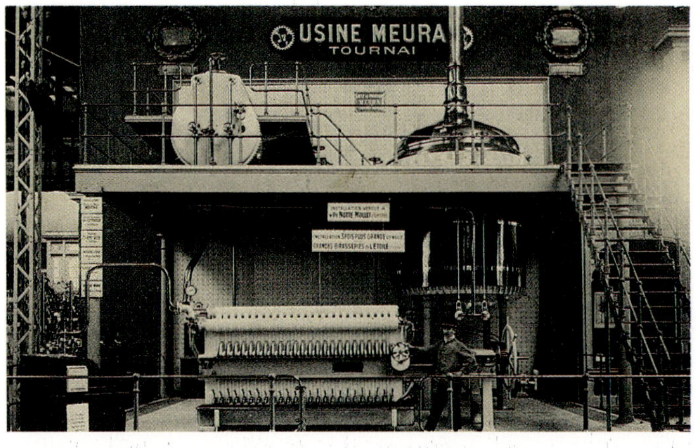

At the Brussels Universal Exhibition of 1910 the Meura brewing hall was destroyed by a fire.

There followed an International Exhibition in Antwerp, in 1909, and then the Universal Exhibition of Brussels, in 1910. The latter show hardly had a chance. The Métropole pavilion, which housed the breweries of Métropole and Wielemans-Ceuppens, was engulfed in flames. Some weeks later, another fire ravaged the brewery section, destroying a certain number of stands and installations, such as the brewing hall shown by the Meura company from Tournai. However, and despite the lively interest shown in the display by German brewers, a Grand Prix diploma gave some recompense to all the Belgian brewers.

The Charleroi Exhibition, in 1911, was characterised by the sumptuous allegoric group which the architect Patris made for the brewery section. This taste for allegory in decoration, perceptible in many of the earlier exhibitions, disappeared with the Universal and International Exhibition in Ghent (1913). The design of the brewery pavilion was entrusted to the architect De Heem. It was a time for efficiency. It was necessary to inform the greater public, and it was also advisable to provide the brewers with solid arguments for the defence of their industry. The Buffet was a vast rectangular complex where the best beers of the country were for sale, to "prove the high merits of Belgian beers, their equality to foreign beers, and indeed their superiority." Placed in the four corners, small kiosks had the role of showing "by means of tableaux, statistics, and diagrams, the merits of the beer." Two stands were occupied by the Federation of Breweries, two others by the Institut Supérieur de Brasserie in Ghent and the École Supérieure de Brasserie in Leuven. All around were exhibitors of raw materials and equipment.

This succession of great exhibitions sometimes hid from view their true destiny. Many thought that universal exhibitions would involve considerable expense without offering any professional interest, while specialised exhibitions could be useful. It was forgotten that "universal exhibitions put different people in contact who thus learn to know each other better. They contribute for the most part in this way to the maintenance of peace." (*Le Petit Journal du Brasseur*, 1911). It was a precarious peace, since they did not prevent the war which was about to break out.

SOME SIGNIFICANT DATES

• **1900:** a Law prescribed the bilateral obligations of the "contract of work".

• **1903:** a Law required the payment of damages for accidents at work. It came into force in 1905.

• **1905:** a Law established rest on Sundays.

• **1906:** the manufacture, transport, and sale of absinthe was banned on penalty of fines, and of imprisonment.

• **1909:** on the death of Léopold II, Albert I came to the throne.

• **1909:** a Law established obligatory military service for one son per family.

• **1910:** the light comedy by Frantz Fonson (Brussels 1870-1924) and Fernand Wicheler (Brussels 1874-1935), *Le Mariage de mademoiselle Beulemans*, was staged in Brussels. The action took place in part in the Brussels establishment "Bières en bouteilles Beulemans", sole depository for Belgium of "Glasgow Stout". It was organised around Suzanne Beulemans, and her father, a truculent brewer whose career is compromised by the loves of his daughter.

The piece, which put forward the *kœkebrœck*, rather tasty Brussels language, found great success in Belgium and abroad.

• **1912:** a Law abolished licence duty, established a tax on opening, and increased the duty on alcohol.

• **1913:** the General Strike, launched by the POB (Belgian Workers Party), had a huge following. It wanted the abolition of the plural vote in favour of universal suffrage, and only led to the appointment of a commission to examine Electoral Law. On the other hand the strikers obtained satisfaction, with the introduction of obligatory primary education.

• **1913:** on the instigation of the Head of Government, Charles de Broqueville (1911-1918), a Law made military service obligatory in general.

The light comedy success *Le Mariage de mademoiselle Beulemans* inspired post cards which Belgian soldiers sent when they were allowed in 1914-1918.

AN ORIGINAL MEAL

On the occasion of a banquet given in 1902 for the annual meeting of the Circle of Brewers of Boom, a menu on the theme of beer, and at the very least unusual, was served to the guests. It was:

« Huîtres congressistes
Consommé à moût clair
Corbeilles fermières à la drèche
Turbot sauce en fermentation
Pommes non germées
Filet de bœuf non moisi, au bisulfite
Tête de veau en tortue, sans queue ni tête
Râble de chevreuil filant
Homards désinfectés
Salade sèche
Glace à 0,17 1/2 % centigrades
Desserts glucosés, au sucre interverti
Fruits non fermentés
Café au sel de feu burggrave
Vins de première trempe. »

Not very mouth-watering names.... But without doubt succulent dishes, because the festivities were a great success!

THE BELGIAN BREWERY IN 1912

Province	Number of breweries	Average output per brewery
Antwerp	350	76,000 kg
Brabant	511	121,000 kg
West Flanders	592	53,000 kg
East Flanders	700	50,500 kg
Hainaut	685	52,000 kg
Liège	115	45,500 kg
Limbourg	152	24,500 kg
Luxembourg	66	30,500 kg
Namur	165	31,500 kg

THE HAZARDS OF BREWING

The fire, in 1913, at the Het SAS Brewery in Boortmeerbeek, shows the extent of damage suffered by the brewers. These disasters were often caused by fires in the maltings and grain dust in the conveying equipment.

Some important breweries created their own mutual insurance companies. This was the case with the Wielemans Brewery in Brussels in 1913; its mutual company remained autonomous until 1947.

For a long time, brewers were preoccupied by the various hazards to which they found themselves exposed in their businesses.

On the first level was the danger of fire. It was all the more reason to be feared, as communes did not always have adequate fire-fighting equipment available. For example, in 1896, an important brewery in Neufville, near Soignies, which belonged to the local burgomaster, M.Caulier, disappeared in flames without anyone being able to intervene. The locality did not possess a pump.

From 1876, brewers joined together to face up to this major risk. Confronted with increased premiums demanded by insurance companies, they created the "Combined Breweries Fire Insurance Company", the headquarters of which was in Brussels, and which was administered by the top personalities in the brewing industry. The most important breweries and maltings very soon joined this company. Its most advantageous tariffs and the fact that claims were ruled upon by brewers, sensitive to the problems of their own profession, contributed to this success.

Another hazard was linked with the activity itself: accidents. Brewers had of course been confronted with this problem and, following trials, had been condemned to indemnify their workers. After the Law of 24th December 1903 and Royal Decrees in 1904, which regulated insurance for accidents at work, the Belgian brewery industry considered setting up a mutual insurance company for breweries. The plan was not unanimously received. In 1905 some came up with the idea of an insurance to which all the brewers in the same region would be affiliated, so as to obtain both reasonable premiums and the best cover. But nothing ensued. It was not until 1912 that the necessity of uniting materialised. This was the creation, in Brussels, of the *Caisse Patronale de l'Amelioration et des Industries à faibles dangers*, a communal insurance fund for accidents at work. Its Chairman was a Liège brewer, Marcel Ortmans, also President of the General Association of Belgian Brewers. Its Board of Directors was, for the most part, composed of brewers such as Georges Damiens (Ixelles), Fernand Piron (Ghlin-lez-Mons), and Prosper Wielemans (Brussels).

Years of service in a brewery could be rewarded by a watch, such as those given by the Chasse Royale Brewery in Brussels.

SOME STAGES IN THE HISTORY OF THE BREWERY

• **1900:** with the help of the Paris Universal Exhibition, there was held, in the French capital, a Franco-Belgian Brewery Congress. The event was important, matters of high scientific content being dealt with there.

• **1900:** in Heidelberg, Gustave Eismer and Bernard Fischer perfected the first stillage intended for malt-house floors.

• **1900:** the filter press for wort made its appearance.

• **1901:** a Law amended the 1885 Law on productivity, regulating work at the mash-tub, and determined the means of establishing gravity.

• **1902:** the three first producers of beer were Germany, the United States, and Great Britain.

• **1903:** the American company Pfaudler Vacuum Fermentation Company, of Rochester, made the first enamel tanks, for fermentation and for storage.

• **1904:** the Commercial Court decided that any Belgian Brewer is authorised to use the word "Munich" for beers of his manufacture.

• **1907:** winner of the Nobel Prize for Chemistry, for his work on fermentation, the German Eduard Buchner demonstrated that fermentation depended on enzymes. Among other enzymes, he isolated *zymase*, extracted from beer yeast.

• **1908:** the First International Refrigeration Congress was held in Paris.

• **1909:** the Danish chemist Soren Peter Lauritz Sorensen, Director of the Carlsberg laboratory, discovered the "pH" indication for evaluating the acidity of a substance. From then on, it would be possible to control the stability of beer better.

• **1910:** the First International Brewers' Congress was organised by the General Federation of Belgian Brewers, in Brussels, Participants included scientists from America, such as Dr. Francis Wyatt, chemist and President of the National Academy of Brewers in the United States, and from Germany, such as Professor Dr. Delbruck, Director of the Research and Education Institute for Brewers in Berlin.

The same year, a First National Congress was organised by the National Federation of Beer and Carbonated Water Merchants of Belgium, in Brussels. From deliberations it was revealed that the creation of professional unions or syndicates was necessary.

• **1913:** The Federation of Central Café-Owners decided to do away with porters, to demand a minimum gravity and to have the right to control beers chemically.

SPLENDOUR AND THEN DECAY

It was on the eve of the Great War that the Grandes Brasseries de l'Etoile (The Star), in Brussels, disappeared. The decision to liquidate the company was taken in August 1913. And recovery attempts were in vain. The collapse of this huge enterprise was inevitable.

Some years earlier, nothing would have suggested its eventual demise. In 1910 the company had acquired a plant located on the quai de Mariemont, alongside its brewery in Brussels, in order to enlarge it. Transformations had occurred in the brewing hall of the Bornhem factory, its own top-fermentation plant.

The Grandes Brasseries de l'Etoile had, moreover, taken over nine tenths of the shares in the Brasserie Bavaro-Belge, endowed with two plants (Brussels and Antwerp), and almost all the shares in the Le Lion Brewery in Antwerp. They had participated in the incorporation of the company "Les Grandes Brasseries du Hainaut", and bought the capital of the Brasserie de la Joncquière, in Wanfercée-Baulet. This is not to forget their technical and administrative assistance in forming the "Grandes Brasseries" in Rio de Janeiro and Bucarest, assistance which brought them founders shares in return.

"A share in the Grandes Brasseries de l'Etoile is considered to be of first order and its rate of 595 is still attractive. [...] We know very well that the profits are enormous and permit any calculation," one could read in the *Fourmi*, in September 1910. In fact the situation was more flourishing. This is demonstrated by the considerable increase in sales of beers as regards the previous year: more than 109 per cent for the plant in Brussels, and more than 57 per cent for that in Bornhem. Insolvency was for this reason quite unexpected.

The effort which was demanded by reconstruction was significant, as is shown in this poster. In the background, the halls of Ypres immediately after the Great War.

THE TURBULENCES OF THE GREAT WAR

From 1913 the economy was under somewhat of a shadow. And then war broke out. Belgium was not prepared. Concerned about protecting its neutrality in any possible Franco-German confrontation, it had in 1913 adopted, on the initiative of its Head of Government, Charles de Broqueville, a Bill providing for the development of its armed forces over the course of the four or five years to come. The conflict thus arose rather prematurely.

Although the country still had faith in its immunity, a general mobilisation was decreed on 31st July 1914. The German ultimatum demanding the passage of German troops over Belgian soil, in order to march on Paris, involved taking on Belgium. "Belgium will, by whatever means in its power, reject any attack on its rights," was the advice of the Crown. The Belgian frontier was violated on the morning of 4th August. At the head of his army, King Albert I conducted operations. After a withdrawal to Antwerp, the Government withdrew to Ostend, then France. During the Battle of the Yser, the opening of the sluices of Nieuwpoort and the flooding of 25,000 square metres allowed the German hold to be saved from one region, between the Yser and the French border. The King and Queen settled there for the duration of the war. The occupied Belgian territory came under the control of a German Governor General.

On the occasion of the National Festival on 21st July 1914, the League of Brewers and Merchants of Brussels Beers demanded of the Mayor that he organise the free distribution of faro "via" the Manneken-Pis. This was refused, for fear that it should not reproduced the disorders which a similar distribution had caused twenty years earlier (*Brussels Pêle Mêle*, 15th July 1914).

Like other sectors of the economy, brewing endured a terrible ordeal. Of course, in the free zone to the West of the Yser, a hundred breweries and four industrial maltings escaped destruction. Furthermore, this region supplied hops from Poperinghe and winter barley from the polders. But, in the occupied territory, the situation was much different.

The City of Liège put up a long resistance to the German army and slowed its advance.

Avis	**Bericht**
Les circonstances actuelles et les mesures prises par la Corporation des Brasseurs, nous obligent de *supprimer* la vente des bières *"Gueuze et Kriek"*, le *mardi et le vendredi.*	De huidige omstandigheden en de maatregelen genomen door de Corporatie der Brouwers, verplichten er ons toe, *geen "Gueuze en Kriek" te verkoopen* den *Dinsdag en Vrijdag.*
Drij-Pikkel.	*Strombeek-Bever.*

On their way, the Germans pillaged some breweries and took their beers for the troops (above). The empty casks were often recovered for maturing sauerkraut or for building floating pontoon bridges.

Severe control over breweries

The activities of the breweries was very soon disrupted. From May 1915, the Germans occupied certain breweries taken near the front, in order to store beer imported from Munich and to brew according to their method. Taking into account the rarity of fuels and of raw materials, the price of beer never ceased to rise. It was fixed by the German authorities. On the other hand, in December 1915, all the Belgian brewers had to answer a questionnaire issued by the Germans and which proved very inquisitive about the operation of their businesses.

The year 1916 was hardly any better. In fact, it was decided that the distribution of raw materials would be carried out according to the declarations of 1915, favouring the large breweries which had profited from the situation to increase their production. The General Federation of Belgian Brewers opposed this decision and won their case. The year of reference would be 1913. Thus the rights of small breweries could be safeguarded.

But in November 1916, a fatal blow was struck upon a number of breweries. The Office of Control of Breweries, installed by the Germans, forced the creation of the Brasseries Centrales and undertook to close 90 per cent of the existing breweries to hasten the removal of copper equipment, requisitioned for the manufacture of shells. This decision caused dissension among brewers, which worsened when it was seen that the first lists, on which the Federation had no right to look, had been revised and that the number of Brasseries Centrales had increased. Less scrupulous brewers took advantage, to the detriment of their more honest colleagues.

The Février Brewery, in Momignies, even served as an abattoir during the war.

From 1917 control was reinforced. Breweries counting more than a dozen workers had to apply for authority to operate. The production of beer was then destined, for the most part, for the occupying troops. The requisition of businesses became an everyday event. For example, the Meura company, which made boilers, had to carry out repairs for the German artillery.

In this economic context, of rigour and dependence, the occupiers played on the peculiarities of the two communities, Flemish and Walloon, the better to rule. And in 1917 Belgium was reorganised administratively, distinguishing on the one side Flanders, with Brussels as its capital, and on the other Wallonia, with Namur as its capital.

A major cause for concern: raw materials

In March 1915, a temporary association of Belgian brewers and maltsters, independent of the General Federation of Belgian Brewers was created under the auspices of the National Committee for safety and food. This committee, born of private initiative, had been founded in Brussels in August 1914 to provide for supplies to the population, and its existence was tolerated by the German authorities throughout the war. The first task of this temporary association was to gather funds for the importation of barley. The association, supported by the Ghent Brewery School, solicited a supply of barley through the *Commission for Relief in Belgium*, a body established in London with the purpose of providing food commodities in Belgium. It was agreed that 15,000 tonnes of malt would be conveyed each month to Belgium, on condition however that the General Federation of Belgian Brewers, which would purchase the malt, would not resell it to the occupiers. Difficulties followed. There was a lack of boats, the Dutch government refused any sort of grain on its land, the temporary association had to repay its subscribers, and so on. And the Germans ended up controlling the distribution of the barley. On 15th July 1915 a central office for the seizure and distribution of barley, the *Gersten-Zentrale*, was created in Brussels.

The proportion of barley granted to the brewers rose at first to about 30 per cent of the amount declared to the Excise in 1913. Then it diminished rapidly and, in 1917-18 it was no more than 10 per cent. On the other hand, the grain harvested, especially maize, was distributed in higher quantities.

As for the other ingredients of beer, their supply was less difficult. Hops were not in short supply, and their quality was consistent. Sugar remained available, at a reasonable price, in free trade, thanks to imports from Holland. However, at the end of the war, its cost became prohibitive.

Lastly there was yeast. The beers produced were, of course, exempt from ills, because they were not nourishing enough to maintain life in micro-organisms. But the problem was that yeasts weakened and refused to come out through the bung in the barrel. Therefore they used bottom-fermentation yeasts, which, too weak, fell prey to microbes, putrid beers multiplying. To remedy this insufficiency of nitrogenous materials, which nourished yeasts, they added rootlets in the mash-tun, that is to say barley germ which a degermer removed after drying. This practice was already in operation in the lambic breweries before the war.

The beer of war

On the side of the Belgian army, the morale of the men was raised with a beer sold near the infantry trenches and artillery zones. This drink, which did not exceed 3°, was not always very good, because it was difficult to make a fine beer with the chlorinated water of the coastal region. Besides, the breweries being small and not allowing sufficient storage, the beer was always very young.

Despite these imperfections, the brewers did not succeed in answering demand. Numerous bar-owners found themselves searching for beer. It was therefore necessary to import beers from England, France, and Switzerland. English beer was available in the English sector. French beer came from Saint Dizier. It kept well and was of a good gravity, this soon being regarded as a threat to the discipline of the troops. It was thus banned, and replaced by beer from the Swiss brewery of Cardinal, from Fribourg. This beer was sold in the establishments of La Panne.

The Quillacq Brewery, in Dunkirk, as shown in this letterhead from 1898. H. Bogaert collection.

The Brasserie Dumortier et Fils, situated in Comines (Hainaut), was destroyed during the war.

At the beginning of 1918, the Belgian stores, wishing to increase the production of beer, rented for one year the Quillacq Brewery and the Verleye Brewery, both situated in Dunkirk. The Verleye Brewery only served three or four times. Near the Quillacq Brewery, which was a military brewery until the Armistice, there was a plant which shelled peas. It was decided to convert it into a maltings, but this was not completed by the end of the war. Also barley, arriving via Dunkirk, was prepared at the Beanert Maltings in Furnes. After from ten to fifteen days, the beer, which was 3°, was transported to the army billets, where it was sold at 15 centimes a glass.

Towards the end of the years of conflict, the situation in the brewing industry was disastrous: requisitions, destruction, dismantling of installations, and so on. Raw materials and fuel were absent. Recovery would be slow, reorganisation delicate. "And now we work! It is the only consolation on offer, the only remedy for so much pain." This exhortation to work, by George M. Johnson in the first edition of *Le Petit Journal du Brasseur* after the war was, in some way, the motto for the years of reconstruction which followed.

INGREDIENTS OF SUBSTITUTION

The difficulty in obtaining raw materials caused brewers to use other ingredients.

• roasted beet seeds replaced roasted malt or served as a colouring for dark beers.

• potato skins were also used. Before the war brewers without doubt had recourse to potato starch, in the form of starch syrup.

• beet husks were used, but without much result. The pulp swelled in the tank, filtration of the must proved difficult, and... the beer had a taste of beet.

• beans likewise became ingredients in beer, but in low quantities, taking into account the disagreeable smell which they developed on maceration and which they gave to the beer. This use of vegetable is very old, and La Cambre mentioned it in his treatise of 1856.

Finally, use was made of houblonnette, a fermented product composed of boiled water, a little sugar, a little alcohol, and hops. This virtual beer without malt was healthy and nutritive. Drunk from the barrel, it presented an agreeable taste. A slight bitterness resulted from the hops. But put in bottles the houblonnette became petillant and frothy after 10 to 12 days.

During the course of the war, the Mark prevailed. Thus, in 1916, a brewer had the idea of establishing a conversion table from Belgian Francs to Marks

THE DIFFICULTY IN OBTAINING RAW MATERIALS CAUSED BREWERS TO USE OTHER INGREDIENTS

From 15th to 18th July 1915, the Germans demanded that all businesses possessing copper equipment must declare it. On 24th November of the same year, the rumour went round, in Brussels, that the copper would be seized. On 27th November an inventory was required of the brewers. The General Federation of Belgian Brewers asked for an explanation from the Governor General, who replied to it in these terms:

"Sir,

"Further to your letter of 26th of last month, it is brought to your attention that the inventory of copper existing in breweries was for the sole aim of having a rapid glance at what is there. The aim is not to take the copper from the brewers and thus damage manufacture. The army administration will have to be forced to requisition the copper apparatus which does not serve in manufacture.

"As it is recognised that Belgian breweries still make great use of copper equipment, in Germany, because of its non-economic method of manufacture, it has long been replaced by other equipment. It may happen that the army administration also takes this copper. But this will only happen on exchange of copper apparatus for other, not causing any possible damage to manufacture.

"On this occasion, I would like you to know that a special office will be set up for the purchase of copper from breweries. The price paid cash by this office will be higher than that which might be made after requisition. It is therefore in the interests of the breweries to sell existing copper on its order at this office. In this event apparatus actively being used can be replaced by others, thus to obtain this copper at the higher price of the purchase office.

Signed, Baron von Bissing, General."

On 20th December 1915, the metallurgic company Pfaffenberger Brothers, in Brussels, informed the brewers that they were charged by the Governor General to acquire "equipment in cooper and alloys of copper, bronze, and brass, as well as equipment in aluminium, nickel, antimony, and so on, located in breweries and distilleries." This company, "appointed experts in the matter", specified that the Governor must proceed with these purchases, "to avoid possible arrests in its being carried out" and that it was necessary "as far as possible to keep the brewing industry at its high level." The purchase prices were fixed. Finally and an important detail, "If this method of acquisition did not give the Governor General the expected result, [...] the payment will be made at the time of requisition by the military authorities in "requisition vouchers". The prices then remained to be fixed later by the Minister of War in Berlin.

In June 1916, an engineer was appointed by the General Federation of Belgian Brewers as an adviser during the review prior to the removal of copper. And it was on 30th December that a circular indicated the classification of the different metals. Class 35 concerned brass, with beer tops and siphon heads, class 38 special equipment for brewing and malting (for example mash and brew boilers, pipes, heating coils, and refrigeration units). But the Germans did not stop there, and on 16th March 1917, it was necessary to make a new declaration relating to industrial copper, which this time included copper from churches and State establishments.

Brewers replaced copper tanks with iron tanks. Here, such a substitution at the Hurion Brewery in Cul des Sarts (Namur).

BREWERY HORSES

Until the appearance and general use of modern means of transport, lorries and so on, brewers provided for delivery of their products on horse-drawn vehicles. This was hard work, because the load was heavy, and animals had to be chosen with very great care. At the beginning of the century, *Le Petit Journal du Brasseur* gave strong advice as to the choice of a horse. "One must not lose sight of the fact that 'without feet there is not a horse' is a dictum true for all services in which one depends on this animal, but above all for that of the brewer who needs rapid haulage over all sorts of ground." it stated in the edition for 27th October 1911.

But beyond this necessity to buy judiciously, it was also necessary to take great care of the horse, and this was a not insignificant burden on the business. Feed had be comforting and refreshing. If oats were the basis of nutrition, barley and treacle had to be used as a complement. At Forest-lez-Bruxelles, the company of Knudsen Brothers made a mixture of brewers' grains and molasses, dry brewers' grains being recommended for equine feed. According to specialists, the minimum amount of daily feed required by a good brewery horse consisted of four kilos of hay, four kilos of straw, five kilos of oats, four kilos of barley, and a kilo of roots. With the First World War it of course became impossible to provide animals with such rations. There were no oats and barley. The breweries received barely enough barley to operate. Roots and brewers' grains came therefore to make up a bigger proportion of the feed.

Belgian horses were preferred by brewers. However the development of bottom-fermented beers and the growth of bottled beers, accelerated the rhythm of deliveries and it was necessary to have horses suitable for rapid transport. Henceforth they had to pull some 2,500 kilos of useful load and to cover an average of 30 kilometres each day. Horses of a certain weight were therefore used, solid without being massive, and capable of working at trotting speed. Of course the Brabant horses were still used, although less. Other breeds entered the lists. The Boulonnais, vigorous and energetic, was to be bought at a lower net cost than the Belgian horse, but the slowness of their training meant they were neglected. The large draught horses of the Nord, or Belgian of an improved breed, descendants of the Bruges, the Brabant, or the Ardennes, established themselves. They proved to be excellent brewery horses, even if some proved unsuitable for work at a trot. Finally, certain brewers replaced some of their horses with mules. The experience was not satisfactory, since, outside the fact that at least three mules were needed to do the work of two horses, the paved roads were not convenient for the hoofs of these animals, more suitable for bumpy and stony roads.

Beyond their eminently utilitarian role, these teams were a form of advertisement for brewers and beer merchants alike. It was therefore important that they were noticed when travelling around towns. Vehicles in gay colours, and with brilliant fittings, horses superbly harnessed, and drivers usually wearing uniforms; this advertisement was relatively easy and very effective! But then came the lorry, which appeared in the world of beer around 1907, and which at the beginning of the Thirties, finally imposed itself, relegating the horse to its place in the history of brewing.

In 1880, the brewers took part in a Cavalcade organised on the occasion of the Fiftieth Anniversary of the Birth of the Belgian State. Their float was the most imposing.

THE BELGIAN DRAUGHT HORSE

The improvement of the Belgian breed of draught horses, from 1886, was motivated by the interest which the Americans then showed in these animals. From the middle of the 19th century, European draught horses had been sent to the United States, especially Percherons. But soon the French breeders were not enough to supply them and so bought the grey Belgian horses, only to pass them off as Percherons. This being perceived as a deception, the Americans bought the horses themselves in Belgium. It was then that the Belgian Government decided to devote 200,000 Francs to promoting breeding.

On the eve of the Great War, the Belgian draught horse enjoyed a world-wide reputation. All the major countries benefiting from climatic conditions close to those of Belgium bred them. Thus, in 1913, 35,600 Belgian horses were exported. The largest customer was Germany which furthermore, during the course of the war attempted to appropriate the breeding. Numerous requisitions were made. The horses were not always destined for the front, but transported to German breeding centres where farmers were able to acquire them at preferential rates. At the end of the conflict, even if France and Belgium had been able to get back a certain number of horses, the Germans had saved the best for breeding. To prevent a similar situation being repeated, the Belgian Government banned, in the Twenties, the export of any first quality horses. The principal breeding farms were then in the region of Binche.

The name of Binche remained closely linked with brewery horses. Not only did this city provide the setting for a famous horse market at which there was no lack of brewers. But in its vicinity a number of establishments made carts. This enabled purchasers of animals to set off fully equipped.

Today the Palm Brewery sponsors the Belgian stet-horse race, thanks to the stables of the estate of Diepensteyn.

Brewery vehicles largely took part in team contests, which were formerly the custom. The *Cart Horse Parade*, which took place in the capital, was particularly famous. "The horses are dolled up, rigged, bedecked with ribbons, rosettes in national colours or the colours of Brussels, the harnesses are new, the fittings gleam, the vehicles are painted in light even delicate colours, some drivers wear white gloves. It is spruce, beautiful, very gay, [...]." Henry Codvelle described the 1908 parade. This counted brewers among its organisers: Prosper, Paul and Marcel Wielemans, from Brussels, as well as Félix Gossens, from Assche. The teams from the Kœkelberg Brewery and the Wielemans-Ceuppens Brewery were among the most sumptuously fitted out.

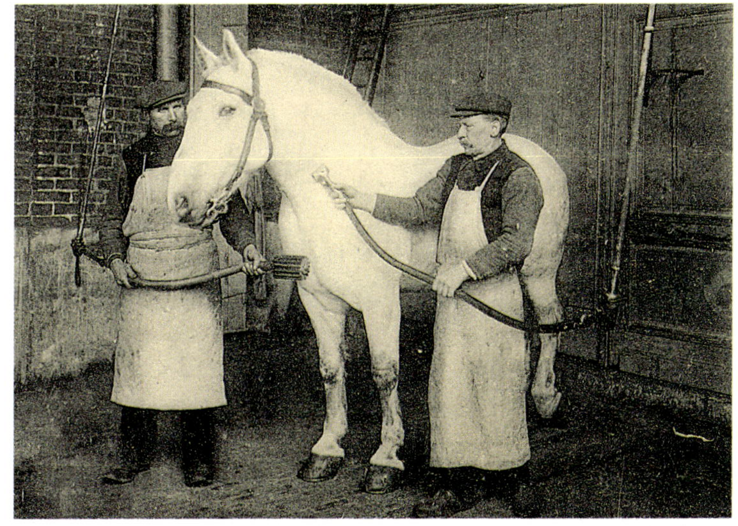

Fully aware of the more modern methods of maintaining horses (electric brushes and shears), the Brussels brewery of Wielemans took First Prize in the harness "Concours" in Brussels in 1906.

THE YEARS OF RECOVERY

The brewing industry had, of course, suffered from the war. After the conflict, the brewers took up life again, but their means of production were sorely tested. In fact, they had often lost all or part of their equipment. Beside that, a scarcity of raw materials and fuel curbed recovery. The figures speak for themselves: the total in 1913 neared 200 million kilos, but in 1919 was only some 40 million. An acute work crisis (nearly 500,000 unemployed at the end of the war), strike movements, late payment of war damages, and so on; the circumstances hardly seemed to presage rapid renewal. All the same, by 1920, the number of unemployed had fallen to 50,000, the Belgian economy was taking off again, and in 1924 it even exceeded its pre-war level. Belgium was more or less the only country to have benefited from such economic recovery.

A new brewing direction

However, the behaviour of the population with regard to beer was changed. Home consumption had fallen. The cause of this change was increasing bar consumption and above all inexpensive wine. Of course, only low gravity beers were involved in this development. Strong beers were not affected. Evidence the English beers which were invading the market. Profiting from the difficulties encountered by their Belgian colleagues in manufacturing this type of beer (for want of raw materials), the English brewers introduced in Belgium beers of a gravity often above that of the beers sold in Great Britain. "The English beers, bocks, and specials, have regained their pre-war gravity, while bourgeois and everyday beers are still under the influence of practices from the time of the occupation. These are not beers, but herbal teas of which the gravity before fermentation does not exceed 1° to 1.5°. The public no longer wants it: it requires, and there is good reason, a strong beer, digestive and fortifying. There was no need to satisfy it by resorting to the strong gravities of special beers, but it has enough of dishwater, it wants the quality it bought before the war, that is to say beers of 3° to 4° in gravity. As much as a beer of 4° is nourishing, beneficial, digestive, and stimulating to the appetite, a beer which is too weak is insipid, indigestible, and disgusting." So said *Le Petit Journal du Brasseur* in January 1920.

Some brewers exploited workers' movements for commercial ends.

In order to face up to this situation there was a solution: to raise the gravity of Belgian beers. But how was this to be achieved? How to obtain the consensus of brewers, in the context of a divided industry - 1,908 breweries in 1920? The General Federation of Belgian Brewers was active there. Thus, in 1921, in order to place a deadline on the sale by certain less scrupulous breweries of pseudo-English beers which were no other than beers of low gravity, raised by caramel and saccharine, it introduced a guaranteed gravity of English-type beers, made according to conditions imposed and of which the original gravity on the legal Belgian hydrometer attained or exceeded 5 degrees. A marque could henceforth be affixed to bottles and casks.

Otherwise, the ideas at the beginning of the century of Louis Van den Hulle were adopted by Léon Verhelst, Professor at the École de Brasserie in Leuven. The conference which he aimed at the Federation, on 5th September 1920, headlined the centralisation of the breweries as the sole means of resolving the problem and of checking foreign competition. It was necessary to construct a new bottom-fermentation brewery, in dealing with the damages of war. This way of seeing things had its adherents. In Ghent, thirteen breweries formed the Belgica central brewery, in the former brewery of Akkergem. In Eeklo, the Kruger Brewery was formed from the combination of nineteen breweries!

The name of the architect Adrien Blomme (1878-1940) is directly linked with the history of the Brussels brewery of Wielemans. In fact, this disciple of Frank Lloyd Wright and of the "liner" style, concentrated on aerodynamism of form, brought back, in the Twenties, the concept of the brewery villa, in Ixelles, of the Metropole Cinema, and a part of the Hotel of the same name, as well as the completion of a brewing hall in the brewery (1931).

This architect likewise built: the mine-workers' village in Winterslag (1912-1930); the Val de La Cambre (1924-1932) in Brussels; the establishments "Aux Armes des Brasseurs" and "La Frégate", in Brussels.

His son, Yvan, also worked as an architect, for the Wielemans family.

The Belgian brewing industry took the inevitable path of concentration, and no one seems to have perceived this development better than Léon Verhelst. "If the small breweries disappear or diminish in importance, on the other hand the large ones multiply and develop gradually. It is the indication of a new direction in our industry. The tastes of the clientele become more refined so that as the well-being of the masses increases the people become used to beers of quality, and they are able to buy them. The ever more heavy burdens upon breweries force us to turn to small economies, which only allow the performance of industrial work. These are all circumstances which force upon us, in spite of ourselves, a development to which neighbouring countries have already conceded. It seems we are taking great steps towards industrial manufacture, of which the present form is bottom-fermentation."

The chauvinism of the Thirties

In 1930 Belgian brewing once more occupied an important place in the economic life of the country. There were 1,500 plants, and 20,000 workers. Each year more than 300 million kilos of cereal were dealt with. Bottom-fermented beers had taken precedence over those of top-fermentation. Not very widespread in the countryside before the war because it was considered as a luxury drink, it was henceforth consumed in large quantity by village populations. As for spontaneously-fermented beers, they had lost favour and represented no more than 5 per cent of the overall beer production.

The fall in beer consumption was accentuated at the beginning of the Thirties. Yet despite the increase in taxes and the cost of raw materials the price of beer remained reasonable. But social habits had changed. People went less to the café, and more to the cinema or dancing. Sparkling drinks, lemonades, and table waters, were increasingly successful. Besides, the world crisis stemming from the crash of the New York Stock Exchange on 1929 began to be felt in Belgium. Once again industrial production fell, plants were closed, the working population was affected by unemployment, purchasing power was reduced, and consumption diminished.

In order to allow the breweries to overcome this new period of difficulty, some advocated the grouping together of various bodies relating to beer in a central organisation, named for example the "Commission for the defence of drinks". Others opted for the exclusive

consumption of national beers. "We suffer from a malady which one calls snobbism for drinking foreign beer," declared Edmond Damiens, Secretary of the Brewers' Consortium, in *Le Petit Journal du Brasseur*, in August 1930. This "chauvinism" was echoed in the 1930 Exhibition.

In the years 1935 and 1936 the devaluation of the Belgian Franc particularly affected the small and medium-sized breweries, since if the sale of their products took place within the country, they purchased their raw materials outside it. The considerable increase in the price of grain (close to 100 per cent) aroused the reaction of the brewers. Some demanded a readjustment of the sale prices of beer, others regarded any increase as inopportune, since it was still remunerative for them. In fact only the breweries which had available large stocks of raw materials could face up to it.

The beer industry suffered, as it did before the war, from disloyal competition, even fraudulent procedures. The introduction of a certain discipline was agreed. The Consortium urged its members to renounce price competition in favour of quality competition, thus undermining foreign imports. On its side, the General Federation of Belgian Brewers sent out a circular showing the anarchy which ruled with beer prices and the non-observance of decisions taken.

Centenary celebrations

In 1930, on the Centenary of the Belgian State, two exhibitions were organised, one in Antwerp, and one in Liège. Some would have preferred a grandiose Universal Exhibition: "here we have satisfaction granted to different local interests which hardly seem to understand that the dispersal of effort will ruin the entire project." Thus *Le Petit Journal du Brasseur* expressed its disapproval in April 1926. But the period, marked by economic and financial crisis, hardly lent itself to an international event which, apart from anything else, would risk favouring the importation of foreign beers, as had been the case at the beginning of the century. It was time for the Belgian beer industry to affirm its power and its ability to rival even the most important foreign breweries.

It was from this point of view that the Flemish International Colonial, Maritime, and Art Exhibition in Antwerp was created, and laid out over fifty hectares. The breweries occupied an elegant stucco palace, in a modern style, a huge 750 to 800 square metres, surmounted by a tower twenty five metres tall. The Brussels architect Charles Verhelle, a former pupil of Horta, was its designer. Four to five hundred people could drink beer in the vast serving room, and on the terraces which surrounded the pavilion. The representation of Belgian brewers was also to be observed at the Liège International Exhibition (Major Industry, Science and its Applications, Old Walloon Art). An appeal had been made to the Brussels architects René and Robert Théry. The Belgian Union of Coppersmiths showed a brewery in operation, equipped in the most modern and advanced manner. As in Antwerp, in the first rank of breweries present were: Wieleman-Ceuppens (Brussels), Vandenheuvel and Company (Brussels), Caulier (Brussels), Bavaro-Belge (Brussels), Chasse Royale (Brussels), Impérial (Brussels), and the Brasseries d'Ixelles (Brussels-Ixelles).

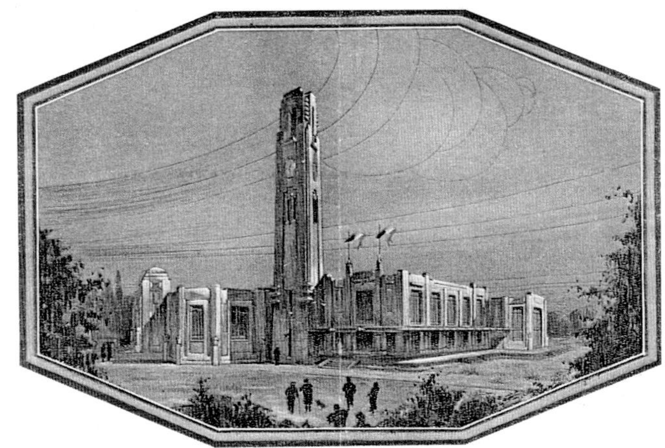

The imposing "Palais de la Brasserie" at the Centenary Exhibition in Antwerp in 1930.

Other shows ...

"The economic struggle looms more and more harshly and without doubt, in the years to come, all the nation's forces will have to be joined, not only to maintain an atmosphere of calm within the country, but also to develop the field of our commercial activity beyond our frontiers and to take from abroad that part it already occupies in our own commercial field. It is quite certain, to arm us better and to permit us more surely to achieve our aim, that our leaders have wished, in this hundredth year of Independence, to realise these two International Exhibitions in Antwerp and Liège", declared Léon Wielemans, President of the General Federation of Belgian Brewers, on the opening of the brewery "palace" in Liège.

"The return to prosperity is dependent upon a larger circulation of merchandise," affirmed the King in

1935 when he opened the Universal and International Exhibition in Brussels. In the "Palais de l'Alimentation", the Belgian breweries occupied the aisle to the left of the superb pavilion designed by Charles Verhelle. Eight to ten hectolitres of beer were tasted there each day, even twenty to twenty five on Sunday. This allowed a better targeting of public taste, for bock (50 %), superbock (41 %), dark Munich-type beer (4 %), gueuze (4 %), and stout (1 %).

The years which followed were marked by other exhibitions. There was, in 1937, the Brewery Exhibition in Ghent, where one found the breweries of Meiresonne, Impérial, Liebært, Wielemans-Ceuppens, Piedbœf, Du Bois-Mertens, le Chevalier Marin, and so on, as well as numerous makers of equipment and bottles. Above all there was, in 1939, the First International Brewery Salon, which was held in the setting of the Centenary Palace in Brussels. J. Lamot, Deputy Director of Brasseries Lamot and General Commissioner of the Salon, explained its aim thus: "Everyone knows that our fermentation industries, and in particular brewing, have gained considerable importance from a national point of view, and that in Belgium we find the most modern and the best equipped breweries in Europe.

"For the general public, our show will be especially instructive. It will be an interesting education as much for the consumer as for the publican."

The accent was placed on the nutritional value of the "liquid bread" which is beer, The exhibitors came from eight countries to participate in the event. Breweries, maltings, producers of raw materials, makers of machines and equipment used in the manufacture of beer, its conservation, its distribution, its sale, and so on, were there. An artistic contest was organised by the General Federation of Belgian Brewers, with, as its aim, the illustration of a menu on the theme of "we drink our home beer".

The Salon was held despite the war situation. In a radio appeal, King Léopold III had asked non-mobilised citizens to pursue their everyday tasks in order not to place in danger the economic activity of the country. Nevertheless, if the Salon was a great success, beyond the borders of the country it did not have the desired effect.

SOME SIGNIFICANT DATES

• **1919:** the National Industrial Credit Company was created. The loans which it awarded to industrialists enabled them to endure the wait for payment of war damages.

• **1920:** Income Tax was introduced.

• **1921:** a Law instituted the eight hour working day, and the forty eight hour week.

• **1926:** retirement insurance was established for workers.

• **1927:** net Supertax on income came into force.

• **1930:** a Law governed insurance for old age and premature death.

• **1932:** a Law established progressive excise duties, in relation to brewery production.

Point of sale beer-coolers made their appearance.

• **1934:** a Royal Decree fixed the conditions of regulation of commercial credits between Germany and the Belgo-Luxembourg Economic Union. Among other provisions, sums due for the purchase of German goods imported into the Union, the Belgian Congo, and other territories under Belgian mandate, had to be paid on maturity in Belgas to the Banque Nationale de Belgique.

• **1934:** after the death of Albert I, Léopold III took the throne.

SOME STAGES IN THE HISTORY OF THE BREWERY

• **1921:** brewers used the first cooling tanks, with double envelopes and cold water circulation.

• **1923:** a Royal Decree regulated the application of the eight hour day in breweries.

• **1924:** brewers used the first centrifuges for the treatment of wort, after refrigeration. Their maker was the company Alfa Laval.

• **1927:** a heat exchanger henceforth permitted the cooling of the wort in closed circuit, preventing any infection. The maker of these was the company Alfa Laval.

• **1928:** Josef Indeken, of the Alken Brewery, launched the first Belgian pils, the *Cristal.*

• **1929:** the first continuous closed-circuit pasteurisation trials are carried out in Great Britain.

• **1929:** the Brewery Workers and Employers Mutual Insurance Company was founded by Edmond Damiens.

• **1930:** stainless steel began to be used in brewing equipment. Cardboard filters were perfected.

• **1931:** a Royal Decree banned male plants in hop fields.

• **1932:** influenced by Prohibition in the United States, the Government envisaged increasing the tax on beers. A huge demonstration took place in Brussels: maltsters, brewers, and café-owners were present. The plan was abandoned.

• **1935:** responding to an appeal from the Queen, the General Federation of Belgian Brewers asked for a contribution from all brewers: 25 F for brewers declaring less than 25,000 kg., 50 F for between 25,000 and 50,000 kg., etc.

• **1935:** the Haacht Brewery absorbed the Brasserie Bavaro-Belge, surviving from the Grandes Brasseries de l'Étoile. Having its plants in Brussels and Antwerp, in 1922 it occupied fifth position behind the breweries of Artois (Leuven), Wielemans-Ceuppens (Forest), de Hæcht and Saint Michel [Vandenheuvel] (Brussels).

• **1936:** breweries applied the eight hour day, and paid holidays.

• **1937:** at the Brewery Exhibition in Ghent, Usines Vandergeeten showed the *Rola* racking, for racking away from the air, and which specifically did not have a collector. This racker took its name from its inventors, the engineers Rosier and Laneau.

Before the war, Belgian hop-growers had seen their position shaken by foreign imports. The situation only got worse. At the end of the 1920's, production of hops fell from 50,000 to 6,000 quintals, which scarcely corresponded to a half of the needs of the country. The regions of Poperinge and Alost were severely affected.

In 1928, for the first time, the General Federation of Belgian Brewers had recourse to the cinema to promote the consumption of beer. The film, entitled *Pourquoi buvons-nous de la bière...?* ("Why do we drink beer?"), and composed of a set of five animated drawings, was projected at the Coliséum in Brussels. It closed on a shot of the collective propaganda poster, *Buvez de la Bière* ("Drink beer"). Drawing: Victor T'sas.

A PROCESS TO SHORTEN THE MANUFACTURING TIME OF BEER

Invented at the very beginning of the 20th century, by Dr. L. Nathan, perfected after the Great War, and developed by the Institut Nathan S.A., in Zurich (Switzerland), the *Nathan System* marked a veritable Revolution, from the Twenties, in the manufacture of beer. The equipment involved the sterile refrigeration of the wort, and the cold sedimentation of the mixture, then the main fermentation in closed tanks of a cylindrical-conical shape, the yeast being recovered in the cone below. Then the secondary fermentation is substituted by an accelerated finishing process by treatment with carbon dioxide. The advantages of the system were the guarantee of absolute sterility in the course of the process and a reduced time of manufacture. Each fermentation tank has a double envelope permitting control of fermentation (raising or lowering temperature). Furthermore, this device avoids refrigerating the entire building as was the case before.

In Belgium, several breweries applied the process. For example, the Brasserie du Lac, in Bruges, used it from 1922. On the other hand, thanks to its closed circuit, the Nathan System especially suited breweries in tropical countries, where heat and bacteria were the worst enemies of beer. The Belgian Congo *(see pages 145-149)* was the first to adopt it. The breweries in Léopoldville and Elisabethville, were both erected in 1926 with a complete installation of this type.

Despite its considerable advantages, the process only achieved success after some delay, because of the increased investment which it represented, and the bad quality of aluminium. The perfection of stainless steel played in its favour, as did the use of concrete which allowed the design of functional premises.

AVERAGE OUTPUT PER BREWERY (in kilograms)

Year	Output
1912	62,000
1913	63,600
1924	86,500
1925	90,000
1928	116,300

THE "TWO LITRES" LAW

The Law of 13th August 1919 forbade the consumption, the sale, and the offer, even free, of spirituous liquors (genever) to be consumed on premises accessible to the public. Traders other than retailers retained the right to sell spirits for consumption away from their establishments on condition that each sale was of at least two litres.

This Law, which was consistent with the fight against alcohol among the working classes, was due to the Minister Émile Van der Velde. The brewing industry had to suffer the consequences, because, to re-establish a balance in the budget, the Minister tripled the excise duty on beer. On the other hand, the absence of genever in cafés was of benefit to beer, to the extent that it urged brewers to make strong beers, beers to which the Belgian brewing industry owes its present reputation.

It is interesting to note that this famous Minister, who occupied the political limelight for more than half a century, effectively from 1885 until his death in 1938, was the grandson of an Ixelles brewer, Guillaume Van der Velde.

THE PACKAGING OF BEER

In this "fin de siècle", when packaging no longer attracted the same sort of attention, one tends too often to forget the difficulties that industrialists encountered in the past, confronted in the presentation of their products for sale. Barrels and jugs were for a long time the only containers for beer. The first bottles were of stoneware. Brewers used them until the middle of the 19th century, because glass objects were then heavily taxed. Furthermore the quality of glass was mediocre. This explains why the English company Whitbread, which was one of the first to resort to this type of packaging, only adopted them after 1868. The glass was blown, and the bottle sealed with a cork stopper.

At the very beginning of the 20th century, Belgium bought its bottles from abroad. The glass there was superior, and price less high. Thus, in 1902, in more than five million kilograms of bottles imported, three quarters came from Germany, and the rest from Holland. However, at the same time Belgian production was growing, thanks to the Jumet glassworks, near Charleroi. This enterprise rapidly became one of the most important glassworks in the world, with a production of some fifteen million bottles.

In 1936 the first bottles were used which were decorated in painted enamel. The label no longer existed, the position of the labeller was abolished, and the brewer could thus compensate for the supplementary charge which came to be imposed upon him by the Law on paid holidays. The process was nonetheless onerous because, with each new law on packaging, it was necessary to print new bottles. It ended by being abandoned, to the benefit of the label.

Pages of a catalogue from the glass-works of Vilain-Hans et Cie, in Lodelinsart (Hainaut), around 1914.

The uniform of a worker in the bottling department at the Piedboeuf Brewery in Jupille (Liège), around 1935.

Research undertaken in 1953, to perfect a new material, more high-performance than glass, and carried out by the Belgian company Solvay, lead to PVC (polyvinyl chloride), of which industrial production was only possible ten years later. This material was blessed with many virtues: absence of toxicity, transparency, opacity to ultra-violet light, lightness, and so on. It was therefore tested for the packaging of beer. The capsuling of bottles was done with classic crown-corks. And in 1963 the first bottles in rigid PVC, intended for beers and sparkling drinks, were shown at the *Kunstoffe* ("artificial materials") International Fair, in Düsseldorf.

The matter of corks...

At the beginning, there was the cork stopper. This was replaced by the screw-top in 1865. Invented by the firm Barret and Ellers, the *screw stopper* was extremely successful in England. Then came the *bottle stopper* (a mechanical stopper) in 1877, after which the cap *(crown cork)*, designed by Painter in 1892. It facilitated the opening of the bottle and permitted the best conservation of the beer - the mechanical stopper allowed air to pass through its rubber washer.

Sorting corks at the firm of Gaston Béguin, in Marchienne-au-Pont (Hainaut), at the beginning of the century.

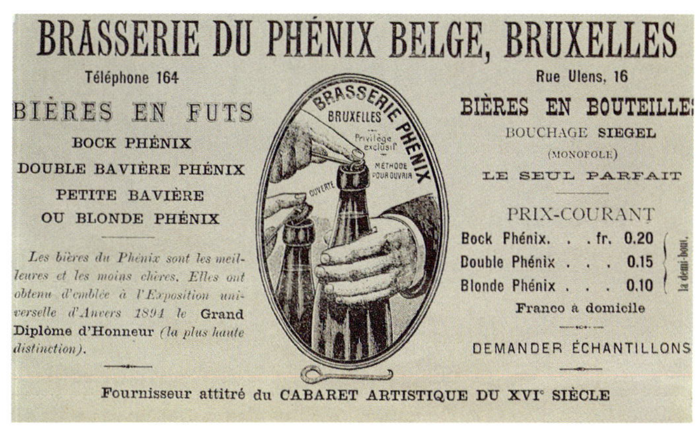

Several caps followed. The *Loop Seal*, composed of rings, required a hooked bottle-opener. The Brasserie du Phénix Belge, in Brussels, was already using it in 1896. It was abandoned because it did not provide a perfect hermetic seal. For the same reason, the *Aluminium Stopper*, provided with a larger ring, and which did not necessitate a bottle-opener, did not have a long career.

But it was in fact the crown cork which won. Used by the English brewery Whitbread from 1908, it pervaded the beer industry after 1918.

Beer in cans

The beer can made of tin appeared controversially in the United States at the beginning of 1935. However its success was dazzling, despite its price being higher than that of the bottle. It is true that its advantages were considerable. Besides its maximum capacity at a lighter weight, it was good for handling, it eliminated risks of breakage, removed the problems of returns, facilitated storage, provided for a reduction in transport costs, and so on.

Following the Second World War, this mode of packaging progressed, and in the Sixties it shared the American market with glass, in equal proportion. Gradually aluminium partly or completely replaced tin. However, Europe reserved a rather reluctant welcome for this new packaging, and even today, beer in cans remains in the minority.

Of course, the appearance of the beer can evolved from the time of its invention. The first cans brought to mind the "Miror can", and were sealed with a cap. The packaging had been created by the firm CCC (Continental Cap Company) and was called Cap Sealed.

Deposits on packaging, Decree of 25 November 1941, came into force on 15 December 1941 *(see page 70)*

In Belgium, the Ekla beer, from the Vandenheuvel Brewery in Brussels was packaged in this way.

Top plate cans were commercialised later. Yet the first contract for the Cone Top had been signed with CCC in 1935. The reason for this delayed launch was the necessity to provide an adapted can-opener. This type of can was used until the middle of the Fifties.

FROM ONE CRATE TO THE OTHER

The transport of bottles necessitated an adapted container, and this was first of all the wooden crate with dividers. Around 1910, it became more solid, lighter and easier to handle.

Wooden crates "aged" rather badly, and plastic cases successfully replaced them. This material in effect presented the qualities of resistance (to very high pressure, shocks, and bad weather), safety (its smooth surface eliminated risks of injury), and lightness (its weight varied between 1.3 and 2 kg, while the wooden crate weighed from 3 to 5 kg). With easy maintenance, a far longer life, and a more attractive appearance (thanks to colour), the new cases were economically interesting. Renson and Company, of Montignies-le-Tilleul, were the first to make them a speciality. They took an Oscar for packaging in 1963. But it was the company D.W.Plastic, located in Bilzen, which became the leader in the market.

This type of wooden case was manufactured at a case-makers. In the Thirties, Caisseries Jean Van Campenhout, whose factories were in Kœkelberg-lez-Bruxelles and Erembodegem-lez-Alost, made a name for their cases intended for bottled beers. Their trump, the "Heineken Case", without compartments, much lighter, less of an encumbrance, more resistant, which saved time in placing the bottles and considerably reduced the risks of breakage.

At the end of the Second World War, spectacles celebrating the Resistance took place in many places. Here, in Frasnes-lez-Couvin (Province of Namur).

THE RISKS OF DISINTEGRATION (1940-1945)

On this beer label produced by the Vander Linden Brewery, in Hal (Flemish Brabant), in honour of the Fifteenth Scottish Division, all the towns which they liberated are mentioned.

Faced with the rise of Nazism in Germany, Belgium took a position from 6th March 1936 rescinding the military accord which, since 1920, had linked it with France in the event of German aggression. This accord did not win unanimous support, since the Flemish saw in it a risk of French tutelage, and the socialists advocated demilitarisation and a policy of peace. It was an accord which, on the other hand, had lost its "raison d'être" following the commitments made at Locarno (1925), and the evacuation of the Rhineland by the Allies (1930).

The day after this abrogation, History accelerated. Hitler had his troops enter the demilitarised Rhine area, thus violating the accords of Locarno. Anxious to protect its territory, Belgium opted for neutrality and a policy of "free hands", which contributed to calming worried or hostile minds and to restoring national unity. This policy of independence, which received a mixed reception on the part of the English and the French, and rather a favourable greeting on the German side, had as its main objective the reinforcement of military equipment from a dissuasive and defensive point of view.

Gradually, in the feverish climate of a country in full rearmament, there emerged the cloud of war. In 1939, *Le Petit Journal du Brasseur* published advertisements and articles connected with the threat of conflict. There was a question of reinforcing brewery buildings, acquiring gas masks, exclusively using sirens for civil alert. And, on 8th September, one could read an appeal to the country by Léopold III, while England and France had declared war on Germany, five days earlier, when they had taken an aggressive stance on Poland. But Belgium could only preserve its neutrality for a short time. On 9th April 1940, Germany invaded Denmark and Norway, then on 10th May, Holland, Belgium, and Luxembourg. The terrible memory of the Great War was present in everyone's mind. This aggression triggered panic in the civil population and led to an exodus for the French border, hampering military movements, in the face of a rapid and well-organised German army. On 18th May, the Government, supporting the solidarity of the Belgian army with the Allies, settled in France, while at the head of his troops, the King continued to fight. The battle of the Lys was concluded on 28th May with capitulation. The country was occupied, the people divided in their options.

The brewing industry, which was then the third industry in the country, had to adapt to these circumstances, following the example of other sectors of the economy. The reduction, by 10% to 15%, in the gravity of beers in stock before the declaration of hostilities enabled them to compensate for the rise in the price of malt, fuels, and raw materials, in the case of bottom-fermented beers, because this was what was given to the troops. In May 1939, the Minister of Economic Affairs asked brewers and maltsters for a commitment to have available in a permanent fashion a stock permitting six months of normal manufacture on the basis of previous excise and gravity declarations. It is interesting to observe that, taking into account the panic and the mobilisation at the German border, only the provinces of Liège and Limbourg registered a rise in beer production, of 2.2 % for the first and 40.6 % for the second. The other Belgian provinces suffered a fairly significant fall, of around 20 %. We should note, in passing, that the mobilisation in Limbourg contributed to the pils *Cristal Alken* being recognised in the rest of the country!

The invasion of Belgium by the German troops urged the General Federation of Belgian Brewers and the AssBra (Belgian Association of Brewers), on 10th May 1940, to unite in one single body. Some days later, maltings became associated. And this regrouping took the name of General Association of Belgian Brewers and Maltsters. The difficulties encountered during the course of the First World War, repeated themselves. Brewers searched for barley in Anatolia, in Chile, in California, and in Morocco, but their shipment proved impossible. On 31st December 1940, the German authorities imposed upon them the constitution of General Group No. 9 (National Corporation for Agriculture and Alimentation), which united the breweries, the maltings, the distilleries, and the drinks sector in general. The talk was again of weak yeasts, rootlets, and beet husks. On 22nd July 1941, saccharine, which had provisionally been banned, was authorised once more. Circulars, dispensations - the brewers were drowning in paperwork.

But, unlike what happened during the Great War, the Germans did not dismantle businesses and left the brewers their working tools. Of more than 1,000 brewery enterprises active in 1939, 758 remained at the end of 1944. Likewise, and contrary to 1914, the gravity was identical for all beers placed on sale, that is to say 0.8°, with the exception of gueuze for which a gravity of 1.7° was allowed. The General Group No. 9 carried out an average of fifteen checks a day and expedited eight hundred and fifty brew cards each month.

On the other hand, after capitulation, the Brussels Stock Exchange did not lose confidence and share prices rose. For example:

RATE		
	Brasserie de Haecht	Brasserie de Kœkelberg
10th May 1937	2,175	2,875
9th May 1938	1,855	2,915
9th May 1939	1,475	2,840
9th May 1940	1,275	2,320
27th December 1940	2,100	4,650
31st December 1941	3,275	6,700

Of the 600,000 prisoners counted on 28th May 1940, only 225,000 remained in the autumn of the same year. From November 1940 to March 1941, 79,114

AN IMPORTANT DECREE

The Decree of 25th November 1941, making deposits obligatory on packaging items, resolved the problem of theft of bottles and cases. Henceforth a special mark was affixed to each type of packaging indicating that they were secured. It was a mention of "returnable", followed either by the year in which the amount of deposit had been fixed, or the price fixed by the scale in force. The proportion of loss of packaging items was 2 %. Furthermore, the possession and use of packages belonging to others was prohibited.

When the Decree came into force, the deposit on bottles was 1 F for those of 25cl or 33cl, 1.5F for those of 50cl and 2F for those of 75cl or 1 litre. The deposit on cases was 11F.

A sorting depot existed in Antwerp from 1906. This Decree considerably developed its activity, since it "managed" some 50,000 bottles per month in 1942. This was a model for the numerous depots in which bottles were henceforth sorted.

The necessity of sorting, brought about by this new regulation, caused, immediately after the war, the standardisation of cases and bottles, a standardisation demanded by the costs of special moulds, of bottles and of handling.

CAUTIONNEMENT
DES EFFETS D'EMBALLAGE

Arrêté du 25 Novembre 1941.

CASIER CAUTIONNÉ 11 FRS.

Cautionnement remboursé moyennant remise en BON ETAT du matériel portant étiquette INTACTE.

B[RIE] BOONE & C°, S.A. LESSINES - Tél. 323

Flemish prisoners returned home. In playing the card of favouritism towards the Flemish, the authorities of the Reich aimed at creating a gulf between the two communities. The Walloon brewers found themselves deprived of man power, and, of market. In the small villages above all, they had recourse to the racking of beer coming by train or by gas lorry from the North of the country, near the linguistic border. As for makers of brewery equipment, some had to close their businesses, their staff having been mobilised or taken prisoner. Thus the factory of Louis Bœl-Marlier, situated in Rancourt, and specialising in brewery tanks, disappeared in August 1940. Other manufacturers worked to increase their activity in Belgium, to the extent that until the war, two thirds of their clientele were abroad. This was, for example, the viewpoint taken by the thermal equipment company Wanson, from December 1940.

During 1942 the attitude of the occupier hardened, as much in regard to the Jews as against those who resisted forced labour in Germany. Active resistance began to build up. Hardships worsened. Steel, notably, was lacking. Aluminium was then considered for pipes and pumps. On the other hand, brewers no longer found caps. The quantity of sheet metal was insufficient. In exchange for scrap iron and steel, one could nevertheless obtain vouchers for the acquisition of sheets of new ferrous metals for the manufacture of caps. Mechanical stoppers thus appeared which were adapted for capped bottles. As for raw materials, the lack of them became ever more acute. In 1941 one counted 75 % of amylaceous material and 25 % of sugar. In 1942 the ratio was 60 % to 40 %. And in 1943 it was estimated at 52 % of amylaceous material, 28 % beet, and 20 % sugar - a distribution of raw materials which only increased the animosity between the large breweries and the small. The latter regarded themselves as wronged. The accumulation of matters for disagreement ended in 1947 in the creation of the Association of Small and Medium-sized Family Breweries of Belgium.

In the face of the disaffection of clientele and the risks of disintegration of the brewing industry, it was necessary to become more organised. Pierre Morren, Acting Managing Director of the Brasserie de Kœkelberg, had the idea of gathering together in a college, for the duration of hostilities, of some bottom-fermentation breweries in order to combine their savoir-faire in producing the beers of war, which were palatable and good. In this way the breweries of Alken, Artois, Chevalier-Marin, Kœkelberg, Léopold, and Piedbœuf were united. But, despite the attempts not to bend before the economic slump, the future of the Belgian brewing industry remained uncertain. In January 1943, at the general meeting of the Association of Engineers, arising out of the National Institute of the Fermenting Industries, George Damiens, in his presidential address, raised the following question: "What will be the situation of the Belgian breweries when the torment

After the Liberation, the Lootvoet Brewery in Overijse (Flemish Brabant) made RAF beer, in honour of the Royal Air Force.

which still breathes on the world is soothed, and we can again hope to return to normal activity?"

Now at that time there were still long and painful months before Liberation. On 2nd September 1944, thc allied troops entered Belgium. On the evening of 3rd September, they liberated Brussels, and by the middle of the month the country was almost completed freed. Belgium then experienced a completely different situation to the one left by the First War. Of course there was a collapse in production, hardship, and so on. But immediately after the war there was a commencement of deliveries to the allied armies in Germany which was paid for in hard currency. Besides, American loans, and profits drawn from the Congo - thanks to uranium sold to the Americans for atomic bombs - contributed to this recovery. The brewing industry benefited, to say the least. It could very quickly buy Canadian or American barley. It was a privilege not seen in France, where beer was dependent upon barley reserved for the population's daily bread. In this period when, because of weak beers, France gained the reputation of producing "small beers", the Belgian brewers acquired a name for quality.

The greatest danger for Belgian beer in the immediate post-war period, was the widespread consumption of cola, influenced by the American soldiers. From there, table beer at 0.8°, with its "saccharine taste", could not compete with cola or the sodas, adopted by children. It therefore disappeared from the family table, and in consequence the brewer lost contact with young customers.

Pre-war beermats are all the more sought after by collectors since the German authorities put them on the list of objects for recovery (sheet metal, cartons, etc.).

A BEER SOUVENIR

Jacques Schuermans, brother of a Kortenberg brewer, left for England after the rout. In 1941, a member of the resistance was listening to Radio London following the Belgium-Holland football match. The name of Jacques Schuermans was mentioned. The resistance fighter immediately informed the brewer, his brother, and the whole village listened in. Jacques scored a hat-trick!

At the end of the war, a Belgian type beer was called *Jacques* by the Schuermans Brewery, as a memento of this achievement.

Left: the "V", emblem of the Allied Victory, was overprinted on labels of the Duvieusart Brewery, in Nivelles (Walloon Brabant).

Right: Allied bombardments in Germany inspired the Van Assche Brewery, in Liezele (Province of Antwerp).

DECLARATIONS BY BELGIAN BREWERIES*

1939	177,090,142
1940	126,266,137
1941	26,183,007
1942	27,426,286
1943	23,795,261
1944	27,505,119

* in kilograms of raw materials.

A BREWER'S SON SADLY REMEMBERED

Son of a brewer, born in 1906 in Bouillon, in the Belgian Ardennes, Léon Degrelle inherited from his father, a provincial councillor and very catholic, a deep-thinking gift for words and ideas. He embodied the ideal of the young Christian in a troubled era, when youth was attracted by extremism, be it fascism or communism.

Christ Roi - Christ Rex (Christ the King) was the name of the movement he ran, an inspirational movement, initially Christian, which never hesitated to be political, even going so far as denouncing, at a Congress of Courtrai, the political-financial implications of the Catholic party and to attacking the President of the Federation of the Catholic Circle, Paul Segus. The elections in 1936 brought him twenty one seats. Degrelle sought a reconciliation with the Flemish movement V.N.V. which had achieved a similar result. But their points of view diverged somewhat. The Degrelle party wanted to dominate Belgium, while the V.N.V. rather more wanted independence for Flanders. As a result, their "alliance" was not always ideal.

During 1936, Degrelle, worried by the scheming polititians, took on the hyper-capitalism of the large breweries. His electoral speech flattered the café-owners and their clientele. Belgium then counted some 100,000 café-owners and around 1,500 brewers, representing a fifth of the male electoral body. The politician was not successful in attracting the sympathy of these café-owners, because they only remembered some of his articles, appearing in the movement's review *Rex*, advising strongly against the consumption of beer. The journal *Le Cafetier Belge* thought it opportune to publish an article, "Café-owners and Politics", which recommended that they abstain from politics, their trade not allowing them to bring out their own political personalities.

All this disturbance around the person of Degrelle resulted in a bitter failure - four seats - in the 1937 elections, especially as the Primate of Belgium, Cardinal Van Roey, had recommended that his faithful vote against him. And Degrelle soon foundered beneath fascism and collaboration. On 27th September 1944, he was condemned to death for contempt, by the Council of War in Brussels, for carrying arms against his country, supplying arms to the enemies of the State, and so on. The indictment was multiple. But Degrelle ended his life in exile in Malaga (Spain), where he died in 1994.

A USEFUL INVENTION

In 1942, the engineer Édouard George invented *Glissocaps* which enabled the problems of re-usable caps (failure to move, lifting, and loss of rare and expensive caps, cracking of irreplaceable bottles, loss of precious beer, etc.) to be done away with. The apparatus could be adapted to any capper.

He also perfected a machine to recycle caps.

THE TRICKS OF RECOVERY

The O.M.A. (Office of Mutual Aid), charged with the liquidation of American forces' war stocks, counted, among the material for sale, a certain number of barrage balloons used against enemy aircraft and V1's. These "dirigibles" were useful to some brewers, who fermented their beers in closed tanks, in recovering the gas. The balloons were therefore utilised as gas reservoirs.

STELLA
ARTOIS

ENCORE MEILLEURE QU'AVANT GUERRE
UNE BIERE RICHE ET FINE
NON PASTEURISEE

(5381) IMPRIMERIE CEUTERICK, 66, rue V. Decoster. Louvain

After 1945, the war time products were forgotten.

THE TIME TO REGROUP

All sorts of difficulties and restrictions mark the first post-war years. At the beginning of 1946, there remained no more than 753 breweries in operation, while there had been 1,143 in March 1938. Some had closed their doors, others had given up manufacture and concentrated on the distribution of beers brewed for them elsewhere. The supply of barley was poor and the transport of products posed problems (the increase of railway tariffs and the slowness in obtaining motor lorries promised by the State). In addition, the consumer, having drunk beers of 0.8° during the war, turned to other products of better quality.

The return to normal

Very quickly, Belgium escaped rather better than its European counterparts, thanks to its colony in the Congo, and the production of coal processed and sold at a low price as a boost. The brewing industry followed the trend, and beers recovered their "normal" gravity from December 1945. This desire to reconstruct manifested itself in production which was only 20 per cent down on that of 1938. But top-fermented beers did not achieved the success hoped for. Pale beers of the *Export* or *Pils* type were preferred.

In spite of the economic expansion, the amplification of industrial activity, and the increase in purchasing power, the Fifties were a rather dull time for the Belgian breweries. Certainly by 1955 they had already risen well, and occupied fourth position in world rankings for production. The rise in the cost of raw materials, the increase in salary costs, the burden of taxes, so many factors favoured the concentration of means. Thus, in all industrial sectors, under the impulse of holding companies, regroupings took place (iron and steel, glass, textiles). It was the medium-sized breweries which were affected the most by this phenomenon of merger, the costs of national distribution being heavy in relation to the competition. The small breweries with tied cafés within a very small radius around the point of production turned the corner, thanks to Export, Pils or Dort! These breweries got by with regional specialisation. Already in 1955, among more than 500 breweries, one hundred accounted for 90 per cent of total production. Several breweries held out the hope of a boost

from the Universal Exhibition in Brussels in 1958, but this proved false. The exhibition only fostered the taste for luxury beers (*Dort*, Danish *pils* beers). An attempt at regrouping special beers was made in 1954, with the "Community of Special Beers". But the trend was irreversible. The strikes of 1960 did not put things right. Between 1965 and 1973, the number of breweries fell by 30 per cent.

Belgium experienced a growth of 5 per cent in the years from 1960 to 1973, and the well-being which resulted from it changed the economic environment. The national market for beer was stagnant. The consumer was turning towards wine, luxury beers, and spirits. The eminently competitive context (television was not available to small brewers as an advertising medium), the lack of financial means from which small business suffered, as much to face up to increases in salary costs as to provide for development, the change in the mode of distribution of beer, the reduction of deliveries to home, an increasing role for supermarkets, where the best known brands, having greater means of publicity, got in right from the outset. Many closed and

Label for the last bottles from the Ghlin Brewery, closed following the restructuring of Interbrew.

sold their land or buildings, in towns for large commercial complexes; in the country, for fire-stations and refuse depots, etc. Others developed by providing for the demands of the time: Moorgat with *Tuborg*, and Palm with *Carlsberg*.

All this explains why, at the end of the Seventies, seven breweries controlled 75 per cent of production and why the two largest, Artois and Jupiler, accounted for 51 per cent. Artois achieved its first million hectolitres of production in 1960, two million in 1966, three million in 1969, and four million in 1973.

The evolution of tastes

The increase in the price of a barrel of oil, in 1973, brought an end to the economy of growth and changed still more the face of the Belgian brewing industry. The Belgian economy slowed down. The consumer searched more and more for the quality aspects of lifestyle and an increasing interest appeared for regional speciality beers. Artois experienced a fall in its production in 1974. Cafés dedicated to speciality beers cropped up all over the country: Coeur de Bœuf, La Houblonnière and Le Père Faro in Brussels, Hopduvel in Ghent, Brugs Beertje in Bruges. An exhibition in Bokrijk brought to light a rich past which gained the awareness of the consumer. This induced some brewers who had been slow to create new top-fermented beers. Between 1981 and 1986, the number of beers doubled. An organisation of consumers was formed, "The Objective Beer Tasters", to denounce certain abuses (label beers, the use of the word Trappist for abbey beers, etc.)

Honey was also used before as an ingredient.

The Lefèbvre Brewery returns to tradition with its *Barbar* beer.

In the face of this revival of the craft in the "Year of Beer" (1986), Artois (Leuven) and Jupiler-Piedbœuf (Jupille) announced their desire to merge. *Jupiler*, created in 1966, had progressed so quickly and Artois had stagnated, with under-exploited equipment and sound finances, so that a synergy had to be created. This synergy, with a rationalisation of distribution, production, and marketing, provided the funds for the purchase of the Labatt Brewery in Canada, for the sum of 56.7 billion Belgian Francs (with 23.1 billion of own funds), the largest sum paid by a Belgian business for the purchase of another. This operation restored a dynamism to the Belgian brewing industry which could well profit from the international renown it had and would have. Interbrew became a scout spreading the image of Belgian beer throughout the entire world (Interbrew is at present in eighty countries).

Belgium therefore stands on the first rank of exporting countries. 50 per cent of its production is exported, and this corresponds to 3.2 per cent of world exchange (with 0.2 per cent of the world's population). It is an exemplary brewing industry which makes a considerable contribution to maintaining the balance of payments. And there are the satellite sectors as well, since of the 666,159 tonnes of malt produced, 71 per cent is exported.

There are new challenges on the horizon. Beer suffers at a European level from taxation which is discriminatory when compared with that on wine, with different tariffs according to country. Furthermore, beer and spirits are the scapegoats for all social ills, while greater tolerance is granted to other euphoric products. New products, such as cola (Coca Cola had been introduced in 1940, but ruled after 1960) and iced teas, and the abolition of obligatory military service (30,000 new conscripts each year) cut the breweries off from any contact with youngsters. All that survived were the universities, but economic had cut the budget of the student, and even he preferred quality to quantity. The hopes for beer without alcohol or with a very low alcoholic content were soon dashed, with only a minimal share of the market.

Table beer was presented in the homes of eulogists of beer like Jacques Brel.

The response of the Belgian brewers was not long in coming. Faced with abbey beers, one found: Bière de Château (Van Honsebrouck Brewery), and Bière de Ferme (Strubbe Brewery). A return to certain traditional products, like spelt (Silenrieux and Blaugies Breweries), or honey (La Binchoise and Lefebvre Breweries), began. New beers saw the light of day: tea beers (Lindemans Brewery), in view of the rise of iced tea and the Christmas Glühkriek (Liefmans Brewery).

Recognition of the quality of Belgian beers is international. Thus, the American trade magazine *The Malt Advocate*, in 1995, designated the raspberry lambic beer "Mariage Parfait" (1986), by Frank Boon, as the best beer sold in the United States. At the 1995 World Beer Championship in Chicago, the Binchoise Brewery won the gold medal for its *Bière de l'Ours*, and the title of World Champion for its *Spéciale Noël*.

There are high rewards and a guaranteed future for a sector representing 4.5 per cent of all those employed, and where the investments of recent years were proving profitable.

If the brewery culture has always been rather "macho", women have nevertheless been the target of one brewery, letting fashion influence the clothes worn by its advertising pin-ups. Opposite left, advertisement for Op Ale dating from 1969, and an advertising panel for Real influenced by Brigitte Bardot (1964).

TOWARDS A FEDERAL BELGIUM

For a long time, under different French rules (Dukes of Burgundy, Royalty, French Revolution and Empire), the Flemish community, independent of Belgium, had to face up to the monolingual French speaking (despite the freedom of language guaranteed by Article 23 of the Constitution) of the administration, the government, justice, and the army. This monolingualism was created as a barrier against the Netherlands, by the French speaking bourgeois of Flanders and Wallonia, since it was only in 1838 that the Netherlands signed, in London, the final determination of Belgian territory.

This monolinguistic position and national cohesion was met in the verses of the song La Bière, by Antoine Clesse (La Haye 1816 - Mons 1889):

"Flemish, Walloon,
These are only forenames,
Belgium is our surname."

The Flemish movement revolved around writers such as Henri Conscience, with his book De Leeuw van Vlaanderen ("The Lion of Flanders", 1938), which brought out the struggle of the Flemish against the French, and depicted the Battle of the Golden Spurs in 1302 (celebrated by the Flemish community on 11th July each year). Their demands resulted in the Law of 22nd May 1878, with regard to use of the Flemish language in administrative matters: "In the provinces of Antwerp, Western Flanders, Eastern Flanders, and Limbourg, as well as in the district of Leuven, the notices and communications which officers of the State address to the public will be given in the Flemish language, or in both Flemish and French languages."

However, in 1903, a Flemish brewer, blamed the General Association of Brewers, in *Le Petit Journal du Brasseur*, for not addressing his Dutch speaking members in Flemish, and thus lacking their support for their professional demands. Later the problem of excise declarations in Flemish by the brewer and transcribed in French by excise agents was raised in 1909, by another Flemish brewer.

In order to establish the idea of strict linguistic equality, and to create a Flemish university, it was necessary to listen to a speech by King Albert I on 22nd November 1918. In any event in 1919 the case of the Flemish activists during the war threw approval on the Flemish movement. A crystalisation of the Flemish took place with the pilgrimage of the Yser around the monument to the memory of Flemish soldiers who died in the Great War. Organised by the obedient Flemish, the pilgrimage became a means of linguistic protest. It was necessary to wait for the Centenary of Belgian Independence in 1930 for various measures being taken to resolve the problem. In 1930 the University of Ghent was made Flemish and the French section transferred to the Institut Supérieur des Fermentations of Ghent in Brussels. Laws required the exclusive use of Dutch in Flanders and French in Wallonia, in schools and the administration (1932), justice (1935), and the army (1938). In 1937 an amnesty was voted for activists. Thus two monolingual regions were created.

After the Second World War the situation allowed the different demands of the two communities to be clarified.

First it was the "Royal question", with popular consultation concerning the return of King Léopold III in exile. He was reproached for his attitude during the conflict, his marriage to Liliane Baels in 1941, while 65,000 Walloon soldiers were held in Germany. The result of the consultation gave a national average of 57.7 per cent in favour of the King's return, 72.2 per cent in Flanders, 48 per cent in Brussels, and 42 per cent in Wallonia, where those against won in the industrial regions. Léopold III abdicated in 1951, following riots provoked by these results.

In the second place, the majority of Flemish were in favour of Catholic secondary education, while the majority of Walloons advocated lay education. Another important point was that in 1960, Wallonia saw its heavy industry decline, and the ageing of its population be accentuated. Wallonia represented 33 per cent of the Belgian population in 1961. The proportional representation system placed in evidence the Walloon minority in the Chamber of Deputies: 76 out of 212 in total, with 104 for Flanders and 32 for Brussels. Lastly, demands were different according to the community. In the North, the creation of a nationalist party, the Volksunie, which wanted cultural autonomy and advocated federalism as a pair: Flanders and Wallonia. In the South, demands were of a more economic nature.

These positions led to the University of Leuven being made Flemish in 1968, and to the revision of the

Constitution in 1970, which granted cultural autonomy, in 1971, a process of regional autonomy applied slowly, with four regions, a Brussels region as capital, a Flemish region, a Walloon region, and a German-speaking region.

Following this development, certain data relating to the communities changed. The creation of several micro-breweries in Wallonia reconstructed the brewery infrastructure which had disappeared after 1945. On the other hand, Flanders possessed the brewery museums of Alveringen, Antwerp, Bocholt, Poperinge, and Brussels. Wallonia spoke to the 2nd Collector (Roland Desmecht) to realise the "Espace Duvieusart" in Nivelles in 1998 following negotiations which did not succeed in saving a unique didactic ensemble on a single site in Romedenne, a brewery-maltings and hop-field of the 19th century, and documentation sold to the Grand Duchy of Luxembourg, and to the French museums of Nicolas de Port and Ville sur Illon. As for Romedenne, in 1997 a museum dedicated to the transport of beer will open its doors on the disused site.

Thus, if the Belgian sovereign is often presented as a symbol of union, it is the same thing for beer, only some 15 per cent wanting the separation of the two communities into nations. If the approach is different (beer brotherhoods the majority in Wallonia, and groups for the defence of beer the majority in Flanders) "The 24 Hours of Beer", in Antwerp in the autumn, unites all the brewers and consumers of Belgium, just like the fairs in Ghent in November and Marche in March, for professionals. All of Belgium is united by beer, and can sing more often the words of Antoine Clesse, in place of a foreign "Ein Prosit"!

A full glass, my good friends,
In drinking it, the beer should sing!
A full glass, my good friends,
The beer of the country should sing.

However it should be noted that three problems still had not been presented for consensus opinion. The first was the amnesty demanded for Flemish activists from 1940-1945. The second was the incorporation into Limbourg of the six communes of Fourons (where the French have advanced since 1932) - they were exchanged with Mouscron and Comines, majority French speaking, from the province of Eastern Flanders, incorporated in Hainaut. The third rested in the fact that certain Flemish, faced with an ageing population and an economy in decline in Wallonia, claim the federalisation of social security.

SOME SIGNIFICANT DATES

• **1944:** a system of social security was created: obligatory insurance for all employees provided cover for all the main risks (unemployment, age, sickness, and invalidity).

• **1944:** Belgium, the Netherlands, and Luxembourg created the Benelux Union, a customs union which would come into being in 1948.

• **1945:** the pasteurisation of beer in bottles by electronic process made its debut.

• **1947:** Verzele discovered the iso-humulone, which permitted the measurement of bitterness in beer.

• **1948:** the Union of Belgian Breweries in Export (Unibex) was created.

• **1949:** Belgium joined the North Atlantic Pact (NATO). An integrated military organisation was put in place.

The Meteor, the Belgian Army's first fighter plane, arriving at Chièvres in 1951.

• 1951: King Léopold III abdicated. Baudouin I, his son, succeeded him.

• 1956: the first Wieze Oktoberfeesten in Wieze, where many English met, and who on the same occasion visited other breweries. These festivals stopped in 1984.

• **1957:** the European Economic Community (EEC) was created, uniting Germany, Belgium, France, Italy, Luxembourg, and the Netherlands.

• **1958:** Brussels welcomed the Universal Exhibition. On this occasion, the National Radio Institute (INR) made its first television broadcast. Television became a part of everyday life and changed the habits of consumers, as well as the advertising approach of brewers.

• **1959:** Miss De Coninck, from Watou, became the first lady engineer-brewer in Belgium, taught at the Brewery School in Leuven.

• **1960:** strikes took place throughout the country, caused by the measures taken to sort out national finances.

• **1960:** Independence was proclaimed in the Congo.

• **1967:** Belgium welcomed the headquarters of the Supreme Headquarters Allied Powers in Europe (SHAPE).

• **1970:** VAT (value added tax) was introduced in Belgium. This caused the Artois brewery to use computers.

• **1970:** Constitutional revision ended a unitary State. "La Belgique de papa", was the expression used by the

Minister G. Eyskens.

• **1974:** the Artois group saw, for the first time since 1945, a fall in production from 8,815,764 hectolitres to 8,346,362 hectolitres, while Jupiler increased its production from 5,016,020 hectolitres to 5,383,561 hectolitres.

• **1977:** in his book *The World Guide to Beer*, the Englishman Michael Jackson brought out the quality of traditional Belgian Beers.

• **1978:** the French group BSN took a shareholding in the Alken Brewery (followed later, in 1980, by the Anglo-Belge Brewery, and, in 1988, the Maes Brewery).

• **1978:** the Belgian brewing heritage interested people more and more. The "Gambrinus Belgique" was to be the first collectors' club.

• **1979:** a movement for the protection of traditional Belgian beers, "Bières Traditionelles Belges" (BTB), was born in Brussels.

• **1982:** in Bokrijk (Limburg), an exhibition was held, "Bieren en Pintelieren", where special beers given pride of place were to be discovered by an audience from all over Belgium.

• **1983:** the Law on spirituous liquor abolished the prohibitionist Van der Velde Law (1919). The sale of alcohol was henceforth allowed in cafés having a licence.

• **1984:** a movement aimed at the defence of beers and consumers was formed: the *Objectieve Bierproevers* (Objective Beer Tasters).

• **1986:** taking into account the success of the exhibitions in Bockrijk, in 1982 and 1983, the CBB proclaimed 1986 as the "Year of Beer" in Belgium.

• **1986:** the Artois Brewery and the Piedbœuf Brewery (Jupiler) merged, later to form the Interbrew group.

• **1986:** the "International Week of the Brewery" Exhibition in Antwerp allowed visitors from abraod to discover Belgian beers.

• **1986:** one of the first brewery museums, in Willebrœck, was sold to Dutch brewers.

• **1987:** Interbrew opened theme bars in Tours (France), the Hœgaarden, and the Brussels Café.

• **1987:** ecologists participated in the formation of government for the first time.

• **1988:** the demolition of the brewery of Wielemans-Ceuppens in Forest (taken over by Artois in 1978) provoked the first attempt to save a brewery building, resorting to industrial archaeology.

• **1988:** the Italian Carlo de Benedetti launched a public offer to buy Société Générale, the largest Belgian holding company. This shook Belgian patriotism and brought out the fact that Belgian capital was gradually falling into foreign hands. The holding company finally fell under the control of the French Indo-Suez group.

• **1989:** following the Interbrew decision to close its production centres in Mechelen (Lamot), Merchtem (Ginder-Ale), Mont Saint Guibert (Vieux-Temps), Ghlin (Brassico), and Eeklo (Krüger), a strike lasted 34 days. This was a phenomenon without precedent in the history of Belgium.

• **1991:** deposits were introduced on beer casks.

• **1992:** the brewers and the CBB supported the formation of the Arnoldus group to promote responsible consumption of beer, with the slogan "a beer brewed with knowledge should be drunk wisely".

• **1993:** the sudden death of King Baudouin I, caused great dismay. (After the shock of the Société Générale on the Belgian economy, here was the disappearance of the symbol of unity of the Belgian people). His brother Albert (Albert II) succeeded him.

• **1994:** on 1st December, the maximum alcohol level permitted to drivers fell from 0.8g to 0.5g of alcohol per litre of blood. The basis of alcohol per litre of air went from 35mg to 22mg.

• **1995:** Interbrew took over the Labatt Brewery in Canada, and became the fourth brewer in the world after Annheuser-Busch, Heineken, and Miller.

• **1995:** the first attempts at fermentation for 24 hours at the C.E.R.I.A. in Brussels, with a yeast of on which was passed wort from the De Dool Brewery, for 24 hours.

Prime Minister Jean-Luc DeHaene, then Minister of Transport, caricatured for a low-alcohol beer, served at the Hopduvel in Ghent.

IN PURSUIT OF UNION

As we have seen previously, it was the in the Middle Ages that trades organised themselves, and guilds made an appearance *(see page 28)*. Brussels had its guild of brewers, very closely linked to communal life. Established from the 17th century in a building on the Grand Place, this corporation was powerful until the French Revolution which, in 1795, by the Le Chapelier Law, put an end to the guild system. It was not until Belgian Independence that freedom of association was reborn. An association of brewers was founded in Brussels in 1831, which did not delay in playing an important role. Other organisations were established here and there around the country. But it soon appeared vital, for greater efficacy in protection of the trade, that there be some sort of guild organisation on a national scale.

The spirit of solidarity manifested by the brewers on the occasion of the Orban Law was closely connected with the creation of the *General Association of Belgian Brewers*, in 1869. Its principal preoccupation was the excise system, which the brewers demanded be revised. On this point, as in other fields, the Association kept the brewers informed, and stepped in to arbitrate on possible problems. Its task was also to distribute scientific studies to its members, and to represent Belgian breweries abroad.

At the turn of the 20th century, the General Association of Belgian Brewers combined some 450 of the 3,223 existing breweries. Numerous brewers' associations, regional and local, were founded, and they were directly affiliated. This development brought the transformation of the Association, in 1909, into the *General Federation of Belgian Brewers*. In the following year the Federation counted 1,400 brewery members. On 25th July 1914 it was recognised as a professional union.

In the torment of the Great War, in March 1915, the *Belgian Consortium of Breweries* was formed in parallel, in Brussels, joining the large bottom-fermentation breweries, a good third of all Belgian breweries. Its objective was the improvement of beer by competition as to quality. Its means were to fix prices and standardise the categories of beer. From its side, the Federation carried on with its task. It had to protect a certain number of top-fermentation breweries, which saw their beers losing favour, in the face of a growth in beers of the Pilsen or Munich type. Rivalry between large and small breweries was accentuated. And it was necessary for the Federation to modify its system of voting in order that the Consortium accept affiliation - each brewery henceforth had one additional vote for every 100,000 kg of flour used, up to one million, and one additional vote for every 500,000 kg above one million.

From then, the large breweries exercised a predominant role in the Federation. The small and medium-sized businesses felt some disquiet about it. Hence their desire to create, in 1931 in response to the increase in excise duties, a *Group of small and medium-sized Partisan Breweries for Progressive Excise Duties*. The following year this group became the *Group of Small and Medium-sized Breweries of Belgium*.

Nevertheless, during the Thirties, the necessity of a union was really obvious. To protect common interests - notably in the face of accumulating taxes - a certain number of brewers wished to regroup the various organisations referring to beer in a central body, which would have to be named, for example, the "Commission for the Protection of the Drinks Industry."

Events quickened. On the eve of the Second World War, the Consortium withdrew from the General Federation of Belgian Brewers. On the other hand, as soon as the action for progressive excise duties ended, the *Group of Small and Medium-sized Breweries of Belgium* craved affiliation to the Federation. Then, after the Liberation, a genuine desire for union manifested itself "so as to provide for the representation and the protection of the general interests of breweries in relation to the constituted authorities, in order to form for the needs of the embryo a professional and economic organisation for a long time envisaged by the government and to prepare better for a return as desired to a freer economy," as it was explained by Paul Van Cauwenberge, Permanent Secretary of the Federation in 1947. This concern to unite, the better to restore the brewing industry, gave birth to the *Directorate* of Belgian Brewers. In this Directorate, the Consortium (now called AssBra, "Belgian Association of Brewers") was represented by two delegates, and the Federation, with some 690 members, by four.

It was still not the time for perfect cohesion. In fact, members of the Federation, in disagreement with it, split to found the *Association of Small and Medium-sized Family Breweries of Belgium* (APMBFB), inspired by the pre-war grouping. Certain breweries could not choose between the Federation and dissidence. The activity of some provincial associations or local circles was practically wiped out. The disappearance of a great number of breweries had, for a large part, contributed to this disaffection.

AssBra, APMBFB, and the Federation... Belgian breweries were not always represented coherently. It was on 15th December 1971, that this was at last achieved. Around the three existing professional associations was created the Confederation of Belgian Breweries (CBB), with a common office and secretariat. This Confederation fixed as its object, "to combine all the breweries located in Belgium and to create, to maintain, and to develop the spirit and the links of solidarity between them," as well as "to protect the general interests of Belgian breweries." Its activity was at a national level, but also on an international scale. It comprised two sections: that of the small and medium-sized breweries, which joined the businesses of which annual production was less than 400,000 hectolitres, and that of the industrial breweries, which concerned companies with an annual production of more than 400,000 hectolitres.

An office for the service of beer

Created in 1951, the National Commission for the Retailing of Beer made way, in 1975, for the National Office for the Retailing of Beer (ONDB), which itself was renamed in 1994, as the "Belgian Office for the Service of Beer". This body organises sales examinations, and awards diplomas. Café-owners whom, through its inspectors, it "recognises" for the quality of retailing and service of the beer, are authorised to affix a plaque bearing the logo of the Office.

See Arnoldus Group, p. 81 ; *Unibex,* p. 159.

PRESIDENTS OF THE GENERAL FEDERATION OF BELGIAN BREWERS

1869	M. Paris	Binche
1882	O. Tystermans	Brussels
1885	P. Grosfils	Verviers
1887	G. Fevrier	Sombreffe
1888	E. Herbos	Brussels
1890	P. Grosfils	Verviers
1891	O. Van Der Molen	Antwerp
1893	P. Grosfils	Verviers
1894	A. Mertens	Kruibeke
1897	D. Lannoy	Menin
1898	A. Mertens	Kruibeke
1900	Ch. Heyndrickx	Lodelinsart
1903	M. Ortmans	Liège
1906	G. Lamot	Mechelen
1910	P. Wielemans	Brussels
1913	F. Piron	Ghlin
1920	E. Van den Schrieck	Tirlemont
1926	V. Cordemans	Antwerp
1929	L. Wielemans	Brussels
1932	L. Van Mele	Gand
1935	M. Carlier	Frameries
1938 (6 mois)	C. Van Breedam	Mechelen
1939	J. de Gesst	Courtrai
1945	G. Deryck	Tubize
1949	G. de Blieck	Alost
1953	X. de Jonghe	Willebrœck
1960	A. Vander Stricht	Ghend
1966	P. de Boeck	Brussels
1973	R. van der Schueren	Wegnez
1976	L. de Weerdt	Bruges
1977	C. Pepersak	Brussels
1984	M. van den Bogaert	Antwerp
1990	O. van der Ghinste	Kortrijk

PRESIDENTS OF THE CONFEDERATION OF BELGIAN BREWERS

1971	C. P. Wielemans	Brussels
1974	P. de Boeck	Brussels
1977	M. van den Bogaert	Brussels
1983	R. van der Schueren	Wegnez
1989	J. Martens	Bocholt
1992	P. De Keersmaeker	Kobbegem

VICE PRESIDENTS OF THE CONFEDERATION OF BELGIAN BREWERS

1992	R. Vaxelaire	Waarloos
	D. Van der Haegen	Silly

The future King Albert II, on a visit to the Brewers' Hall in 1993. At his side, the President of the Confederation of Belgian Brewers, P. De Keersmacker. C.B. document.

BELGIUM AND ITS BREWERIES

Abbaye Notre Dame de St. Rémy
Rue de l'Abbaye, 8, B-5580 Rochefort
Tel : 084/ 21 31 81

Abbaye des Rocs
Chaussée Brunehaut, 37,
B-7387 Montignies-sur-Roc
Tel : 065/ 75 99 76

Abbaye de Scourmont (Chimay)
Rue de la Trappe, 294,
B-6464 Forges-Les-Chimay
Tel : 060/ 21 30 63

Abdij der Trappisten Van Westmalle
Antwerpsesteenweg, 496, B-2390 Malle
Tel : 03/ 312 92 22

Abdij St. Sixtus
Donkerstraat, 12, B-8640 Westvleteren
Tel : 057/ 40 03 76

Brasserie d'Achouffe
Route du Village, 32, B-6666 Achouffe
Tel :061/ 28 81 47

Alken (Alken-Maes)
Stationsstraat, 2, B-3570 Alken
Tel : 011/ 31 27 11

Het Anker (John Martin)
Guido Gezellelaan, 49, B-2800 Mechelen
Tel : 015/ 20 38 80

Les Artisans Brasseurs
Place de la Station, 2, B-5000 Namur
Tel : 081/ 23 16 94

Artois (Interbrew)
Vaartstraat, 94, B-3000 Leuven
Tel : 016/ 24 71 11

Brasserie d'Aubel
Rue de Battice, 93, B-4880 Aubel
Tel : 087/ 68 70 29

Bavik - De Brabandere
Rijksweg, 33, B-8531 Bavikhove
Tel : 056/ 71 13 79

Belle Vue (Interbrew)
Rue DelanoyStraat, 58-60,
B-1080 Sint-Jans-Molenbeek
Tel : 02/ 412 44 11

Belle Vue (Interbrew)
Quai du Hainaut (Henegouwenkaai), 33,
B-1080 Molenbeek Tel : 02/ 412 44 11

Belle Vue (Interbrew)
Chaussée de Mons (Steenweg naar Bergen), B-1600 Sint-Pieters-Leeuw
Tel : 02/ 412 44 11

De Bie
Stoppelweg, 26, B-8978 Watou
Tel : 057/ 38 86 66

La Binchoise
Faubourg St. Paul, 38, B-7130 Binche
Tel : 064/ 33 61 86

Bios - Van Steenberge
Lindenlaan, 25, B-9940 Ertvelde
Tel : 09/ 344 50 71

Brasserie de Blaugies
Rue de la Frontière, 435,
B-7370 Blaugies Tel : 065/ 65 03 60

De Block
Nieuwbaan, 92,B-1785 Peizegem-Merchtem Tel : 052/ 37 21 59

Bockor
Kwabrugstraat, 5, B-8510 Bellegem
Tel : 056/ 21 65 71

Brasserie du Bocq
Rue de la Brasserie, 4, B-5530 Purnode
Tel : 082/ 61 07 80

Boelens
Kerkstraat, 7, B-9111 Belsele
Tel : 03/ 772 32 00

Boon
Fonteinstraat, 65, B-1502 Lembeek
Tel : 02/ 356 66 44

Bosteels
Kerkstraat, 92, B-9255 Buggenhout
Tel : 052/ 33 22 82

Brasserie de Brunehaut
Rue des Panneries, 17, B-7623 Brunehaut
Tel : 069/ 34 64 11

Cantillon
Rue Gheude (Gheudestraat), 56,
B-1070 Anderlecht Tel : 02/ 521 49 28

La Caracole
Côte Marie-Thérèse, 86,
B-5500 Falmignoul Tel : 082/ 74 40 80

Caulier
Rue Sondeville, 132, B-7600 Peruwelz
Tel : 069/ 77 04 34

Clarysse
Krekelput, 16-18, B-9700 Oudenaarde
Tel : 055/ 31 17 21

Cnudde
Fabriekstraat, 8, B-9700 Eine
Tel : 0055/ 31 18 33

Contreras
Molenstraat, 115, B-9890 Gavere
Tel : 09/ 384 27 06

Crombé
Hospitaalstraat, 10, B-9620 Zottegem
Tel : 09/ 360 02 40

Deca Services
Elverdingestraat, 4, B-8640 Woesten-Vleteren Tel : 057/ 42 20 75

Devaux
Rue de l'Église St. Philippe, 1,
B-5600 Philippeville
Tel : 071/ 66 63 47

De Dolle Brouwers
Roeselarestraat, 12b, B-8600 Esen-Diksmuide Tel : 051/ 50 27 81

Domus
Tiensestraat, 8, B-3000 Leuven
Tel : 016/ 29 18 68

De Dool
Eikendreef, 21, B-3530 Helchteren
Tel : 011/ 52 29 99

Geuzestekerij Drie Fonteinen
H. Teirlinckplein, 3, B-1650 Beersel
Tel : 02/ 331 06 52

Dubuisson
Chaussée de Mons, 28, B-7904 Pipaix
Tel : 069/ 66 20 85

Dupont
Rue Basse, 5, B-7904 Tourpes-Leuze
Tel : 069/ 67 10 66

Brasserie Ellezelloise
Guinaumont, 75, B-7890 Ellezelles
Tel : 068/ 54 31 60

Eupener Bierbrauerei
Paveestraße, 12-14, B-4700 Eupen
Tel : 087/ 55 47 31

Eylenbosch (Alken-Maes)
Ninoofsesteenweg, 5, B-1703 Schepdaal
Tel : 02/ 569 14 78

Facon
Kwabrugstraat, 27, B-8510 Bellegem
Tel : 056/ 22 07 69

Fantôme
Rue Preal, 8, B-6997 Soy
Tel : 086/ 47 70 44

La Ferme au Chêne
Rue Comte d'Ursel, 36, B-6940 Durbuy
Tel : 086/ 21 10 67

Friart
Rue d'Houdeng, 20, B-7070 Le Roeulx
Tel : 064/ 66 21 51

't Gaverhopke
Steenbrugstraat, 187,
B-8530 Harelbeke-Stasegem
Tel : 056/ 25 86 70

Gigi
Grand-Rue, 96, B-6769 Gerouvillle
Tel : 063/ 57 75 15

Girardin
Lindenberg, 10, B-1700 Sint-Ulriks-Kapelle Tel : 02/ 452 64 19

De Gouden Boom
Langestraat, 45, B-8000 Brugge
Tel : 050/ 33 06 90

Haacht
Provinciesteenweg, 28, B-3190
Boortmeerbeek Tel : 016/ 60 15 01

Hanssens Geuzestekerij
Vroenenbosstraat, 15, B-1653 Dworp
Tel : 02/ 380 31 33

Hoegaarden (Interbrew)
Stoopkensstraat, 46, B-3320 Hoegaarden
Tel : 016/ 76 76 76

Huyghe
Brusselsesteenweg, 282, B- 9090 Melle
Tel : 09/ 252 15 01

Jupiler (Interbrew)
Rue de Visé, 243,
B-4020 Jupile-sur-Meuse
Tel : 041/ 62 78 00

De Keersmaeker (Alken-Maes)
Lierput, 1, B-1730 Kobbegem
Tel : 02/ 452 47 47

Kerkom
Naamsesteenweg, 469,
B-3800 Kerkom-St.Truiden
Tel : 011/ 68 20 87

De Koninck
Mechelsesteenweg, 291,
B-2018 Antwerpen Tel : 03/ 218 40 48

Léfèbvre
Rue de Croly, 54, B-1430 Quenast
Tel : 067/ 67 07 66

Leroy
Diksmuidseweg, 406, B-8904 Boezinge
Tel : 057/ 42 20 05

Liefmans (Riva)
Aalststraat, 200, B-9700 Oudenaarde
Tel : 055/ 31 13 92

Lindemans
Lenniksebaan, 1479, B-1602 Vlezenbeek
Tel : 02/ 569 03 90

De Loterbol
Michel Thijs Straat, 58, B-3290 Diest
Tel : 013/ 32 36 28

Louwaege
Markt, 14, B-8610 Kortemark
Tel : 051/ 56 60 67

Maes (Alken-Maes)
Waarloosveld, 10, B-2550 Waarloos
Tel : 015/ 30 90 11

Martens
Reppelerweg, 1, B-3950 Bocholt
Tel : 089/ 47 29 80

Meesters
Hoogstraat, 50, B-1570 Galmaarden
Tel : 054/ 58 84 80

Le Miroir
Place Reine Astrid (Koningin Astridplein), 24-26, B-1090 Jette
Tel : 02/ 424 04 78

Moortgat
Breendonkdorp, 58,
B-2870 Breendonk-Puurs
Tel : 03/ 886 71 21

Brasserie d'Oleye
Rue d'Elmette, 39,
B-4300 Oleye-Waremme
Tel : 019/ 33 04 35

Old Bailey
Kerkplein, 6
B-8880 Sint Eloois Winkel
Tel: 058/ 50 07 28

Brasserie d'Orval
Orval 2, B-6823 Villers-devant-Orval
Tel : 061/ 31 12 61

Paelmans
Brockakkerstraat, 1
B-9230 Wetteren
Tel: 093/ 69 50 97

Palm
Steenhuffeldorp, 3, B-1840 Steenhuffel
Tel : 052/ 30 94 81

Poncelet
Route de Charleville, 72,
B-5575 Gedinne
Tel : 061/ 58 85 54

Brasserie de la Praile
Rue de la Praile, 3, B-7120 Peissant
Tel : 064/ 77 16 43

Riva (Riva)
Wontergemstraat, 42, B-8720 Dentergem
Tel : 051/ 63 36 81

Roberg
Rodebergstraat, 46, B-8954 Westouter
Tel : 057/ 44 62 14

Brasserie Rochefortoise
Rue du Treux, 43, B-5580 Eprave
Tel : 084/ 37 80 84

Rodenbach
Spanjestraat, 133, B-8800 Roeselare
Tel : 051/ 22 34 00

Roman
Hauwaert, 61, B-9700 Oudenaarde-Mater
Tel : 055/ 45 54 01

De Ryck
Kerkstraat, 28, B-9550 Herzele
Tel : 053/ 62 23 02

Brasserie de Silenrieux
Rue Noupré, 1, B-5630 Silenrieux
Tel : 071/ 63 32 01

Brasserie de Silly
Ville Basse A, 141, B-7830 Silly
Tel : 068/ 55 13 51

De Schuur
Gobbelsrode, 75, B-3220 Kortrijk-Dutsel
Tel : 09/ 223 60 01

Slaghmuylder
Denderhoutembaan, 2, B-9400 Ninove
Tel : 054/ 33 18 31

De Smedt
Ringlaan, 18, B-1745 Opwijk
Tel : 052/ 35 99 11

St. Bernardus
Trappistenweg, 23, B-8978 Watou
Tel : 057/ 38 80 21

St. Jozef
Itterplein, 19, B-3960 Oppiter
Tel : 011/ 86 47 11

Steedje
Schoolstraat, 45b, B-8460 Ettelgem
Tel : 059/ 26 50 30

Sterkens
Meerdorp, 20, B-2321 Meer
Tel : 03/ 315 71 45

Straffe Hendrik (Riva)
Walplein, 26, B-8000 Brugge
Tel : 050/ 33 26 97

Strubbe
Markt, 1, B-8480 Ichtegem
Tel : 051/ 58 81 16

Timmermans (John Martin)
Kerkstraat, 11, B-1701 Itterbeek
Tel : 02/ 569 03 58

Brasserie de la Tour
Rue Chera, 9, B-4180 Comblain-la-Tour
Tel : 041/ 69 14 87

De Troch
Langestraat, 20, B-1741 Ternat-Wambeek
Tel : 02/ 582 10 27

Union (Alken-Maes)
Rue Derbèque, 7, B-6040 Jumet
Tel : 071/ 35 01 33

Van Den Bossche
Sint-Lievensplein, 16,
B-9550 Sint-Lievens-Esse
Tel : 054/ 50 04 11

Van Eecke
Douvieweg, 2, B-8978 Watou
Tel : 057/ 42 20 05

Van Honsebrouck
Oostrozebekestraat, 43,
B-8770 Ingelmunster
Tel : 051/ 30 34 14

Vander Linden
Brouwerijstraat, 2, B-1500 Halle
Tel : 02/ 356 50 59

Vandervelden
Laarheidestraat, 230, B-1650 Beersel
Tel : 02/ 380 33 96

Brasserie à Vapeur
Rue de Maréchal, 1,
B-7904 Pipaix-Leuze
Tel : 069/ 66 20 47

Verhaeghe
Beukenhofstraat, 96, B-8570 Vichte
Tel : 056/ 77 70 32

Villers
Liezeledorp, 37, B-2870 Liezele-Puurs
Tel : 03/ 889 88 00

Walrave
Lepelstraat, 36, B-9270 Laarne
Tel : 09/ 369 01 34

Wieze-Anker
Nieuwstraat, 1, B-9280 Wieze
Tel : 053/ 21 52 01

CLUBS

Brasserie Hobby Club
c/o Saive Freddy
Rue Defuissaux, 93, B-7301 Hornu
Tel : 065 / 77 89 82

Cervesia Tormacum
c/o Detournay José
Rue d'Ormont, 20b, B-7540 Kain
Tel : 069 / 21 42 45

Gambrinusclub van België
c/o Vandermotten R.
Brusselsesteenweg, 47,
B-3080 Tervuren Tel : 02 / 767 67 86

Vlaamse Klub van Bierattributen
c/o Goeman Rony
H. Consciencestraat, 37,
B-9308 Hofstade-Aalst
Tel : 053 / 21 39 58

West-Vlaamse Bierviltjes en Attributen Club
c/o Vandenborre Léonard
General Deprezstraat, 154,
B-8530 Stasegem
Tel : 056 / 21 31 86

Camra (Brussels)
c/o Stephen D'Arcy
Rue des Attrébates, 67
B-1040 Brussels
Tel: 02 / 736 72 18

THE OBJECTIVE BEER TASTERS

Created in 1984 in Berchem, the Association of *Objective Beer Tasters* aims to protect and to promote the heritage of the Belgian breweries. Its main aim was first of all to fight against the disappearance of small traditional breweries, and to make consumers aware of the requirements of quality in beer. For some years it looked to make known the range of artisanal beers. Thus it organised each year the "24 Hours of Special Belgian Beer", a major beer festival in Antwerp, where the brewers came to give tastings of their products. In 1994, 45 brewers were present, with 123 beers, of which 90 were served from the barrel.
Office address :

De Objectieve Bierproevers
Postbus 32, B-2600 Berchem 5
Tel : 03/ 232 45 38

NOORDZEE
MER DU NORD
Oostende
Oudenburg
Steenbrugge
St Idesbald
Brugge
Alveringem
Westvleteren
Poperinge
WEST-
VLAANDEREN
1/256
Pittem
Roeselare
Ieper
Kortrijk
Comines
OOST-VLAANDEREN
1/283
Gent
Wetteren
Ename
Oudenaarde
Mater
Zottegem
Aalst
Asse
Dielegem
Bornem
Westmalle
Antwerpen
ANTWERPEN
1/346
Lier
Tongerlo
Mechelen
Grimbergen
Aarschot
VLAAMS
BRABANT
1/675
Bruxelles
Brussel
1/391
Park
Leuven
Halle
Lembeek
Wavre
BRABANT
WALLON
1/675
Tournai
Silly
Cambron-Casteau
Thieusies
Nivelles
Villers-la-Ville
Mons
Stambruges
Le Rœulx
HAINAUT
1/341
Charleroi
Namur
Floreffe
Rocs
Bonne Espérance
Aulne
Châtelet
Maredsous
Romedenne
Chimay
FRANCE
Flemish Region
Walloon Region
German Speaking Region
Brussels Region - Capital
Provincial Border
Regional Border

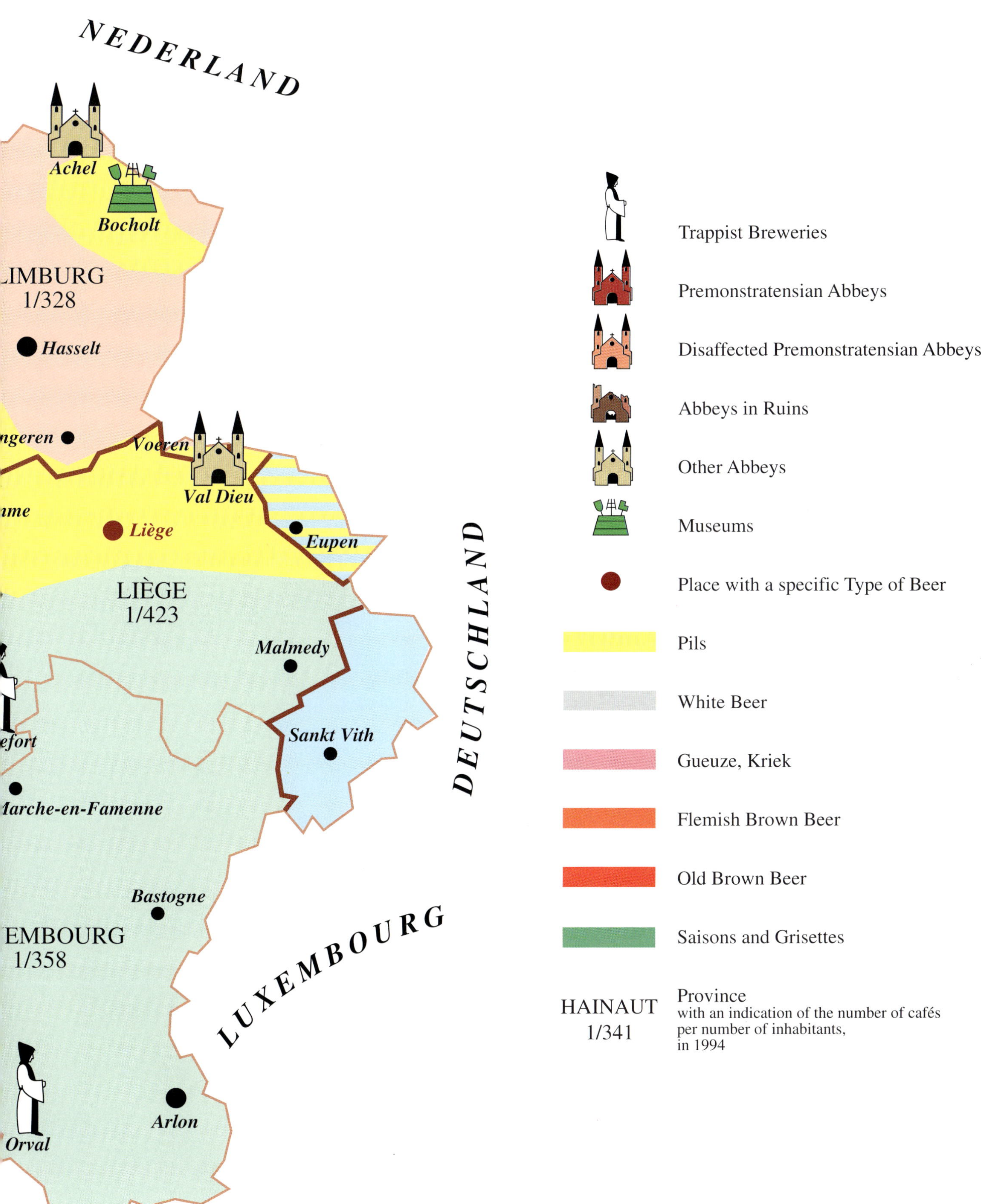
NEDERLAND
Achel
Bocholt
LIMBURG
1/328
Hasselt
Voeren
Val Dieu
Liège
Eupen
LIÈGE
1/423
Malmedy
Sankt Vith
Marche-en-Famenne
Bastogne
EMBOURG
1/358
Arlon
Orval
DEUTSCHLAND
LUXEMBOURG
Trappist Breweries
Premonstratensian Abbeys
Disaffected Premonstratensian Abbeys
Abbeys in Ruins
Other Abbeys
Museums
Place with a specific Type of Beer
Pils
White Beer
Gueuze, Kriek
Flemish Brown Beer
Old Brown Beer
Saisons and Grisettes
HAINAUT
1/341
Province
with an indication of the number of cafés
per number of inhabitants,
in 1994

"Belgian" Beer

Alarmed by the success of English beer in Belgium, at the very beginning of the 20th century, the teachers at the various brewery schools decided to create a "Belgian" beer. The learned professor Henri Van Laer, in particular, had produced the idea that the country, famous for the diversity of its brewing production, should provide a type of modern beer capable of appealing to the most delicate palate. A Contest for the Improvement of Belgian Beer was organised on the occasion of a brewery exhibition which took place in Brussels, in the Golden Jubilee Hall, in December 1902 and January 1903.

The characteristics of the beer called "Belgian" were to say the least imprecise. Raw materials were left to the choice of the brewer, on condition of course that they corresponded to the provisions of the legislation currently in force. Original gravity was to be between 4.5 and 5° Belgian, therefore more than that of all the beers which the consumer neglected. It was to cost 15 to 20 centimes a glass, foreign beers being around 30 centimes a glass.

Entries to the competition were not very numerous. It turned out that the constraint upon entrants to provide a description of manufacture had been an obstacle to participation. And this clause was removed in 1904 for the second exhibition and the Contest for the Perfection of Belgian Beer (the title had changed a little!). The following year, the Universal Exhibition in Liège was the setting for a new competition. Seventy three brewers entered, with fifty seven top-fermented beers, seven bottom-fermented, and nine of spontaneous fermentation. The winners were, for top-fermentation, the Melsbrœck Brewery, for its cask beer, and the Binard Brewery, of Châtelineau, for its bottled beer - from whence came the renown of the *Belge Faleau*, which it brewed. As for bottom-fermentation, the Artois and Kœkelberg brewerie won joint first prize, the first with its Munich, and the second with its Bock. Lastly the spontaneous fermentation beers were illustrated by the Bontemps Brewery, in Brussels.

The beer from the Binard Brewery, of an *ale* type, was dazzlingly successful. Several breweries in the region imitated it. *Belge* was made by Delbruyère, Masureel and Fauconnier in Châtelet, by the Union Brewery in Jumet, by Dussart in Gilly, Heyndrickx in Lodelinsart, and Bavery in Couillet. *La Belge* from the Delbruyère Brewery, created in 1888, became the most famous, however. It was to be taken over in 1955 by the Union Brewery from Jumet, which, in 1964, was absorbed by Watney-Maes. The last brews date from 1978, when special beers were experiencing a revival.

The *Vieux Temps* from the Grade Brewery was originally a *belge*. In Brabant the beers took the name of *spéciale* (*Spéciale Palm*, for example) or of *ale (Ginder Ale*, *Horse Ale*, *Op Ale)*. After the Second World War, the brewers of lambic, low on reserves, produced this type of beer: *Spéciale Heyva* (Heyvaert Brewery, in Asse), *Spéciale Néval* (Nève Brewery, in Schepdaal). Some brewers did not hesitate to establish a comparison with British products. "A true Belgian pale ale", could be read in the publicity material of the Aliés Brewery, the Union Brewery, and the Dussart Brewery.

Taking into account its national success, the Delbruyère Brewery even had a depot in Brussels.

BEER

» En chaque enclos, l'été ; l'Hiver, sous chaque Toit,
Où la province
S'attable, au jour le jour, et boit,
Le Bourgmestre est prince
Mais le brasseur est Roi.

» Sa Brasserie, elle est là bas, lourde et fumante
Et la chaleur s'active, et les brassins fermentent ;
Et lui-même surveille, et du geste et des yeux,
Le moite et sourd travail de l'eau avec les feux.

» Une odeur d'orge,
Soudain, dès qu'on franchit son seuil,
Serre la gorge ;
Les gros chevaux sont lourds d'orgueil
Et, quand ils passent,
Avec leur char avec cent tonneaux,
Sur la Grand'Place,
Ils font trembler plus d'un carreau
Qui, dans le soir, scintille
Aux fenêtres en or du Vieil hôtel de Ville.

» L'homme est hospitalier, facile et cordial ;
Dans sa maison au long trottoir, près du canal,
La bière,
À celui qui la boit devant un feu vermeil,
Semble sortir en robe de soleil
Du creux des verres.

» Sa femme saine et grasse, et ses enfants replets ;
Dans un coin de la cour, à l'ombre des ramures,
Elle-même, les mois d'été, puise aux baquets
Et verse aux boulangers les mousseuses levures ;
C'est son modeste orgueil, quand est meilleur le pain
Et puis, le soir, quand la lampe brûle, ses mains,
Calcul après calcul, s'acharnent à poursuivre
La piste des erreurs au taillis du Grand Livre.

» Et d'année en année, en s'aidant tous les jours,
La femme ardente au gain, et l'homme âpre aux négoces
Cueillent les lourdes fleurs des fortunes précoces ;
Ils ont acquis, aux angles clairs des carrefours,
Vingt maisons à pignons, dont les larges enseignes,
À celui qui s'en va ou s'en revient, renseignent
Quelle bière éclatante et vivante on y sert.
Oh ! la pinte vidée, à la hâte, en plein air,
Et l'orgueil de sentir au fond de soi descendre
La sève en or des grains et des houblons de Flandre !

» Voici quinze ans bientôt que le brasseur travaille
Et que la vie, avec ses vœux et ses souhaits,
Se serre, ici, là bas, partout, entre les mailles
Qu'il noue en chaque rue autour d'un cabaret ;
De faubourg en faubourg, son renom règne à l'aise,
Dès qu'il paraît, il paie à boire et dûment boit,
Et sa parole alors est parole de poids,
Et son geste est suivi aussi loin qu'il les mène.

» Si bien que la boisson qu'il vend chaque semaine
Se répand dans la ville, orientant vers lui,
De maison en maison, les cœurs et les esprits ;
Elle est la force lourde et la lente pensée
Dont s'émeuvent encore les cervelles tassées ;
Et tels jours de scrutin où le pouvoir a peur,
Elle est celle qui chauffe, à feu brusque, l'ardeur
Que renferment les fronts joyeux ou taciturnes ;
Et c'est elle toujours qui glisse entre les doigts
Le vote alerte et franc ou le vote sournois
Que chacun jette, avec sa passion, dans l'urne.

» En chaque enclos, l'été ; l'Hiver, sous chaque Toit,
Où la province
S'attable, au jour le jour, et boit,
Le Bourgmestre est prince
Mais le brasseur est Roi. »

(Émile Verhaeren, *les Villes à Pignons, 1909.*)

Émile Verharen, Belgian poet in the French language, lived from 1855 to 1916 in Roisin, in the Honnelles region, near the present day brewery of Abbaye des Rocs. The *Villes à Pignons* poems are one fifth of the anthology *Toute la Flandre* (1904-1911), a work in which the poet recalls the country of his birth.

This enamel plaque made by the Haacht Brewery in 1938, bears witness to the importance given by brewers of the time to raw materials. The sower of barley appears as a symbol.

THE VARIOUS INGREDIENTS...

THE FIRST CONSTITUENT,

MALT

It is barley, a cereal of the gramineae species, which is transformed into malt. The two great species used in brewing are: two row barley, or common barley *(Hordeum vulgare)*, of which the everyday have the names Triumph, Menuet, Prisma, and Alexis, and six row barley, or winter barley *(Hordeum hexastichum)*, of which the most common varieties are called Clarine, Capri, and Plaisant. Certain varieties are sown in autumn ("winter" barley) and others in the spring ("spring" barley). All are harvested more or less early in the summer. The work of the maltster consists, therefore, in the first place, in carefully selecting the barley, according to these criteria, but also in taking account of other characteristics, which are the origin of the grains (maritime or continental), their rate of humidity (it should be approximately 16 per cent), and their grade.

The first stage in the "disintegration" of the barley into malt is the soaking of the grains in water, an operation in the course of which the complex molecules change into more simple molecules with the effect of enzymes (or amylases), thus promoting the development of the germ. The humidity of the grain should attain a rate of approximately 45 per cent.

During malting, the barley is germinated. The nature of the nitrogenous materials changes, the grain becomes more crumbly, its diastatic power increased (Wielemans-Ceuppens Brewery, before 1914).

A **grain of barley** is composed of three elements:

- the *endosperm*, rich in starch, in albumin, and in gum;
- the *husk*, which protects the germ on malting and contributes to filtration during brewing;
- and the *germ*, which is the living element of the grain.

Barley contains 10 to 20 per cent water and 80 to 90 per cent dry materials, among which are carbon hydrates (at the rate of 60 to 65 per cent), gum-yielding materials, which give viscosity to the wort, a good mousse to the beer and contribute to the roundness of it, albumin, which nourishes the yeast, grass materials, which for their part harm the hold of the mousse, and finally tannins, the influence of which is exercised on the colour and the taste of the beer.

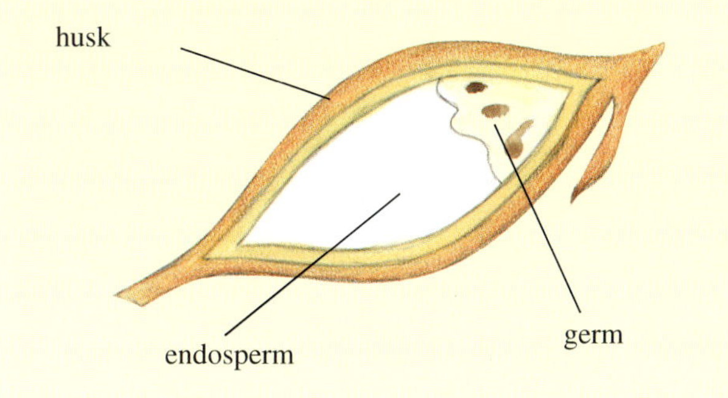

BARLEY FROM HERE AND ELSEWHERE

The River Scheldt was always a great axis for the trade in barley. This was hindered by the Belgian Revolution of 1830, the Dutch forbidding all passage. Althought, from 1833, navigation could be picked up again, it was not until six years later that a treaty introduced a toll, and in so doing settled the delicate question of the right of passage over Dutch territory. Besides this, from the middle of the 19th century, the construction of great metalled roads and the enlargement of the canal network favoured the importation of foreign barleys.

Until 1850, barley came from Russia, the Baltic, and Denmark. But from 1853 the first Spanish barley from the Almeria region arrived in Antwerp. The abolition of customs duties on cereals, in 1872, contributed to the development of these imports. The principal suppliers were then, in decreasing order of importance: the Danube, the Black Sea, Prussia, Russia, and Holland. Soon the preference was for the Danube, for the barley of Moldavia (70 kg per hectolitre) and Bourgas (64 kg per hectolitre). Californian barley was likewise much appreciated, just like the "chevalier" barley from Denmark. This trade generated a rivalry between Antwerp and Rotterdam. In 1914, Rotterdam had twenty six grain elevators, while Antwerp only had four. Administrative slowness and the substandard development of elevators only served to make the difference greater: Rotterdam "monopolised" the trade in grain. The situation was only remedied at the end of the Great War.

During the Second World War, the accent was placed on indigenous barley, and one saw a spread in the cultivation of Kenyan barley, selected spring barley which had already been introduced in the Walloon Brabant.

Today, France (Gâtinais and Beauce) and Germany (the regions of Lower Saxony and Unterfranken in Bavaria) have been superseded. These two countries benefited from rich soils used to cultivate wheat, which provided them with greater output and profits. The two principal suppliers of barley were henceforth Great Britain and Denmark which, taking into account their climate, grew spring barley, perfect for malting. To reduce the costs of transport, maltings were set up near canals and ports.

Of course, in Belgium one still found brewing barley in the region of Luxembourg. But the maltsters deplored the absence of a policy of supply and wished that the government would help in the co-ordination of the activities of the grain merchants and those of the farmers. One stocked a production of two to three months and one only malted two months after the harvest: a well ripened barley gives a better extract of sugar. Otherwise, fertilisers are dreaded by maltsters and brewers. The more there are fertilisers, the more their are proteins and the less there is starch. Proteins produce cloudiness in the cold and render the beer less stable.

So far as winter barley is concerned, it must be recalled that in former times that cultivated in France - in the region of Arras, in Beauce, and in the Vendée - was highly prized, just like that of the Belgian polders, where the soil, rich in humus, gave an excellent output of barley for the brewery. The winter barleys produced to the North of Brugge and in the region of Cadzand were more sought after and their price has much higher. But from the 1930's the urbanisation and the democratisation of holidays by the sea delivered a fatal blow to cultivation in the Belgian coastal regions.

FORMERLY, THE AIR

Thus one indicated the platform of the drying kiln, since originally this part of the drying kiln was covered with a sort of hair fabric. The hair was later replaced by earthenware tiles, pierced with holes, then by metal foil similarly perforated.

The Caulier Brewery, in Brussels, extolled their beer *Perle 28* as being a beer bottom-fermented with 28 kg per hectolitre. Today one uses, for a pils, around 15 to 17 kg per hectolitre. The use of raw grains and better productivity explains this difference.

The second stage consists of the *germination* of the soaked grain. This is carried out on an appropriate floor *(germination area)*. The grain is laid out in a layer with a thickness of approximately 20 cm. The temperature is between 12°C and 15°C, the rate of humidity being maintained in the vicinity of 45 per cent.

As soon as the germ has attained a sufficient length (three quarters of the length of the grain), generally some six weeks later, the *green malt* is subjected to *kiln drying*. It is spread on a metal floor, pierced with slots, in a layer about 10 cm in thickness. With this kiln drying, heating provides for the drying of the barley, of which the level of humidity is reduced to only 4 per cent, and of which germination is in this way stopped. This operation is terminated by a coup de feu or blast of heat, at a temperature in the order of 80°C to 105°C, for 2 to 4 hours. The temperature of the coup de feu determines the colour and the aroma of the malt. The degradation of the nitrogenous material by the enzymes, and a larger content of sugars and amino acids permits the obtention of the varieties of beer which we know. After the kiln drying, the grains are, with the aid of a degermer, cleared of the rootlets which appeared on germination, and then dusted off.

In former times, the trade of maltster was demanding. At first it had to take account of seasons. Too low temperatures curbed germination which on the other hand, in summer periods was too rapid. Then the work, properly so called, was delicate. On soaking, careless turning over of the barley grains, with the malt shovel or rake, caused them to be crushed and generated the appearance of mildew. Even more tiresome is the kiln drying, where workers have to turn the malt at a temperature nearing 120°C. It happens that heating by open flame originally caused fires or the coke, used for this heating, released carbon when the heater, placed under the floor, was not perfectly hermetically sealed. Also, before 1914, there were numerous cases of cancer caused by these emanations! Workers were also exposed to many other accidents. But this was a form of production, often suffering from a lack of strictness and from defective conditions of work, which produced a less than satisfactory malt. Fortunately, the development of techniques came to remedy this, and today matters have changed. Man intervenes hardly at all. The process of malting is carried out automatically. Mechanical turning has permitted the raising of germination to a height of 1 metre and the heating is done by pumped hot air. Labour being reduced, the costs are lowered, and productivity improved.

The maltings sector required increased investment, independent maltings coming into being. This was the case with the Antverp Maltings.

While, at the beginning of the century, nearly 50 per cent of Belgian breweries possessed a maltings - some 130 maltsters worked independently - today the Walrave brewery, in Laarne, is the last to have its own maltings. As for the Artois Brewery, it had two maltings, through its subsidiary Dewolf-Cosyns. At the start of this dissociation between the trades of brewer and maltster, extremely heavy investments in maltings and considerable production were required to reach the threshold of profitability. Nevertheless, present maltings are doing well and Belgium is the second world exporter of malt. It is true that, by virtue of its geographic position at the heart of Europe, the country benefits from an enormous advantage when it comes to the purchase of brewery barley. It has at its disposal the principal varieties of barley (Denmark, South West France, and England).

Other grain in the service of beer

• Young **wheat** is a constituent much prized by Belgian brewers. Non-germinated, it enters into the manufacture of white beers, the beers of Liège and of Antwerp, as well as those of Brussels. Because of its richness in gluten, it gives a cloudiness to the beer.

• A variety of durum wheat, above all known in Egypt, Greece, and Sicily, **spelt** is very little used in brewing, since it contains much gluten and clouds the beer. In the 19th century, in the land of Liège, for a vat of 12.30 hectolitres, one added 250 kg of malted spelt and 300 kg of raw wheat.

• **Rice** replaces malt when this is at a high cost. It is therefore used above all in bottom-fermentation for maximum reduction of manufacture costs and to obtain a

First of all established in Tubize, the De Stordeur plant, specialising in the conversion of maize, saw such growth that they moved to Leuven, next to the main brewing centres.

low price beer. It also has other advantages, however. It makes the beer clearer and improves its colloidal stability since its flour contains little grass material. The quantity used, varies from 10 to 15 per cent. At the present time it is neglected because of its high cost.

• The use of **maize** in brewing increased in the last quarter of the 19th century. Around 1840, the high rise in price of raw materials (around 40 per cent) caused brewers to search for substitutes to malt. Thus they had recourse to maize, generally at a much lower cost (nearly 50 per cent at least). After the American Civil War, America, a major producer of this cereal, promoted it in Europe through missions entrusted, in 1888, to Colonel Murphy. The first degermer for maize was used in London in 1890, by the firm of Gillman and Spencer, who in 1892 assigned the patents to the Keulemans & Windelinckx Maltings, in Mechelen. In 1893 Colonel Murphy praised the use of maize in brewing, in his memorial lecture on the occasion of the International Congress of Chemists, held in Brussels.

The maize industry then developed in Belgium. Among its first "followers" were the Anchor Distillery & Maltings and the Merxem Mills (both in Antwerp). Imports of maize by this port suffice to show the stunning growth of this raw material, from its debut. In 1880, it was 1,083,900 hectolitres and in 1903 7,246,157 hectolitres, while at the same time the import of barley was respectively 1,750,839 and 4,273,833 hectolitres.

The starch in maize gave the effect of roundness and body to the beer. Nevertheless, taking into account the oil which maize contained, one could not use it alone, since the oil destroyed the mousse.

THE VARIOUS MALTS

The European Brewery Convention, created in 1946 and whose General Secretariat was located in Zoeterwoude (Netherlands), fixed a standard measure (EBC) for the analysis, and the determination of the colour of malt, this colour being linked with the temperature of the kiln drying. It distinguished:

• Pils malt or blond malt:

dried at approximately 80°C; 3.5 EBC

• Colouring malts:

- Pale Ale: dried at 85-90°C; 7 to 9 EBC;
- Munich: dried at 100-105°C; 14 to 16 EBC;
- Aromatic: dried at 115°C; 45 to 55 EBC;

The Pale Ale and Munich malt gives body to the beer in maintaining a certain degree of colour. Beside this colouring, the aromatic malt confers aroma and taste to the beer. Compared with caramel malts, colouring malts have great diastatic power

• Caramel malts:

- Carapils: 10 to 20 EBC
- CaraVienne: 30 to 60 EBC
- Caramunich: 140 to 160 EBC

These malts, worked from green malt to obtain amino acids and primary sugars to obtain simple substances, give a very good colloidal and organoleptic stability. They are dried and grilled at 70°C, in drums to liquefy and saccharify the starch in the grain

• Smoked (peated) malt: on kiln drying peat is burned. The smoke which it emanates contains phenol, which settles on the malt. This practice is very old. Otherwise one provides for the soaking of the barley with water filtered by earth loaded with peat, this water containing phenol, and by distillation, gives its taste. Smoked malt is used for whisky and whisky malt beer.

THE ORIGIN OF AROMA

HOPS

A perennial plant of the *cannabinaceae* (canabis) family, the hop *(Humus lupulus)* is characterised by its climbing stalk which attains a height of 5 to 6.2 metres. Only the female plants are cultivated for brewing. Its multi-flowered inflorescences or *cones*, are harvested in August and September according to whether it is an early or a late variety. Their "scales", or bracts, contain their active element, lupulin. This contains bactericidal properties. It benefits the fermentation of beer in preventing the establishment of undesirable microbes. Besides, by virtue of its resin content, it clarifies the beer by picking up materials in suspension. Finally it contributes to the taste of the beer (bitterness and aroma). This taste depends at the same time on the variety of hops used - there are aromatic hops (Hallertau, Fuggles, Saaz) and bitter hops (Northern Brewer, Super Alpha) - and the quality of the lupulin brought into play - between 150 and 700 grams per hectolitre of wort. It should be noted that, in a process of which traces were found from as early as 1653, the drying of the hops in kilns lasts for six to eight hours, at a maximum temperature of 40°C. Today the brewer's preference is for an extract of hops, a concentrate, or pellets. These products are more "clean", with a consistent degree of bitterness, and a price which fluctuates less.

The use of hops in brewing goes back to the Middle Ages. In 1364 the Emperor of Germany Charles IV recommended its use in his Novus Modus *Fermentendi Cervisiam* ("New Law on the Manner of Brewing). The Duchy of Brabant, falling under his authority, was one of the first to use hops, while Flanders, under French tutelage, continued to go for the gruit, a mixture of spices being used to aromatise the cervisia, or ale. Hopped beer thus appeared in 1368, in Leuven and in Vilvoorde, then in 1372 in Mechelen. But this new practice was not unanimously accepted at first. Time was needed for it to become established. For example, in 1524 the Flemish introduced the cultivation of hops in England and it aroused an immediate "raising of shields" by learned scientists who affirmed that this herb, certainly beneficial to the health of the body, proved to be subtly dangerous, since it generated melancholy and mental problems. This medical opposition, which did not only

The cones of the female hops should be virgin. To prevent fructification, it was necessary to do away with any male plant from a large radius around the hop field.

What more surprising spectacle is there than a field of hops? Endless rows of poles, 7 to 8 metres high, intertwined with a network of galvanised wires. Until the beginning of the 20th century plants were grown on wooden stakes, 6 to 11 metres high, which were costly and required more rigorous maintenance. Recourse to wire facilitated cultivation and increased productivity, even if it was still onerous. Plants are less exposed to the wind and at the same time benefit from more light, maturing earlier and more uniformly. Insects, less attracted and less protected than before, were thus less feared. Finally, easier access to the plants allows them to be treated more efficaciously against disease.

manifest itself on this occasion, was a not inconsiderable obstacle to the adding of hops to beer.

For a long time, the quality of the Belgian hop suffered from a poor reputation. In 1848 one could read from F. Rohart that 1.5 kg of Flemish hops was to replace 1 kg of hops from Alsace. It is true that a lack of rigour was often to be observed in the treatment of

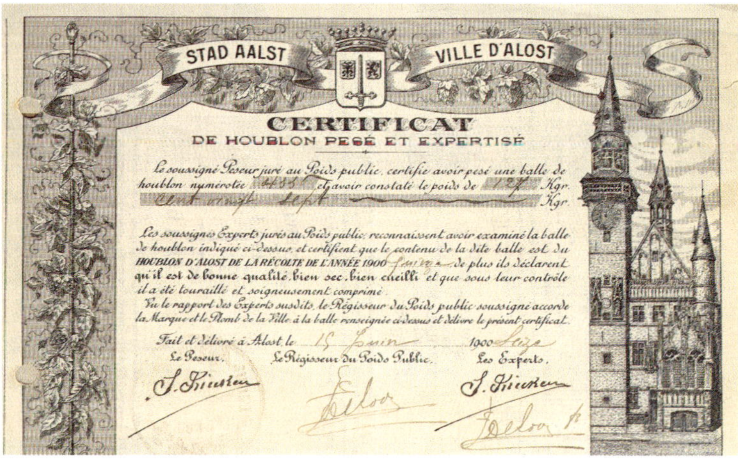

STAD AALST — VILLE D'ALOST

CERTIFICAT
DE HOUBLON PESÉ ET EXPERTISÉ

Le soussigné Peseur juré au Poids public, certifie avoir pesé une balle de houblon numérotée ______ et avoir constaté le poids de 127 Kgr.
Cent vingt sept Kgr.

Les soussignés Experts jurés au Poids public, reconnaissent avoir examiné la balle de houblon indiqué ci-dessus, et certifient que le contenu de la dite balle est du HOUBLON D'ALOST DE LA RÉCOLTE DE L'ANNÉE 1900 ______ de plus ils déclarent qu'il est de bonne qualité, bien sec, bien cueilli et que sous leur contrôle il a été touraillé et soigneusement comprimé.
Vu le rapport des Experts susdits, le Régisseur du Poids public soussigné accorde la Marque et le Plomb de la Ville à la balle renseignée ci-dessus et délivre le présent certificat.

Fait et délivré à Alost, le 15 Juin 1900 Seize

Le Peseur, Le Régisseur du Poids Public, Les Experts.

Hop certificate from the town of Aalst.

hops. Thus in 1881 Professor Damseaux, from Gembloux, wrote to the Home Secretary of the time, "that no part of the gathering and especially the capital operation of drying is carried out with more negligence than in Belgium. With small cultivation where the drying should however be carried out in a perfect manner, it takes place in a most primitive fashion." A defective appearance, an unsatisfactory colour, packing too often short on guarantee seals – these were adopted for the first time in 1833 in Saaz, Germany – etc., so many factors which contributed to a less favourable image.

It was an image which very soon had a beneficial effect for the competition of foreign hops. In fact, while the cultivation of hop fields did not cease to develop, the growth of railways allowed the import into Belgium, around 1850, of German and

In 1905 German hops came freely into Belgium. On the other hand Belgian hops were taxed at 25 Francs on entry into Germany. This provoked a major event in Asse, in which the famous Abbot Daens, defenders of worker's powers, took part. It attracted some 6,000 to 7,000 growers and the hall being crammed full, the Abbot harangued the crowd in the street. He was sentenced to three days in prison!

The precarious position of growers is shown in the photograph above. The Honorary President of the Gilde Groene Belle Monopole distributes subsidies and diplomas to members of the Guild.

Czechoslovakian aromatic hops. In 1855 those from America arrived. Imports increased to a point where in 1882 the Government, anxious to protect national production, sct up a commission charged with studying the means of promoting cultivation. A testing station was created at Aalst which, with Poperinge, supplied hops then highly rated on the international market. Nevertheless, measures had to wait. It was only on 27th February 1931 that a Royal Decree banned the presence of male plants in Belgian hop fields.

In this rather gloomy agricultural context, the industrial development of Belgium came to the fore. The hop field saw its labour force opt for better salaries in the coal-mines of Mons, or the iron and steel works of Liège and Charleroi. After the Second World War, the industrialisation and urbanisation of Brabant completed this disaffection. The hop fields of Asse were emptied of workers.

All these elements struck a blow to the number of farms and the area under cultivation. This was accentuated at the end of the Seventies by the gross revenue per hectare being equivalent to 35 per cent of global cost price. Taking into account the increasing cost price, the hop farm should have at least 5 hectares to be able to maintain modern mechanisation and to reduce the costs of analysis for obtaining a label. This was rare in Belgium.

Another cause of recession in the cultivation of hops was the market speculation on this merchandise, which was so dependent on the variability of harvests each year. The price of hops reflected this through its own variations. This could only discourage the grower, constrained to rough and assiduous labour (some 500 hours per hectare).

Furthermore, a selection of hops corresponding to demand was essential. This was not always the case. In 1980, aromatic varieties represented 62 per cent of the cultivation in the Asse-Aalst region, but only 10 per cent around Poperinge. The rest was dedicated to bitter varieties. The crisis during 1985 and 1986 is explained, in part, by the fact that a third of the harvest was not sold. The bitter variety Brewers Gold, which itself represented 40 per cent of the area under cultivation, ceased to be in demand. Belgian brewers preferred the fine hops Hallertau, Challenger, and Saaz. As for the variety Northern Brewer, it retained a certain favour for the first hopping of the wort. Inevitably a conversion was necessary.

In 1987, on the instigation of Belgium, the EEC granted subsidies for the conversion of fine hops and of very bitter hops Super Alpha during the period from 1988 to 1992. From 1989, Brewers Gold almost totally disappeared, and the area of hop fields dedicated to bitter varieties fell from 83 per cent (in 1985) to 51 per cent. Today the aromatic varieties cover 39 per cent of the area and the Saaz variety remains in the Asse-Aalst region. A new variety already grows in 50 per cent of hop fields, Target.

At the present time, Belgium only produces 0.5 per cent of the world's production of hops and approximately 1.5 per cent of European production. Belgian brewers use on average 25 per cent of Belgian hops and buy the rest abroad.

Concern for quality is now a priority. In 1993, the ONDAH (National Office for Agricultural and Horticultural Markets) introduced a quality label for Belgian hops: "Belgian Quality Hop". The same year, controls were made more rigorous. 6 per cent of hops submitted for inspection were judged to be of insufficient quality. In 1994 only 1 per cent was eliminated for that reason!

THE TIME OF ITINERANT TRADE

Formerly the trade in hops was to say the least picturesque. Merchants took to the roads with their heavy loads. The patron, on horseback, preceded the great cart with its four horses, ready to let the client know of the passage of his team and possibly to negotiate with him on the conditions of sale. These expeditions often lasted several months. Leaving from Stambrugge for example, with a great quantity of hops, merchants took a route towards the black country. The first cargo sold, they got supplies on the way from other places of production, such as Havré, Buvrinnes, Biesmes, or Jupille. Then they took the route to Brussels, stopping at Aalst to reload with hops, then making their way to Poperinge and from there going to France.

THE HIGH PLACES OF BELGIAN HOPS

• From 1537, the Abbey of Saint Bertin in Saint Omer, in France, suzerain of the town of **Poperinge**, judged it right to take measures in favour of the cultivation of hops in this corner of Western Flanders. This was in accord with the Governors of the Netherlands. It therefore founded a college of hop controllers. The regulations were published on 15th November 1573 and amended on 30th October 1648.

This beer takes its name from hops (*hommel* in Poperinge patois), as well as its pronounced bitterness.

From 1,524 hectares in 1880, the area under cultivation fell to 401 hectares in 1940, then to some 320 hectares today. It is a matter above all of bitter hops, but there is a gradual turn towards aromatic varieties.

• The region of **Liège** counted 45 hectares in 1880. Cultivation ceased with the Second World War.

• Stambruges and Saint-Symphorien-Buvrinnes were for a long time the major production centres in the **Mons** region. There was an old tradition of hop-growing in Stambruges and in the region, at Hensies, Pommeroeul, Herchies, Hautrage, Ville-Pommeroeul! A document dated on the 7th Thermidor of year VI (25th July 1798) showed that, among the 591 inhabitants of the town, nine traded in hops. Such families as Gosselin, Manfroy, Haubourdin, Laitem, and Flamme illustrated this. As for the hop fields of Saint-Symphorien-Buvrinnes, they covered 228 hectares at the end of the 19th century, and only one hectare survived in 1952-53. These hops were sold to the Brasserie du Coq d'Or in Verviers.

• Mention is made of hop fields in the province of **Namur** in 1710. It was in 1945 that a certain Samyn, a hop merchant in Poperinge set up in Romedenne.

From 2 hectares in 1945 the area under cultivation exceeded 48 hectares in the Seventies, then fell to 4 hectares in 1985, as a result of an unfavourable economic situation. It should nevertheless be noted that hops were of a superior quality to those of Poperinge and that yield reached 1,500 to 2,000 kilograms per hectare. It should likewise be recalled that the second producer of hops in Romedenne, by the name of Cornette, invented the semi-automatic binding of hop field stakes. This same grower perfected a machine for harvesting hops, at the rate of 15 to 20 plants a minute, which gave a saving of 15 hours' work for every hectare.

• The cultivation of hops has been carried on in the region of **Asse-Aalst** since the 11th century. It was introduced there by the Benedictines of the Abbey of Affligem, founded in 1086. The improvement of hops seems to have been, in these places, a preoccupation dating far back. As early as 1719, regulations specified that "in view of being able to distinguish quality better, one place will be designated in the market for well-picked hops, and another for those which are not so." Half a century later, in 1767, it was prescribed that all hops must pass by the public weigh-bridge, to be examined by sworn experts, and that any merchandise not giving satisfaction would be refused.

In a comparable concern for quality, the Société Saint-Roch was founded in Aalst in 1886, with the object of promoting the improvement of cultivation, picking and drying of hops. Likewise, Louis Tellier, Louis Botte, Victor Derauw, Georges Damiens, Louis Van den Hulle, and Eugène Goffin created the limited company of Houblon Normal in 1893, in Aalst, the object of which was "the development of the transformation of hops to normal hops, as well as everything relating to the conservation of hops." At the beginnings of this enterprise, a patent was taken out in 1883 concerning a process for manufacturing a complete extract of hops. But the real improvement in the cultivation of hop fields was due to the priest of Affligem (Hekelgem), originally from Bavaria, who in 1907 imported into the region the variety known as Hallertau and thus introduced the cultivation of aromatic hops into Belgium.

With a huge 659 hectares in 1880, the region of Asse-Aalst had only 67 hectares in 1941. The area is today some 50 hectares.

The first visiting cards for commercial representatives were "porcelain cards" printed on china clay. This technique, practised from 1840, was abandoned in 1870, because of the toxic nature of kaolin powder.

WHAT IS MEANT BY ... ?

Hop tray. A large sieve serving to hold the draff of the hops after the cooking and the hopping of the wort. Of course, if one uses hop extract, there is no draff.

Hop bail. A large sack made of a rough fabric and containing hops (approximately 150 kg). Formerly, bails were enormous, and of a length corresponding to the width of the horse-drawn vehicle intended for their transport, permitting them to be stacked easily. Today, the hops are strongly compacted by means of presses - their keeping capacity was found to be improved this way - and the bails are small and square.

EBU (European Bitterness Unit). *See page 94.*

Hop pellets. Vacuum-packed granules of pressed hops.

Aged hops. Old hops of which the bitterness is diminished by age. Aged hops are used for the production of lambic, for example. This loss of bitterness conserves the beer's agreeable acid flavour.

A MUSEUM OF HOPS

There is no wonder that Poperinge, with such a long and rich tradition of hops, should be endowed with the National Museum of Hops! It was established in the Stadsschaal, a building constructed in the 19th century, where hops were checked, measured, dried, and put into sealed bails. Equipment and documents allude to the cultivation of hops, through the seasons, as was the practice before the appearance of machinery, at a time when man was the only worker and when the harvest was done by hand.

It is because the hop has been omnipresent in Poperinge for centuries. And each three years the International Hop Festival takes place during harvest, in September. The town is brightened by colourful processions and folklore events, as they famously celebrate their beer *(hommelpap)*.

The next Festival will take place in 1999.

HOPS IN BELGIUM*

1846	2,968 ha
1866	3,960 ha
1880	4,185 ha
1910	2,047 ha
1913	2,405 ha
1920	960 ha
1925	1,277 ha
1927	1,515 ha
1928	1,478 ha
1930	1,030 ha
1931	2,834 ha
1942	506 ha
1950	4,161 ha
1969	1,097 ha
1973	1,220 ha
1979	756 ha
1985	710 ha
1990	372 ha
1994	386 ha

* The hops presently cultivated are as follows :

- Super Alpha : Target (10), Yeoman (11), Northern Brewer (7,5) ;
- Aromatiques : Hallertau (4,5), Challenger (4,5).

A VITAL CONDITION

WATER OF QUALITY

Water plays a predominant role. In former times 10 litres were necessary for 1 litre of beer produced, and today breweries use 7 litres of water for 1 litre of beer.

It is the water which to a large extent decides the type of beer which the brewer may make, since its composition asserts an influence on the product. In the first place, its salt content. A bottom-fermented beer requires a "soft" water, poor in salt, and a top-fermented beer needs a "hard" water, heavy in salt. On the other hand, the distribution of salt has an effect on the degree of acidity of the water (pH); calcium carbonate and magnesium bicarbonate reduce it, while calcium sulphate and magnesium sulphate increase it. Now the lower the pH, the more certain is the beer. Thus it is 4.2 to 4.3 for a pils, and 3.6 for gueuze.

If the brewery has a spring, as was the case in times gone by, it was necessary to guard for variations of output according to the seasons, because this caused changes in the characteristics of the water. Water was corrected by ion exchangers, by adding lime, or by boiling. These processes provoked the growth of quality top-fermented beers in Flanders. There was permission, moreover, to "Burtonise" a water to produce Belgian beers of a *pale ale* type, and thus to avoid the use of a plaster containing iron, which was harmful to yeast and gave a grey colour to the beer.

A second element of which account has to be taken is the nitrate content of the water. In fact any water which contains an appreciable quantity of nitrates and organic materials should be set aside. In certain regions it is sometimes impossible, because of the geographical structure of the land, to find water which is free of these substances. In a number of districts in Flanders and the Campine, devoted to agriculture, the water may not be used in brewing. The surface water is loaded with nitrates and organic materials, and the water in the upper strata - generally sand - has bicarbonate of soda. As far as coastal breweries are concerned, they encounter the problem of water rich in sea salt, which of course gives a bad taste to beer - this hazard brought about the closing of numerous breweries along the coast. It explains why, at the beginning of the 20th century, the Ostend brewers possessed two floating-reservoirs, and fetched soft water from near Damme, on the Bruges-Ostend canal. The voyage lasted three days.

Lastly, long ago there existed another relatively frequent cause of impurity. Some breweries were also farms, and, for this reason, experienced pollution of the water by seepage. Thanks to the development of the motor lorry, which provided for the removal of manure, the risks of contamination could be resolved.

The quality of the water determined the type of beer, according to the amount (in milligrams per litre) of residue (lime, magnesium, sulphate, chlorate) after evaporation

• Pale Ale - English	1,790 mg/litre
• Dortmunder - German	1,110 mg/litre
• Munich - German	280 mg/litre
• Pilsner - Czech	50 mg/litre

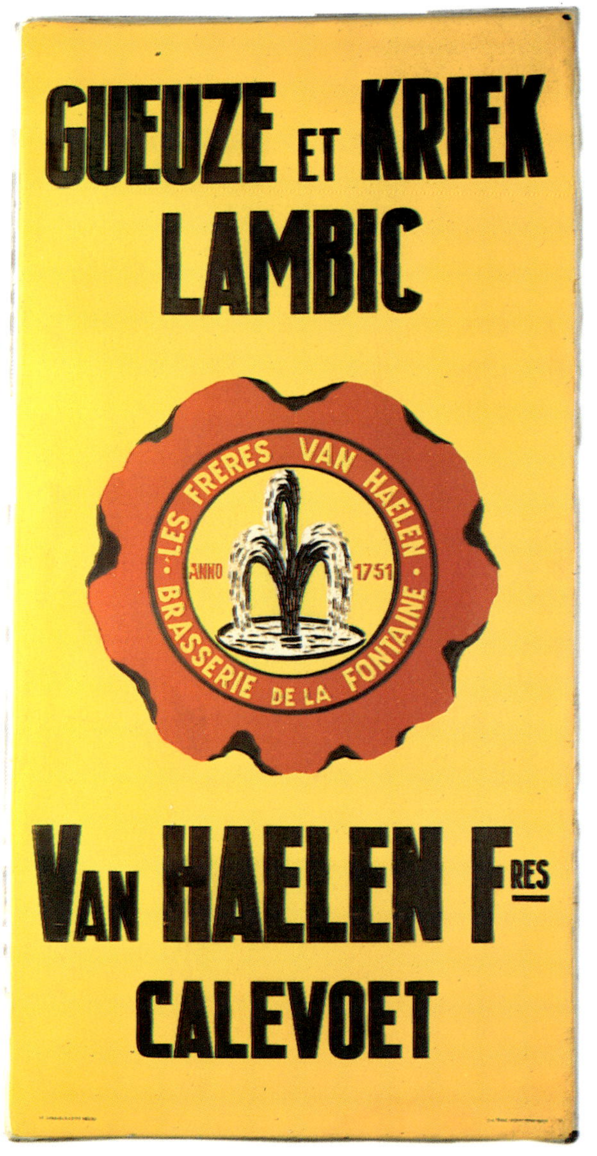

The importance of water in beer... Several breweries recalled it in their names: Source Brewery (Hannicq), in Tubize; Fontaine Brewery (Van Hælen), in Uccle (Calevoet); La Bonne Source Brewery, in Velaines.

Above, an enamelled plaque from 1930.

THE WATER HOUSE, IN ANTWERP

In medieval times, the City of Antwerp experienced grave difficulties with its supplies of soft and drinkable water. And in 1486 a canal was cut for 7 kilometres to bring soft water to the city from Schijn, "captured" downstream from Wommelgem. For the most part established along the Cammerstraat (Kammenstraat - the word *kam* signified "brewery" in old Flemish), the brewers from then on used the water of the canal (later, called the "Canal d'Herentals") for the manufacture of their beer.

At the middle of the 16th century, the enlargement of Antwerp, provided with a Nieuwstad ("New Town") and a new boundary, put such a strain on the communal budget that an appeal was made to a certain Gilbert van Schoonbeke (Antwerp, 1519-1556), a talented town planner and enlightened businessman, to redress their most worrying situation. Major works followed which were aimed at the economic growth of the city. The building of three thousand houses was undertaken. To enlarge the port, new canals were cut. Moreover to reduce the significance of imported beers intended to satisfy local consumption, van Schoonbeke judged it right to develop the Antwerp brewing industry, and he created breweries in the new town, along the brewers' canal.

If Lazare de Schwendi (1522-1583) is better known for having introduced the tokay grape variety in Alsace (France), he was also a faithful servant of Charles V. It was thus that he put down the revolt in Antwerp in 1554, and that he was appointed first Governor of the fortified town of Philippeville. The Devaux Brewery is, moreover, installed in the former stables of the Governor's palace.

But water posed a problem. The solution was rapidly found: ditch water of a quality judged acceptable was led towards a "Water House", which then directed it to the breweries. Built in 1553, this water distribution centre could not function straight away, while ten breweries were already active in March 1554. The pump mechanism was operated by horse. It was therefore necessary to bring the water by narrow boat. It was "taken" principally in the Rupel, at Rumst. This was not without arousing jealousy and discontent among the powerful brewers of the old city - those on the Cammerstraat - who started the rumour that this water poisoned the beer! Van Schoonbeke, it is true, attracted some hostility but the riot which erupted in July 1554, fomented by the rebellious bourgeois, which demanded his death, was not fatal to him. In his description of the Netherlands (1567), Guichardin relates this uprising to an Order according to which only the brewers of the New Town were authorised to manufacture beer from barley. Banned by the magistrates from the city, van Schoonbeke took refuge in the Court, in Brussels, where he was appointed Commissioner of the Royal Finances, but he died suddenly two years later, on a mission to Antwerp. He then lived in 23 rue des Récollets. In the meantime the Water House had begun operation.

In 1562 the City of Antwerp acquired from the heirs of van Schoonbeke the Water House and the six breweries of the New Town. Although it transferred the breweries, it retained ownership of the Water House, and the conveyance of water from the canal (the present Canal des Brasseurs, "Brouwersvliet"). The water was supplied for an annual fee for the maintenance of the installations. From 1581, the brewers fell into the habit of meeting there to deliberate upon their interests, and soon the place also became an office - the Maison des Brasseurs *(Brouwershuis)*, that is to say the head office of the guild.

In 1925, urbanisation and the pollution of water courses led to the brewer Wodon, of Namur, indicating on his letter-head that all his beers were "made with water distributed by the City". The thing is rather rare these days.

Works to improve the system were realised in the 17th century. In the middle of the 19th century the Brussels Company of Brewers modernised it and installed pumps. Hydraulic activity continued until the beginning of the 20th century. In 1903 one could read in *Le Matin*, an Antwerp journal, "Three of the breweries created by van Schoonbeke still exist. They belong to Messrs Hermans, Meeussen and Royers. A strange question arose some years ago. These businessmen, could they be considered as owners of the Water House? A case was begun over it and the Court decided that the real property belonged to the City, but that the brewers had the usufruct of it, that is to say that they could supply water to all the properties situated between the Canal and the rue des Brasseurs and be remunerated in a manner to cover the costs of exploitation. M. Royers having renounced his right, Messrs Hermans and Meeussens remain sole usufructuaries."

It was only in 1933, the last brewery having closed its doors, that the House became a museum, richly endowed with souvenirs of its double activity.

Below: the meeting room in the Brewers' Hall in Antwerp.

INDISPENSABLE

YEAST...

An oval single cell micro-organism, 5 to 10 μ in diameter, the function of yeast is to transform the sugar in the wort into ethyl alcohol and carbon dioxide, with a liberation of energy (heat). The alcoholic content cannot exceed 12 per cent since, beyond that, the yeast dies. To a wort of 12 per cent sugar (Plato) is generally added some 200 grams of yeast per hectolitre in the case of top-fermentation, and approximately 500 grams in the case of bottom-fermentation.

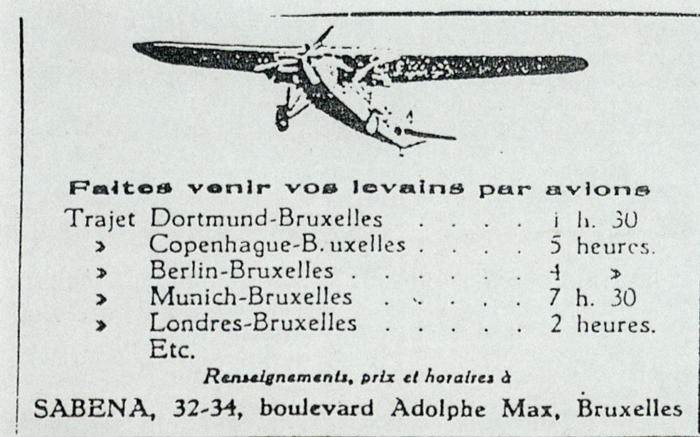

SABENA, the Belgian national airline, contributed to the importation of yeast culture from various foreign beers, needed by the brewers (advertisement c. 1934)

Three types of yeast can be distinguished, corresponding to the three modes of fermentation. In the case of bottom-fermentation, the yeast is of the type *Saccharomyces carlsbergensis*. It works at a temperature between 6°C and 10°C, for 8 to 10 days, and then it is recovered at the bottom of the tank. For top-fermentation, the yeast is of the type *Saccharomyces cerevisiæ*. It works at a temperature between 18°C and 25°C, for 4 to 6 days, and then it is recovered on the surface, by packet. As for spontaneous fermentation, its process is different since wild yeasts are used which are contained in the ambient atmosphere and culture the wort. *(see pages 121 and following pages)*

The principal causes of degeneration of the yeast are as follows:

• a beer of too low gravity. If the material assimilable by the yeast is weak, the yeast cannot benefit;

• a beer made of malt which is kiln dried at too high a temperature and subjected to soaking at too high a heat; the nitrogenous material on which the yeast feeds is destroyed;

The development of railways allowed the delivery, in metal boxes, of yeasts from the house of Hillaert (Ghent), to small village breweries.

• the presence of bacterial germs. From one harvest of the mother-yeast to another, an infection may develop, to the point of introducing in a fresh wort a preponderance of germs. The yeast, poisoned, is impotent and floats to the surface of the half-fermented wort.

In former times, brewers dreaded the wind, which carried bacteria, as well as the autumn (because of decomposition), and the cherry period (because of insects). Today the harvest of yeasts requires less manipulation, and fermentation is carried out in closed vats, which improves the state of the yeasts;

• less hard water, rich in nitrates. In the presence of the acid reaction of the wort, the nitrates give nitric acid.

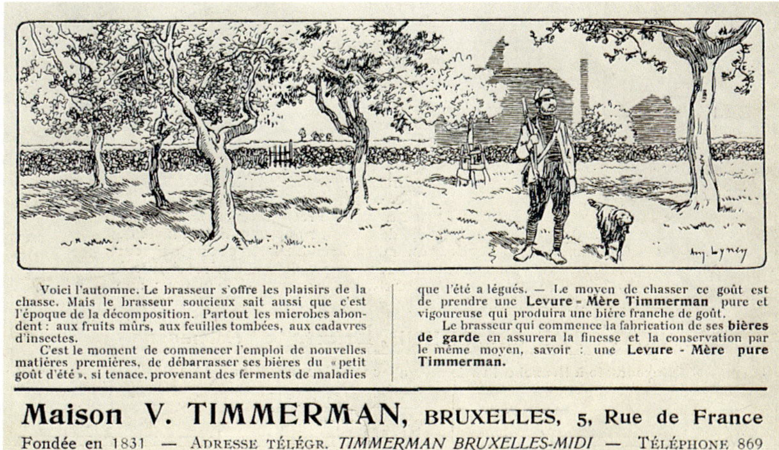

Cherry-picking time has always been rich in infection (warmth and associated bacteria). This advertisement for a pure autumn yeast attests to the fact that the problem is not resolved.

A PROFITABLE TRADE

In the middle of the 19th century, trade in yeast was of considerable benefit to the brewer. A mash-tun of 1,500 kilograms of flour could win him the sum of 500 Francs! Until 1870, the production of yeast represented 12 to 15 per cent of the total figure of beer made.

In 1909 the trade in yeast by the Ieper Association of Brewers rose to some 7,000 kg, with a daily production of around 200 kg, and a price of 10 to 13 centimes per kilogram. This is not surprising when one learns that the volume of yeast after fermentation is four to ten times more than its initial volume.

Brewers' yeast was largely used in making extracts of soups. This treatment was by the Belgian Society for the Use of Brewers' Yeasts, in Aalst. On the other hand yeast was packaged in small pots for the consumer, in which he obtained his precious Vitamin B.

OTHER CONTRIBUTORS

Aromatics. The dried seeds of coriander are strongly aromatic. They are used in the brewing of white beers. The *Grain of Paradise* (or Guinea Pepper) is a sort of cardamom, with a very pronounced perfume, which was much used in the Middle Ages. It is less common today. It is used in the manufacture of faro. Among the other aromatics used are orange and lemon peel (for white beers), ginger, camomile, juniper berries, Panama wood (for bitterness), and beech chips.

Used in minimal quantities these aromatics tend to conserve the beer. Besides, they also communicate to it a character of good taste and render it stimulating to the stomach.

Artificial sweeteners. *Aspartame*, endowed with a sweetening power two hundred times that of saccharose, is used in beers without alcohol or of low alcoholic strength. As for *saccharine*, discovered in 1884 by Dr Fahlberg of the John Hopkin University in Baltimore (United States), it is the sugared substance extracted from coal tar. Its sweetening power is four hundred and fifty times more than that of saccharose. Appearing on the market in 1886, it was presented at the Universal Exhibition in Antwerp in 1894. Saccharine was generally used at the rate of 2 to 3 grams per hectolitre. Today, taking into account the risks which it represents to health, it is forbidden in the manufacture of foodstuffs. In Belgium its use is regulated and reserved to acid beers. Its use should be mentioned on the label.

WHAT IS MEANT BY... ?

• **Residual** yeast: either a yeast which, by settling, rests at the bottom of the tank at the end of secondary fermentation, or a yeast which is recovered by centrifuge. This sort of yeast is not re-used.

• **Broken** yeast: in bottom-fermentation, a yeast which flocculates on fermentation, forms a fault, and precipitates at the bottom of the tank. It is also called *flocculant* or *flocculating*.

• **Dusty** yeast: a yeast which, in the fermenting tank, remains very scattered in the wort and deposits slowly at the bottom of the tank.

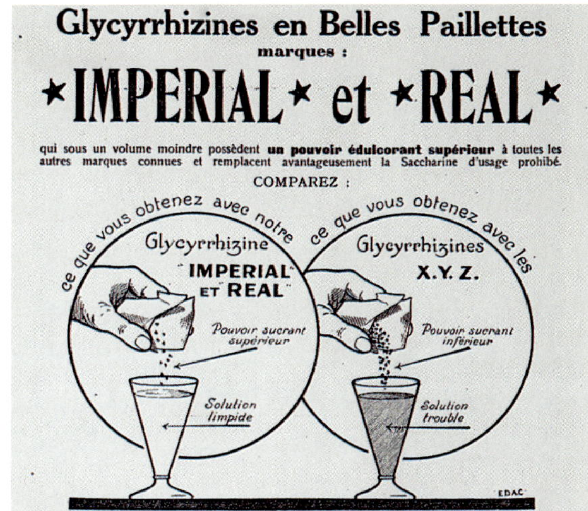

Glycyrrhizine. Glycyrrhizine (liquorice in mauve flakes), and glycyquem (extract of glycrrhizine, of a yellow brown colour), are used to improve the taste and the bouquet of the beer. It has been observed that the addition of liquorice favours the stability of the mousse. Nevertheless, its use is banned in Belgium today.

Gum Arabic. Produced by natural exudation of the Senegal Acacia, it figures among the emulsifying agents and allows the mousse to be maintained.

Sugar. To increase the gravity, with less malt, the brewer adds sugar to the wort (approximately 20 per cent of the total weight of the raw materials). The addition of sugar also intervenes to cause a refermentation. On the other hand, brown candy sugar and caramel are used to colour the beer.

The "sugar" which is used appears in several guises. *Saccharose* is beet or cane sugar, as we commonly know it. *Invert sugar* is the result of the hydrolysis of saccharose. With a more sugary taste than with saccharose, it comprises glucose and fructose (or laevulose) in equal proportions. It began to be used around 1900. It took the name *syrup of inverted* (or *interverted*) sugar when it appeared in the form of a solution of sugar containing at least 62 per cent of dry material, of which more than 50 per cent was invert sugar. As for glucose, which has been well favoured since the 1980's, it is obtained by saccharification of starch (maize, wheat) or of edible starch (potato, cassava). This glucose is called *massé* when it results from the concentration and crystalisation of a strongly hydrolysed juice.

Calcium sulphate. It is used for treating the brewery water before brewing. It is added during boiling, or before. This process is known by the name "Burtonisation", because it is intended to "imitate" the composition of the water in Burton-on-Trent, in England, a water which thanks to its properties is ideal for brewing *bitter* and *pale* ale.

Magnesium sulphate (or **Epsom Salts**). Like calcium sulphate, it is used for Burtonisation. Epsom Salts were once the dry residue of the mineral water from springs in Epsom, in Surrey, England.

FROM MALT AND HOP TO BEER

• Certain varieties of barley have given their name to beers: Kenya to the *Golden Kenia*, from the Huyghe Brewery in Melle; Triumph to the *Triumph Pils*, from Het Hamerken (Gouden Boom) in Bruges; Hanna to the *Hanna Pils* from the Labor Brewery in Mons. Moreover, the *Carapils*, from the Ponselet Brewery in Anderlues, owes its name to the Cara malt used in its manufacture.

• Some varieties of hops have likewise given their name to beers: the *Saaz* from the Cavenaille Brewery in Dour; the *Kent* from the Dubois Brewery in Lebbeke.

Moortgat Brewery collection.

Brewhouse at Rochefort Abbey.

... AND THEIR USE

The brewhouse is a place marked with mysticism, a sanctuary where alchemy works in the making of beer. Whether the vessels be of cast iron, in red copper, or in more modern stainless steel, they are a part of this magic, which often makes one forget that the art of the brewer is a process in several stages, and that each of them has its own significance, even if their aesthetic beauty is not always immediately perceptible.

The first phase is the **grinding** of the malt in the mill *(crusher)*.

Of course raw grain, not malted, like rice, wheat, or maize, also undergoes this operation.

Then comes the **mashing**, that is to say the hydration of the milled malt, which is mixed in two or three times its own weight of water. In former times, a forked shovel was used for this purpose. It has become the brewers' symbol. Today the operation is carried out mechanically. The process is intended to dissolve the substances rendered soluble by germination, in order to obtain a fermentable wort (transformation of the starch into sugar). The enzymes obtained by the malting become active in the water, each enzyme having an optimal temperature for "working". This explains why mashing suffers, on successive soakings, from progressive heating, culminating at 75°C.

Mashing. Ch'ti Brewery collection.

R. Desmecht collection.

From 30°C to 40°C hydration of the enzymes takes place. From 45°C to 50°C the proteases move about and attack the albuminoid material. At this stage the aromatic materials come into action. From 68°C to 75°C, thanks to the work of the alpha-amylases and the beta-amylases, saccharification transforms the flour into maltose, dextrines, and glucose.

A **first filtration** takes place in the mash tun. The wort is left to rest for about an hour. The husks of the malt and part of the material in suspension falls on the grills at the bottom of the tun and serves as a filter - this mass at the bottom of the tank is called the *draff*.

After filtration of the wort, it is necessary to turn this draff in order to permit more efficient washing, in hot water (approximately 75°C), and to take off a maximum extract. Often, the extract which results from this washing is fermented separately to obtain table beers, with a low alcohol content.

A collecting tray recovers the filtered wort which, from there, passes through the heater to be brought to boiling. The **baking**, which lasts for 90 to 120 minutes, even 60 minutes, is meant to evaporate the surplus water, to destroy the enzymes, to sterilise

THE USE OF LIME

Lime has played a sad role in the manufacture of beer, as A. Laurent testified in his *Dictionaire de la Brasserie* (Brussels, 1875). If, at one time, the beers of France and of Belgium were inferior to the beers from abroad, then lime was responsible. Lime was in fact added to the wort in the boiler, either to clarify it or to colour it. It was claimed that lime clarified the beer, because it saturated the acids. It is known, in fact, that the vegetable acids hold the albumin in dissolution. Now to clarify, it is necessary for the albumin to be able to coagulate.

And lime had the role of preservative. In boiling the sugar content in the wort, the beer is rendered bitter and hard, and enabled to keep for a long time.

Outside this effect on the flavour of the beer, lime, in combining with albuminoid substances, confers upon it a disagreeable odour.

the wort, and to make the nitrogenous materials coagulate (cassure). It is during this stage that the hops are added *(see page 95)*, which brings its bitterness and contributes to the sterilisation of the wort. Cassure occurs, composed essentially of nitrogen, tannins and bitter materials which coagulate and appear in the beer in the boiler. One observes: 20 to 70 g of dry trub (cassure) per hectolitre of wort.

Baking may be carried out at high temperature. Normally it is at about 100°C, and under pressure the temperature attains 140°C. According to the temperature and the duration of the baking, the colour of the beer varies.

The moment then comes to proceed with a **second filtration**. In the old days, this operation was done with a hop tray or a separator (wort centrifuge). Since the beginning of the 1980's, a *whirlpool* has been used, a cylindrical container in which the wort is pumped at great speed (8 to 12 m/s) to be projected tangentially: a hollow vortex forms, which allows the sediment to deposit in the middle of the bottom.

The wort is thereafter cooled. Formerly a cooling tray was used, where the beer rested for 20 minutes, in order for the trub to settle. Then the beer streams to the Baudelot pipes where the wort takes in oxygen. This cooler, called "Baudelot" after the name of its inventor, was composed of pipes in which cold water was circulating. At the present time, it is with the help of a plate cooler where the oxygen is infused, a piece of apparatus comprising plates in which liquid coolant circulates in closed circuit. A fine sediment (proteic sediment) appears on this **cooling**. It is eliminated by filtration. One observes: 5 to 6 g of fine trub per hectolitre of wort.

Before beginning fermentation, the temperature of the wort is that of leavening.

A centrifuge for the for the treatment of the wort, from the company Alfa Laval.

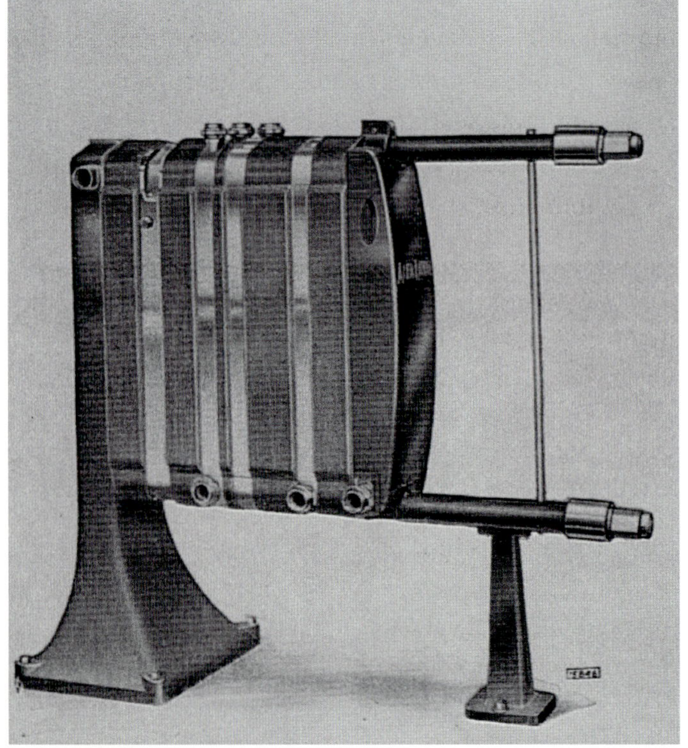

A plate heat-exchanger for cooling the wort in closed circuit, from the company Alfa Laval.

The **fermentation**, in the course of which, under the effect of the yeast *(see page 103)* the sugar in the malt is transformed into alcohol and carbon dioxide, takes place in three stages: the main fermentation, in the fermenting tank; the secondary fermentation, in the maturing vat; and the third fermentation, reserved for beers refermented in the bottle. In the past, the cooled wort was placed in the guilloire tank. Today fermentation begins with the direct addition of yeast in the vat or in the fermentation tank.

One distinguishes two main fermentations:

• *Bottom-fermentation* is carried out at a temperature of 4°C to 13°C for a period of 7 to 8 days. It is a slow fermentation, with a deposit. The yeast falls at the end of fermentation to the bottom of the vat or tank.

The leavening is done with bottom yeast coming from a culture of bottom yeast or recovered from the bottom of the vat. This fermentation suits soft beers which must keep;

• *Top-fermentation* is carried out at a temperature of 15°C to 25°C for a period of 4 to 6 days. The yeast, at the end of fermentation, rises to the surface of the vat or tank. It is more rapid and transforms more sugar into alcohol.

The leavening is done with top yeast coming from a culture of top yeast or recovered from the top of the tank.

Recovery of the yeast is no longer carried out today. In fact open tanks have given way to closed tanks in a cylindrical-conical shape where all yeasts (top or bottom) are recovered, taking into account that, beneath the effects of pressure and cooling, the yeast falls into the lower part. This is the Nathan system, perfected before the Great War, which takes its name from its Swiss inventor.

We have chosen not to deal here with the third main type of fermentation - *spontaneous fermentation* - because it is a particular process, specifically Belgian, and merits separate treatment. *See page 121.*

The double envelopes of tanks permit, through the circulation of hot or cold liquid, the reactivation or the slowing down of fermentation, according to needs. Fermentation is thus best controlled. These tanks have made brewing possible in tropical countries, since there is no contact with the air, a source of infection. Another advantage is that they contribute to reducing the costs of cooling. Previously it was necessary to cool the entire building, while today only the tank in use is cooled.

In traditional brewing the secondary fermentation is carried out here. It is for the formation of carbon dioxide and the disappearance of diacetyl with the taste and odour of rancid butter. In modern breweries the maturing is simply to eliminate proteic sediment and to clarify the beer. The maturing tank is only transitional, before racking.

Filter press (200 l) by Meura.

But the yeast and albuminoid materials remain in suspension. A third filtration is necessary. In the past this was done with a mass filter, that is to say through plates of pressed cellulose paste (cake). Later the cellulose paste was mixed with asbestos. These cakes were re-used, after cleaning. For more hygiene and less handling, the cakes then became disposable.

At the present time a kieselguhr (diatomaceous earth) filter is used. This neutral powder, formed from the debris of marine micro-organisms (diatomes), is very useful for the clarification of beer. It is added to the pumped beer. Retained by the filter, the kieselguhr forms a filtering layer.

A centrifuge may also be used, which at a speed of some 7,000 revolutions per minute permits the separation of the yeast from the beer.

Filtering is in three stages:

1. use of a centrifuge to smooth the beer;
2. simple filtration with a kieselguhr plate filter;
3. filtration with compound and very tight plates, with the possibility of sterilisation.

Racking is done into the bottle, into casks, and even crates. To avoid losses of carbon dioxide and an undesirable oxidation, a back pressure is applied to remove the maximum of air in the cask or bottle on filling.

For a third fermentation yeast and sugar are added on racking. This refermentation is characteristic of the Belgian brewing "art". It necessitates a well equipped laboratory and a hot room to reactivate the yeast. However some brewers achieve similar finesse with filtered beers.

Lastly there is **pasteurisation**, which allows for the beer to be sterilised. By raising the temperature (from 62°C to 63°C) for 30 to 40 minutes, the yeasts and bacteriae which affect the beer are destroyed. In the past, bottles were soaked in a container of hot water, from which came the invention of the bottle crate of galvanised iron which served rather for soaking than for delivery. Today bottles are placed on a metal conveyor-belt which circulates through a tunnel in which hot water is flowing. Pasteurisation can give a bad taste in the presence of air or beneath the effect of temperature being too high. The beer takes on a taste of biscuits or papier maché.

Recently, *flash pasteurisation* has provided the beer with long keeping powers. It is applied to beers intended for export. The beer passes from one tank to another, via an apparatus which heats it to more than 60°C. This technique has the advantage of taking place before packaging, in the absence of air, and for this reason the taste of the beer is not altered.

THE USE OF RAW MATERIALS IN THE BREWERY

(in tonnes)

	1970	1975	1980	1985	1988	1989
Malted barley	151,051	181,386	130,585	194,962	186,083	181,962
Grits of maize	13,003	18,438	9,030	16,755	14,634	15,437
Maize flour	3,642	3,023	5,449	6,106	2,423	156
Broken rice	13,953	14,259	22,167	13,947	15,017	14,263
Wheat	2,829	3,534	2,256	3,171	5,573	5,969
Other farinaceous substances	2,206	881		956	668	2,386
Saccharine	16	14	8	5	2	2
Sugar substances	5,990	6,054	7,427	9,733	10,436	11,134
Hops (+concentrates)	2,334	2,474	2,627	2,444	2,416	2,523
Yeast	35	25	13	36	15	8
Carbon dioxide	1,534	2,387	4,395	8,797	13,481	16,616

FROM ONE CLARIFICATION TO THE OTHER

Clarification is linked with the process of deposit, which begins on cooking the wort.

Clarification in the boiler, called "by deposit", plays an important role in the quality of the beer. Its object is the coagulation of various impurities in dissolution in the wort (residues of malt, gluten, trub, etc.) and which cloud its transparency, as well as their precipitation, in a manner to eliminate them. As the vegetal albumin of the wort coagulates under the effect of heat, there no longer survives enough albumin on adding the hops to produce a new coagulation. An exterior material intervenes then, which dissolves totally in the wort, and in the presence of the tannic acid from the hops, coagulates and effects a clarification.

It is interesting to note that an ancient clarification process used the feet of cows and calves: twelve to fourteen fresh feet per hectolitre of wort. They were placed in a basket or a rack, which was suspended in the wort before or on boiling (according to the wishes of the brewer) and before the addition of hops. The production of gelatine favoured the clarification of the wort. From this practice, a little isolated but very efficient, came the legend according to which heads were thrown into the boiler to make the beer good.

As for **cold clarification**, to refine the wort, numerous substances were utilised: lichens, the pith of young plants originating in India, agar from Japan (extract of seaweed), etc. But of all of them *isinglass finings* have proved to be the most efficacious. These finings come from the bladder of skate and sturgeon, which comprises up to 98 per cent extremely pure gelatine. To dissolve the finings in order to take from them the best part possible, they used to use vinegar. Then tartaric acid came to be preferred, since it did not harm the beer.

Clarification called the **"monks' secret"**, which in the past intervened during fermentation in the barrel, consisted of racking the impurities contained in the beer. For this a solution was introduced into the barrel, composed of dried skate bladders dissolved in tartaric acid.

It was the Brewer Martens de Cruybeke (Antwerp) and M. Laurent, brewery supplier, who, around 1863, divulged this method, which had been born in Holland.

Lastly, **clarification in the maturing vessel** may use wood chips (more particularly, of beech and hazelnut). The use of wood chips is extremely ancient, and after the adoption of the filter, survived for a long time as a special mode of clarification, because it enabled beers to be obtained which were well clarified and softened. Chips were then linked with the filter to work in common. This system is no longer employed today, except in the Anheuser-Busch Brewery in the United States. *Budweiser* owes its special flavour to this.

Other than their considerably relieving the filter, the usefulness of wood chips was to smooth down the action accelerated by the latter, which influenced the quality of the beer in a negative manner (the flavour, the hold of the mousse, etc.). As Marc H. Van Laer clearly explained in *Le Petit Journal du Brasseur*, on 19th May 1933, "The filter acts in a brutal fashion, not simply by its properties of surface absorption, but by a veritable colloidal sifting, which can in certain extreme cases, get as far as the colouring material.

"The action of wood chips [...] is essentially an action of contact, all the more intense given that the surface area of the wood will be more considerable. Their influence on the colloidal structure of the beer will be very much less marked. They will modify its quality correspondingly less than the clarification which would be permitted by a less tight final filtration."

This method was debated for a long time, wood chips being considered as a potential source of infection, and apparatus was perfected, even systems of metals chips, which could be installed in the maturing tuns or tanks. But the bacteriological risks linked to wood chips were eliminated by their being sterilised. And there was an awareness that any material made by man could not replace them. "Wood chip works in beer, it swims, constantly collides with the air and with the bubbles of carbon dioxide, and it contributes thus to maintaining secondary fermentation. Little by little it covers itself with yeast which is deposited on all its sides, and finally it sinks, dragged down by the weight, totally loaded with yeast which remains stuck until racking."

(*Le Petit Journal du Brasseur*, 24th February 1928)

The brewing hall of the De Koninck Brewery, in Antwerp, opened in September 1995.

In certain breweries, like Orval, the hops are partially added in the heating boiler, but also cold in the maturing tanks, which gives a special taste to the beer. This method is much practised in England *(dry hopping)*.

HOW BEER IS BREWED

1 Arrival of the malt flour at the exit from the crusher.

2 The mashing in the mash-tun.

3 Heating boiler.

4 Hopper for the hops.

5 Racker for racking the trub and the hops.

6 Meura filter for filtering the wort.

7 Plate exchanger for cooling the wort.

8 Cylindrical tanks for fermentation and maturation

9 Filtration of the beer by centrifuge before bottling.

10 Tanks of filtered beer before racking.

11 Control room with command desk.

WHAT IS MEANT BY ... ?

Agitator. The mash-tun is equipped with a very sturdy agitator, which stirs the mixture by turning around a central axis. It is fitted with iron hooks, intended to churn up the malt.

Finishing. One must distinguish "finishing" and "blending". One blends accidentally to mask a vice. Blending is a mixture which is made instantaneously. Finishing is a craft, forming a beer (faro, for example). It requires months, even years.

Bung. The hole in a cask by which the beer is introduced.

Cassure. By this term is meant the formation of a rough sediment in the course of cooking. Flakes form on cooling, the wort becomes more clear - this is a sign of quality.

Fining. This operation consists of adding to the wort a coagulating agent so as to clarify it.

Scottish cross. This device is intended to deploy the water for cleaning the draff in the tank-filter. The apparatus presents itself in the form of a cross, above the open tank-filter.

Exterior burner. This apparatus is used for the cooking of the wort or the raw grain. Some wort boilers are equipped with it. The wort is pumped into the heater, then it is heated before being put in the boiler.

Tank filter, or clarification tank. This tank is used for filtration of the mash*.

Guilloire tank. This is an open vat where the cooled wort arrives. There it is scattered with the yeast, then, when the fermentation starts, it is decanted into the fermentation vats. The guilloire tank has been neglected for fifty or so years. The beer passes directly from the cooler into the fermentation tanks. Formerly the guilloire tank often played the role of both cooling and decanting tank.

Mash-tun. Apparatus in which the maceration of the grain takes place. At a certain time, in Belgium, tax was calculated on the basis of the content of this vessel.

Dextrin. This is the state between the transformation of starch into maltose. The dextrin is rubbery and translucent, odourless and tasteless. Unlike sugar, the beer yeast does not act on it. It is the dextrin which makes the beer mellow, with body, and presenting a creamy mousse.

Diacetyl. This product of fermentation allows one to measure the maturity of the beer. Beer contains 0.1 to 0.5 mg of diacetyl per litre. On fermentation the level reaches 0.5 to 0.9 mg per litre. When one can no longer taste the diacetyl, fermentation is achieved.

Diastase. It is the ensemble of the soluble enzymes which one withdraws by aqueous maceration of the germed barley. It is an enzyme which serves as a catalyst for the splitting of the starch into dextrins and sugars. There are natural diastases and others, of microbe or bacteria manufacture.

Draff. This is the insoluble residue of malt - notably the husks - and hops. Because of their richness in proteins and nitrogenous materials, the draff are recovered and sold for the feeding of livestock. From 100 kg of malt one obtains 20 to 30 kg of dry draff, equivalent to 100 kg of good hay, which represents in nutritional value, 60 to 65 kg of barley. The composition of the draff is as follows: 75 to 80 % water, 8.5 % proteins, 10 % nitrogenous material, 2 % fat, 5 % cellulose, and minerals.

Draff is also used in fish-farming. The taste shown by fish for this food has, of course, not left fishermen indifferent. In brewing regions, great use is made of it.

False bottom. This is a perforated metal sheet, which retains the draff* of malt and of hops when the mash* runs from the mash-tun.

Tun. Vat of 2,000 to 3,000 litres, even 6,000 litres.

Waste. This is the loss, the difference between the number of hectolitres contained in the mash-tun and the number of hectolitres of beer sold. Losses are incurred at each stage of the manufacture of beer. The calculation of this loss is used for the tax and excise duty on the beer.

Isobarometric racking. This allows the beer to be drawn off under counter-pressure to avoid the loss of carbon dioxide. This counter-pressure should be the same as saturation pressure. It depends on the temperature of the beer and the saturation (quantity of carbon dioxide in grams).

Krausen. The mass of froth which forms above the open fermentation vat, due to the decomposition of the tannins in the hops and of the albuminoid materials, as well as under the effect of the carbon dioxide which rises to the surface.

Mash. *See Salad.*

Pipe. This vat contains 600 to 700 litres.

Salad. The contents of the mash-tun during soaking. It is also called mash or soak.

The *decoction* method, much used since the use of raw grain, consists, after mashing in the raw material vat, of boiling a part of the mash in the boiling tank, then in pumping it boiling into the mash-tun to raise the overall temperature of the mash. One does not make more than three decoctions during a mash. Another method, *infusion*, consists of gradually heating the whole mash by the addition of boiling water.

Stuickmand. This Flemish word comes from *stuick* ("push") and *mand* ("basket"). The use of the basket goes back rather a long way. Having difficulty in pouring their mash, because they used 50 per cent of wheat flour, the Brabant brewers had recourse to baskets. A basket was pushed into a vat, and when it received the wort, it was taken out, by means of a large ladle to be carried into the boiler.

The practice was not without danger. It frequently happened that workers charged with placing the baskets fell inside. This explains why one brewery in Leuven chose for its name Zœten Inval ("sweetened fall") and for its logo a worker having fallen in the basket.

Gambrel. This utensil, carried on the shoulders by two brewery workers, formerly served for the transport of casks of beer.

Ton. The content of a ton of beer is, on average, 250 litres. It varies according to locality.

Soak. See Salad.

REGARDING COLORATION

Coloration of the wort results mainly from the colorations of the malt and from the cooking, on account of the action of the temperature on the sugar which it holds. It varies in intensity according to whether the boiling is more or less severe, of longer or shorter duration.

In fact, several factors intervene:

- the temperature used for the first soakings
- the period of maceration of this mash
- the proportions of water and grain used
- the nature of these grains
- the type of heater used. Thus a heating by open fire leads to a caramelisation of the beer.

But the coloration may also be in part artificial. Colouring agents are then employed. These are either mineral materials (lime, potassium, soda), or vegetable materials (extract of liquorice, roasted chicory, brown malt, caramel).

WHAT HAPPENS TO THE YEAST?

In the course of fermentation, the yeast reproduces in abundance. Its quantity triples or quadruples. And once the main fermentation has stopped, it is recovered. Checked, and preserved in cold surroundings, it serves for later brews. Each re-use is called a "generation". In the case of top-fermentation, it is removed by skimming the yeast which has risen to the surface. The same stock may serve dozens of times. In the case of bottom-fermentation, the yeast is harvested at the bottom of the tank. The yeasts degenerate very rapidly, and the same stock cannot serve more than eight times.

The remaining yeast is used by the pharmaceutical industry, taking into account its content of albuminoid material and Vitamin B. It also serves in the manufacture of products added to soups, and products intended for the cleaning of copper (with the addition of sulphuric acid).

As for the residual yeast which is deposited on the bottom of the maturation tank (by settlement), at the end of the secondary fermentation, it is not re-used.

A Fifties enamel plaque from the Tielemans Brewery in Aarschot.

BEER IN ALL ITS STATES

THE GREAT TOP-FERMENTED BEERS

BOCK. This beer, with a gravity of about 3° Belgian and a pale colour, assumes the name of *Munich* when its colour is dark.

Originating from the small German city of Einbeck, in Lower Saxony, bock was known in Belgium at the end of the 19th century and was very widespread there until 1914. Bock Artois from the brewery of Artois Leuven was successful in the contest held at the Liège Exhibition in 1905. At the present time, some breweries continue to manufacture this type of beer, among table beers.

The poster by Émile Berchmans, dedicated to the Bock de Kœkelberg (1896) has remained famous *(see page 160)*.

The success of German beers, in the Fifties, forced Belgian brewers to take the words Hops and Malt, following the example of the German expression *"Hopfen und Malz. Gott erhalt's"*.

DORT. This beer, with a gravity of approximately 5.2° Belgian, owes its beautiful pale colour to the caramel malt used in its brewing. Another characteristic is the use of water containing 1 to 1.5 grams of minerals per litre, as in Dortmund.

Following the Universal Exhibition in Brussels (1958), beer of the Dortmund type was extremely popular. Belgian brewers responded to this keen interest by manufacturing the *dort*, and often, to bring it even nearer to the original, they gave it the name of the emblem of the brewery, lengthened by the suffix *bräu*. Thus the Anglo-Belge Brewery in Zulte created the *Rossbräu*, from the German *ross* ("horse"), since a horse appeared in its logo. In a similar effort to "look real", numerous festivals were organised, accompanied by music, in Bavarian style. One of the best known was that in Marche-les-Ecaussinnes (1959).

The success of the dort was staggering. For example, the production of *Rossbräu* passed 45,793 crates in 1957 and 109,427 in 1958, reaching 268,538 crates in 1965. In 1967-68 dort represented up to 50 per cent of the pils production of one brewery! But from the beginning of the 1970's the quality of Belgian pils improved appreciably, and dort slowly became neglected because of its high price. And today, the Silly Brewery is one of the last to brew its dort, the *Silbräu*.

EXPORT. This beer, with a gravity of around 4° Belgian, was very widespread in the immediate post-war period and up to about 1950, a time when pils at 5° saw growth, with the brands of Stella and Jupiler.

MUNICH. This beer, with a gravity around 3° Belgian and a dark colour, is brewed with a water with not much mineral content (0.5 grams per litre).

The *Munich* from the Kœkelberg Brewery won the competition at the Exhibition of Liège in 1905.

PILS. This beer, with a gravity around 5°, is brewed with a water containing very little mineral (0.005 to 0.0075 grams per litre).

Pils originated in Pilsen, in Czechoslovakia, where it was created in 1842. The name *Pilsen* being protected, Belgian brewers gave it the name of pils.

The first Belgian pils was *Cristal*, from the Alken Brewery, in 1927. *Pils Stella*, created in 1928, marked the apogee of this type of beer in the Sixties.

Today, pils represents around 70 per cent of the market in Belgian beers, illustrated by such brands as Stella, Jupiler, Primus, and Maes.

Below left: Draft advertisement for the Piedbœuf Brewery (in the "Thirties"
Below: from *Cella* to *Celci*, the success of Stella attracted a following and similar brands appeared.
Bottom: Advertisement designed by Francis Delamare, in 1928, for the Artois Brewery in Leuwen.

Opposite left: Stella Artois plays such a part in every-day Belgian life, that the socialist party wanted to imitate the brewery's advertising campaign. Nevertheless the poster was never put up!

IN TERMS OF MEASURE

The *extract content of the wort* is the quantity of extract contained in the wort after boiling. It is what one calls "original wort". This wort contains soluble materials (simple sugars, amino acids, dextrins, proteins). Only the quantity of sugar (maltose) is fermentable.

This determination of the quantity of soluble particles present in the wort before fermentation is carried out with the aid of a densimeter. It is expressed according to different methods:

• *Gravity Régie*. A gravity of 1045 corresponds to 4.5 degrees Régie. It is the system used in France.

• The measurement in *degrees Balling*, which expresses the quantity of extract in grams in 100 grams of wort. So a wort of 13°B will give 13 grams of dry residue, when one proceeds to the evaporation of 100 grams of wort. Degrees Balling are obtained by multiplying degrees Régie by ± 2.6.

This beer hydrometer shows all the elegance of the Belle Epoque.

This method, created in 1844, has been replaced by the Plato system, as the international standard.

• The *Plato extract*, measured at 20°C with the Plato densimeter - after the name of its inventor - indicates in degrees the percentage in weight of extract. It is called "original" when it is measured on the wort after boiling, "apparent" when it is measured on the finished beer, and "real" when it is measured on the finished beer from which the alcohol has been isolated by distillation. The real extract is therefore always higher than the apparent extract, the presence of alcohol rendering the measured liquid lighter.

In this work we have chosen to give the "strength" of the beer in legal degrees Belgian. At the boiling vat, the excise take the legal original gravity of the wort of which the temperature has been brought back to 17.5°C, with the aid of the Belgian excise densimeter *(see page 179)*.

It should be noted that, to reduce the temperature to 17.5°C the Vinchent apparatus - named after its inventor - is used. This drawer pump, patented at Frameries (Hainaut), was necessary from the end of the 19th century, in response to the Law of 13th August 1887 on beer excise, which placed an obligation on all brewers "to supply a cooling apparatus agreed by the administration, and legitimate to lower the temperature of the wort to be tested."

The attenuation is the expression in percentage of the value of the transformation of the fermentable extract of the wort in the course of fermentation. One must distinguish:

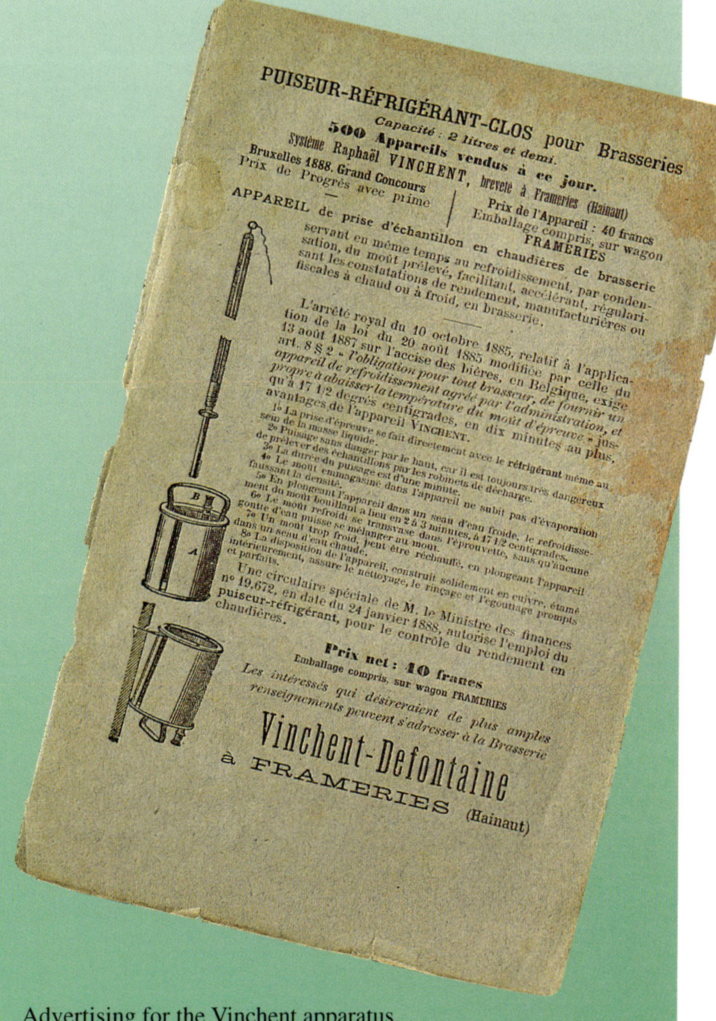

Advertising for the Vinchent apparatus, taken from a brewing directory.

• The *degree of in-tank attenuation*, at the end of the main fermentation. In traditional breweries, it is 10 to 12 per cent less than the degree of maximum attenuation. In modern breweries where there is no longer a secondary fermentation, the degree of in-tank attenuation is equivalent to the degree of maximum attenuation.

• The *degree of maximum attenuation*, at the end of fermentation. In general it is between 65 and 85 per cent.

The alcohol content depends on the content of extract of the wort and on the degree of attenuation on fermentation.

The alcohol content of the beer is expressed either in the percentage of alcohol by weight, or in the percentage of alcohol by volume. It must be noted that, water being heavier than alcohol, one obtains the percentage of alcohol by weight which is lower than the percentage of alcohol by volume.

Lastly, to know the degree of alcohol of a beer, it must be distilled to determine the content of alcohol in the distillate with the help of a Gay-Lussac hydrometer. The measure obtained is slightly less than the gravity Régie of the original wort. For example:

5° Régie = 4.5° Gay-Lussac.

BELGIAN GRAVITY	PLATO EXTRACT
(in degrees)	(in degrees)
2.24°	6°
2.65°	7°
3.05°	8°
3.46°	9°
3.87°	10°
4.29°	11°
4.71°	12°
5.13°	13°
5.55°	14°
5.98°	15°
6.41°	16°
6.84°	17°
7.28°	18°
7.72°	19°
8.17°	20°

Above right: a 19th century beer densimeter, with its wooden case.

ANALYSIS OF STRONG BEERS

	Gulden Draak	EKU 28° (Germany)	Bush Beer	La Bière du Démon (France)	Sanmichlaus (Switzerland)
Legal original gravity	8.64°	11.65°	9.59°	7.53°	11.06°
Plato extract - original	21.06°	27.60°	23.16°	18.56°	26.34°
Plato extract - apparent	3.66°	9.66°	3.07°	0.00°	3.95°
Plato extract - real	7.65°	13.23°	7.01°	3.58°	8.40°
Percentage of alcohol by weight	7.72 %	8.32 %	9.43 %	9.87 %	10.66 %
Percentage of alcohol by volume	9.66 %	10.39 %	11.76 %	12.31 %	13.27 %
Apparent attenuation*	82.62 %	65.00 %	86.74 %	100.00 %	85.00 %
Real attenuation**	66.52 %	52.06 %	69.73 %	80.22 %	68.71 %

* the extract is apparent, in the presence of alcohol
** the extract is real, by the elimination of alcohol

SPONTANEOUS-FERMENTATION BEERS

Spontaneous-fermentation is a purely localised phenomenon. Lambic and its derivatives (faro, gueuze, and kriek) are only brewed within a radius of fifteen kilometres around Brussels. The localities concerned form a cirde: Vilvoorde, Tervueren, Overijse, Beersel, Dworp, Lembeek, Halle, Sint-Pieters-Leeuw, Itterbeek, Schepdaal, Wambeek, Asse, Brussegem, and Wolvertem. Outside this perimeter, none has succeeded in imitating these Brussels beers, of which still little is known of their fermentation process. Research carried out by Professors Van Den Hulle and Henri Van Laer, at the end of the 19th century, tended to explain its mystery, and Van Laer showed that the agents of fermentation were to be found in the pores in the wood of the casks. On these lines, his son, Marc Van Laer, succeeded in isolating the bacterium *Brettanomyces Bruxellensis*, which was found in the air and without which the lambic would not exist. In fact the beers of Brussels are created without the addition of yeast.

Spontaneous fermentation beers demand of the brewer specific qualities, notably a sharp sense of observation and a judicious mind, to proceed with various concoctions of brew, according to which he obtains faro, soft lambic or gueuze. This explains why experience is primordial and why the lambic brewer is rarely inclined to reveal his secrets.

The logo of the Belle-Vue Brewery shows a traditional scene. Before selecting the lambics for the production of faro and gueuze, the brewer formerly had to taste his production. For this purpose he used a 20-litre copper pail, a special hammer (pinhamer), and a glass. He slightly loosened the spyle (tap, in Flemish) - a tapered wooden dowel in the hole made in the top of the cask - and with this hole opened, the beer flowed into his bucket.

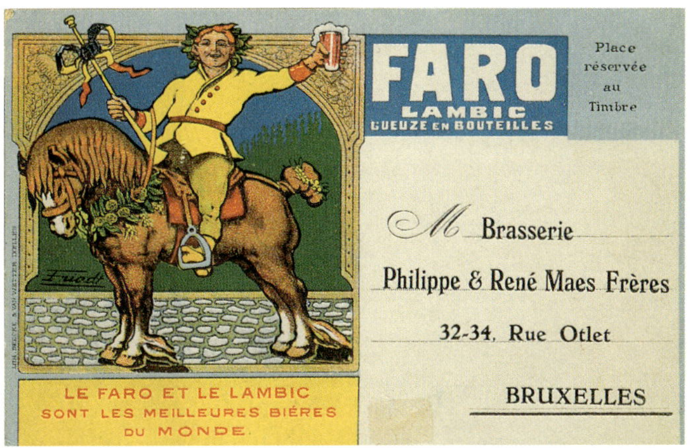

This post card, drawn by Dratz, was intended to revive the fortunes of faro and lambic in 1914.

Tradition and perseverance

Lambic, of which the first written mentions date back to the middle of the 16th century, was for a long time at the heart of the evolution of brewing in the Brussels region. But the arrival of foreign beers, around 1840, came to incite brewers to react, with the manufacture of top and bottom-fermented beers. Furthermore, in the 1860's, several cholera epidemics were attributed to beer brewed with water from the Senne, into which the inhabitants discharged their waste. Consumers therefore neglected lambic and faro. Another factor to explain the recoil from spontaneous-fermentation beers was that for café-owners bottom-fermented beers delivered under pressure needed less care and handling.

In 1910, however, attempts were made to re-establish it, with the help of the Brussels Exhibition. The chemists Victor Denamur and Léon Verhelst placed in evidence the great nutritive value of lambic. A litre of this drink was equivalent to 200 grams of bread, 180 grams of meat, or 72 centilitres of milk. This did nothing. Spontaneous-fermentation beers continued in recession. The economic crisis which preceded the Great War did not favour them. Six breweries closed in the space of fifteen years. Of course, in 1914, a widespread publicity campaign was organised by the association of brewers of lambic, with, at their head, Van Haelen, from Uccle. Its theme was "faro and lambic are the best beers in the world." Nonetheless, these beers did not experience the revival which had been hoped.

Then war broke out, and several breweries ceased manufacture. The casks for maturing the lambic were sometimes even used by the occupier … for the production of sauerkraut.

Before the war, more than a dozen breweries each produced 200 brews of 125 to 150 hectolitres per season, that is to say at least 10,000 tons of 250 litres each year. The situation was very different after the conflict. The total annual brewery use for lambic fell to some 12 million kilograms, which corresponded to approximately 467,000 hectolitres of beer at a gravity of 5.2°.

Production held until the end of the Eighties. Spontaneous-fermentation beers then saw a further fall in popularity, as is witnessed by their annual production, going from 470.000 hectolitres in 1987 to 389,000 in 1990, and then 352,000 in 1991. Their importance in Belgian brewery production did not cease to decline: 2.98 % in 1992, 2.88 % in 1993. It is true that, despite their incomparable perfume, lambic, faro, and gueuze are not enjoyed by cosmopolitan clientele, because of their peculiar taste.

It is nevertheless interesting to note that gueuze on its own constitutes 48 per cent of the entirety of spontaneous fermentation beers, competing with kriek, increasing strongly (45 per cent), and then framboise a long way behind arrived (7 per cent). In fact there exists a gueuze-kriek "rivalry", which results in a considerable consumption of gueuze in Wallonia (80 per cent gueuze as against 10 per cent kriek), while in the province of Antwerp and in Limburg, twice as much kriek is drunk than gueuze.

Lambic: a special manufacture

Pale in colour, and with a gravity varying between 5.2 and 5.6°, lambic combines in its composition 60 to 70 per cent malted barley, and 30 to 40 per cent red wheat from Brabant, as well as aged hops, at the rate of 400 to 600 grams per hectolitre - the proportion was formerly 700 to 800 grams of hops per hectolitre, which gave the beer more bitterness. The Belgian provenance of the hops has its raison d'être: the bitterness of the aged hops of Alsace and Central Europe became stronger, with time, in an acridity which gave a bad taste to lambic, while the hops should lose their bitterness so that the lambic might have that agreeable acid flavour which normally characterises it. A flavour which varies from one brewery to another; here a pronounced lambic character, and there a perfect mellowness. But, beware. It is a mistake to describe its taste as *acetic*, since the term supposes that it is the result of an infection by acetic ferment, and that is not the case.

At the end of the 19th century, Henri Van Laer recommended for lambic strictly equal proportions of malt and wheat. However it was necessary to reduce the quantity of wheat later since it was noticed that, deprived of its husk, wheat hindered filtration in the mash-tub, and that a not inconsiderable quantity of extract remained in the draff. The rural folk of the Brussels region, because of this phenomenon, had shown a keen interest in the draff of the lambic brew, for its rich nutritional value for their animals. Unlike wheat, winter barley, which contained more straw, permitted better filtration. And brewers blended 50 to 75 per cent of malted winter barley with 50 to 25 per cent malted barley.

Carried out during the months of winter, brewing was formerly done thus. Once the mash was completed (that is to say the mixing of the grains and the water at a temperature of 45°C), the *slijmmethode* consisted of taking off the cloudy mixture, sometimes by surface syphoning *(slijm)*, then boiling it in a kettle *(slijmketel)*, and lastly, boiling achieved, pumping it back on the mash. After rest and saccharification, the first soak of the thick wort was drawn off and pumped into the kettle. Following three hours boiling, the hops were added. At the end of this boiling process, lambic was obtained. It then had one or more soaks, less dense, which were called "bière de mars" (or *meerts* - March), because the brew took place in the month of March.

The wort was conveyed to the cooling vessel where it stayed all night to provoke *trub*, that is to say the settlement of the coagulated nitrogenous materials. During this time bacteria in the ambient air (*Brettanomyces Bruxellensis* and *Lambicus*) infected the wort, allowing spontaneous fermentation which then occurred in oak or chestnut casks (tuns of 250 litres, pipes of 650 litres, or vats of 3,000 litres). This slow fermentation, which began after some hours or some days according to the ambient temperature, caused a spurt at the bung-hole (a small hole on the top of the cask) of white froth from the wort. This froth gradually became darker and ended by blocking the bung, thus isolating the wort from any contact with the air. The temperature of the wort varied between 10°C in winter and 25°C to 30°C in summer.

Fermentation then continued for one to three years, either in the brewer's *pakhuis* (beer store) or with the

Faro was formerly contained in jugs. Left, a jug used for serving faro in the Café de La Bécasse, in Brussels. Right, a jug used for shopping at the drinks outlet.

biersteker (beer merchant). It was calm or lively depending on the ambient temperature. Because of the variable capacity of the casks, the wort was sold by weight. The barrels were marked in chalk with a letter (referring to the year), the specific sign of the brewer, the date and the number of the brew.

Two or three weeks later, the beer (*joenk* or *platten*) was delivered in small barrels to individuals and to bars. At this stage its taste was both soft and bitter. It did not have a mousse. It was two or three months before the beer finally became *jonge lambic*. To obtain soft lambic it was sufficient to add a little sugar.

The result of a blend: faro

Formerly, this red-brown coloured beer was only sold in casks. It was obtained by blending, in equal quantities, a lambic of 5.5° gravity and a "mars" at 3°. It stayed in the barrel for around two years. The brewers who carried out this blending themselves were rare. Beer preparers or finishers *(gereedmaker)*, bought lambic and mars from them and produced faro.

In the regions around Liège and Namur, as well as Brussels, faro was much enjoyed. It came to have a moderately sweet flavour and a beautifully bright appearance. Nevertheless it did not please everybody, and even had its detractors, some of whom were famous. Gérard de Nerval discovered it during his stays in Brussels: "The intoxication of the faro drinker only shows itself at first by an increase in noise which is only deafening, and finally by a silent deterioration of the mind." Later, in 1871, during the construction of an arch on the Senne, by the French, the "bad taste" of the beer was attributed to the water used, which was at that time polluted. Following a trip to Brussels, Baudelaire expressed his hostility to faro in his *Amœnitates Belgicæ*, writing especially, "Do you drink faro?" I asked Monsieur Hetzel. I saw a look of horror on his bearded face. "No, never! Faro (I say this without rancour) is beer which is drunk twice." A certain Vaughan, a Paris journalist, responded to this virulence in 1875 with a laudatory verse extolling the virtues of the beer.

Brussels cafés neglected faro from 1924. The progress of gueuze did it harm. Brewers no longer had beers available for the production of faro (other than those which were too young or of second choice), all the others being used for gueuze. Another unfavourable factor was that after the Great War the use of saccharine was tolerated in place of pure cane sugar. Finally a certain snobbism turned consumers away from faro.

It was more than half a century before this beer was re-introduced, thanks to the opening of the café "Le Père Faro" (1979) in Brussels, and the creation of the Confrérie du Faro (1980). Thus today one still finds a whole range of faros, from beers which are extremely acid, slightly sweetened, to highly sugared beers.

The "Champagne of Brussels"

"Lambic and gueuze are only brothers and sisters; the first has received finings and candy sugar, while the lat-

Drawing dating from the beginning of the 1890's.
Brewers of Munich type beer could not "provide" during mid-summer, and faro surfaced again.

ter matures and clears without any finishing off. It is the best beer in the Brabant." Thus A. Laurent defined these beers in his *Dictionnaire de la Brasserie*, in 1875, the first definition known, in fact. Indeed, in his treatise on the manufacture of beer (1856) La Cambre makes no mention of gueuze. This leads to the assumption that its origin is somewhere between 1860 and 1865.

The success of this beer, obtained by the blending of lambics of different ages (one, two, or three years), was both rapid and considerable. In 1897, the Brussels International Exhibition made the beer known, as did various campaigns. The majority of cafés in Wallonia took to serving it. But the provisioning of drinks outlets was not immediate, and the quality of the gueuze varied from one place to another according to the length of its maturation in the cellar. Often it had not matured for more than eighteen or twenty four months in the barrel and scarcely a few months in the bottle. Quite clearly it did not present the crystal clearness, the slightly acidulous taste, and the beautiful creamy and persistent head which should characterise it. The head was abundant and rich. It was necessary to add sugar to make it drinkable. Gueuze is a dry lambic, not sugared. This loss of quality caused a significant decline in the consumption of gueuze.

Entry to the "Vlaamsch Bierhuis" (Flemish Beerhouse) at the Brussels International Exhibition in 1897. A great deal of faro was dispensed there.

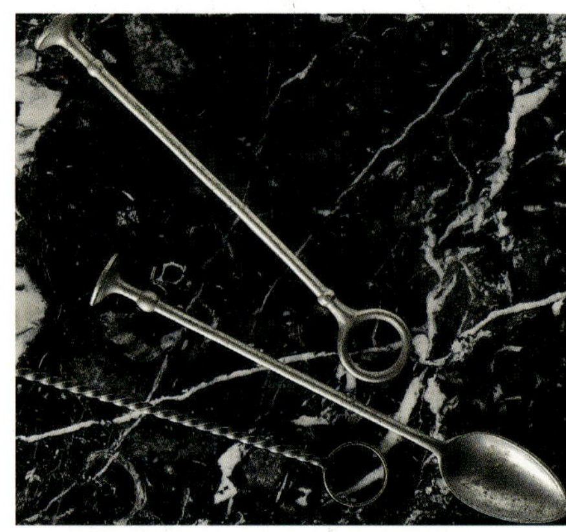
A sort of pestle, the stoemper served to crush the sugar in the gueuze glass to soften the beer.

In the Thirties, brewers were to exploit this "negative" evolution of gueuze. In fact, workers, who had been its principal consumers, deserted foreign bottom-fermented beers which had become very expensive, in favour of gueuze, which the café-owner sold by the bottle of three glasses.

After the Second World War, stocks of gueuze were exhausted once more, and many brewers stopped producing it. Then there was a growth in industrial production. Little lambic came into the composition of the beer. Maize and rice replaced wheat, and the maturation of the wort was more rapid. The gueuze was sugared. Some brewers even bought brews of *pils*, of mediocre quality, which they used for blending in order to reduce production costs.

From 1932 Brussels producers of lambic protested against excise duties being proportional to manufacture. In fact some brewers bought residual beer from outside, and in this way the excise duty did not correspond to final production. And it was this which allowed small breweries to surpass all the large breweries of good gueuze after 1945.

Today the Belle-Vue Brewery has 75 per cent of the market, while the Van Honsebrouck Brewery has 11 per cent and the Mort Subite-Eylenbosch Brewery 6 per cent. Since the closure of the De Neve Brewery in Schepdaal, a desire to "return to basics" has emerged, to which the Belle-Vue and Van Honsebrouck Breweries have responded with non-filtered gueuzes, the first with the *Sélection Lambic Gueuze*, and the second with *Fond Tradition*.

The flavour of fruit

A beer with a red colour, and with 6 % volume alcohol, *kriek* is obtained by adding cherries from Schaerbeek to a year-old lambic. The proportion is some 30 to 40 kilo-

Enamel sheet from 1936. The Belle-Vue Brewery began its activity in the former Vos Kina Brewery.

R. Desmecht collection.

grams of whole fruit (including skin and stone) for a tonne of 230 to 240 litres. This addition generates a second fermentation. At the end of a maceration period of five to six months, the beer is filtered, and then bottled. It improves with ageing, but beyond four to six years it loses its cherry flavour to the benefit of a strong alcohol content.

Kriek was already in vogue at the end of the 19th century, just like raspberry lambic which is made in the same way. These were imaginative beers, so to speak, which only certain bars had the privilege of serving. In the Eighties, taking advantage of the fashion for sweetened drinks and sodas, it regained favour. All manner of varieties of fruit extract came to complement the range of cherries and raspberries which already existed. One can find gueuze with banana, peach, strawberry, plum, and more.

A peach of a beer, from Lindemans Brewery of Vlezenbeek.

DID YOU KNOW ...

• *Lambic* takes its name from the village of Lembeek, situated near Brussels, and which in the 15th and 16th centuries, formed a free zone between the Earldoms of Brabant and Hainaut. The lambic brewers there knew such prosperity that the name of the village became confused with that of the beer brewed. Today the Frank Boon Brewery perpetuates the tradition.

• The origin of the word *faro* is much more blurred. Some hear echoes of faro from Messina being wine which is drunk with added sugar. Others would derive the term from the Castilian *farro*, which indicates "hulled barley". According to others the name was given to the beer by the Spanish because of its colour, which was reminiscent of the wine from the Faro vineyards in Portugal. Others still prefer legend. In medieval times, a certain Hughes, Lord of Kantersteen, near Brussels, did not find beers to suit his taste. So he organised a competition in which several breweries participated. The produce of the Haute Pinte Brewery seemed to him so good that he exclaimed, "Maître Géry Knaps, your beer is marvellous, it is spirited and mellow, it is lusty and show-off ("faraude"). The term faro is derived from this.

• The origin of the term *gueuze* (or *gueuse*) is much debated. Some claim that it is Germanic. In fact, when a certain Van Helmont, from Vilvoorde, discovered carbon dioxide, he called it gas, as opposed to air (*lucht*, in Flemish). On the other hand, the Danes gave water which contained gas and bubbled the name of *geyser*. The adjective *gueuze* therefore signifies "mousseux", or "sparkling with gas". The denomination of *lambic mousseux*, gradually became transformed into *lambic gueuze*. Until around 1940 one spoke of "lambic gueuze en tonneau" for lambic sparkling in the cask. Today this appellation is reserved for lambic mousseux in the bottle.

Another theory takes into account the fact that the Walloons who came to visit the Brussels International Exhibition in 1897 heard the name gueuze given to the beer which pleased them with its taste. The word *gueuse* was then used in foundries to indicate a cast iron ingot in its first smelting. It was a means of remembering the beer. And perhaps this explains why in Wallonia the spelling was originally gueuse while in Flanders it was a matter of gueuze.

• The word *kriek* comes from the Flemish *krieken*, which means "cherries". There is nothing surprising about that. Cherries are used in making the beer of which the complete name is in fact *krieken lambic*.

THE DEVELOPMENT OF LAMBIC GRAVITY

From the analysis of beers presented at international exhibitions, we know the gravity of lambic previously. It was not rare to encounter gravities of 8.4° for lambic and 5.5° for faro. Perhaps this was a matter of special brews, realised for exceptional circumstances. Around 1840 lambic gravity corresponded to 6°. Around 1920 lambic showed 5.5° to 6°. Having experienced the Second World War, a number of brewers made acid beers of less than 5°, which could only suit the making of good faros, by blending. These acid beers today make the quality of a gueuze, as it is loved by purists, enthusiasts for tradition. The gravity varies from 5.2° to 5.6°.

LEGISLATIVE MATTERS

It was not until 1965 that the appellations *lambic*, *gueuze*, and *gueuze lambic*, were defined and protected. In fact a Royal Decree dated 20th May ordered that these names should only be used for spontaneous fermentation beers. On 17th July 1973, a Royal Decree then specified that these same names were only applicable to beers obtained by germination in the ambient air, on cooling the wort on a cooling tray.

No less precise, the Royal Decree of 19th March 1974 provided that the appellations *lambic*, *gueuze*, *gueuze lambic* and *kriek lambic*, could only be used for drinks originating from the spontaneous-fermentation of a wort of at least 11° Plato and a certain acidity. Furthermore their ingredients had to include at least 30 per cent of wheat.

Nearer our own time, the Royal Decree of 17th March 1993 fixed at 51 per cent the quantity of beer obtained by spontaneous fermentation which had to be found in gueuze.

In 1995, finally, within the context of European Law on specificities, certain gueuze breweries issued draft appellations, intended to distinguish *gueuze*, produced by industrial breweries, and *vieille gueuze* ("old gueuze") reserved to traditional gueuze breweries.

True gueuze, non-sweetened, is recommended by doctors for diabetics. By virtue of its perfect attenuation, it contains hardly 0.2 per cent of residual sugars.

THE CHAMPAGNE BOTTLE FOR SERVING GUEUZE

From 1865, glass no longer being considered as a luxury product, taxes on it were abolished. And it became a habit to dispose of champagne bottles as being of no value. In order to re-establish the sale of lambic mousseux, in sharp decline, someone had the idea of using non-returnable bottles.

Gueuze was so successful that the price of champagne bottles increased rapidly. From 9 centimes in 1893, it passed 11 centimes in the following year, then following the International Exhibition which took place in Brussels in 1897, reached 13-14 centimes in 1898! The stock of bottles peaked in 1903, with a price of 9 centimes, because of imports of bottles from Holland and Germany.

GUEUZE, THE SECRET IN THE CELLAR

Once the blend of lambic is completed and the beer racked, the bottles, capped and often wired, are placed in cellars where maturation continues, more or less rapidly according to the nature of the blend (young or old lambics) and the ambient temperature (between 7°C and 12°C). The bottles, lying down, are sometimes marked on the bottom with a chalk line, white for gueuze, red for kriek, which indicates to the client the position to be maintained in his cellar. They rest thus for at least a year, before being sold.

As for the gueuze cellar at the drinks outlet, formerly they often housed 40,000 bottles, and took all the attention of the patron of the Brussels café *(baes)*. He himself tasted the first bottle of a cuvée or batch in order to make sure of its quality before serving it.

An engraving dated 1839 shows us Faro regaling his friends, on the occasion of peace, who are depicted as different types of beer. Produced by the Association of Brussels Brewers, it repeated the theme of an older engraving (18th century), owned by the brewers of Ghent, and which was called "Treat given by Lieven Uytzet".

TOP-FERMENTED BEERS

ABBEY BEERS

Domestic in its origins, the manufacture of beer took shape and became organised in the secrecy of the medieval monastery *(see page 18)*. This tradition of monastic breweries only survives today, in Belgium, with the "Trappist" beers *(see page 128)*, which are authentic abbey beers. This is because the beers called "abbey" are no longer brewed in abbeys. Under this denomination are hidden several individuals. And it is interesting, for example, to place some "abbey beers" in their context in order the better to understand the diversity of origin in their names:

• the name is that of an active Premonstratensian abbey:
Abbaye de Grimbergen, Abbaye de Leffe, Abbaye de Postel, Abbaye de Tongerlo ;

• the name is that of a closed Premonstratensian abbey:
Abbaye de Bonne Espérance, Abbaye de Dielegem, Abbaye de Floreffe, Abbaye du Roeulx (St-Feuillien) ;

• the name is that of an old abbey destroyed in the French Revolution:
Abbaye d'Aulne (De Smedt Brewery), Abbaye de Cambron (Silly Brewery), Abbaye d'Ename (Roman Brewery), Abbaye des Rocs (Abbaye des Rocs Brewery), Abbaye de St Idesbald (Huyghe Brewery), Abbaye de Villers la Ville (Van Liezele Brewery) ;

• the name is that of an active abbey:
Abbaye d'Affligem (De Smedt Brewery), Abbaye de Bornem (Bios Brewery), Abbaye de Maredsous (Moortgat Brewery), Abbaye de Steenbrugge (De Gouden Boem Brewery), Abbaye de Val Dieu (Piron Brewery) ;

• the name is monastic:
Moinette (Dupont Brewery), Divine (Silly Brewery), Cuvée de l'Ermitage (Union Brewery), Witkap (Slaghmuylder Brewery), Pater Lieven (Van den Bossche Brewery), Het Kappitel (Leroy Brewery), Triple Moine (Bocq Brewery), Petrus (Bavik Brewery).

(Premonstratensian abbeys and their beers, see page 18-21).

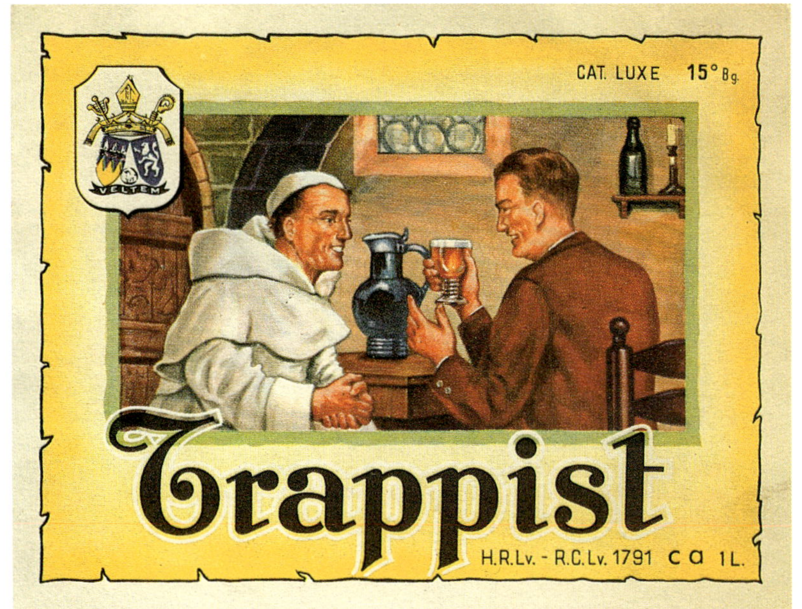

In 1960, the Veltem Brewery near Leuven, owned by the Anglo-Belge Brewery since 1957, brewed a beer by the name of Trappist de Veltem. Anxious to protect the interests of the Trappist fathers, the Orval Brewery instructed a lawyer in the matter. Legal proceedings were commenced. On 28th February 1962, a Judgement by the Commercial Court in Ghent sentenced the Anglo-Belge Brewery to pay one Franc in damages and interest, as well as publishing the Judgement.

The Anglo-Belge Brewery found itself with 9,500 wooden crates, engraved with the name of the beer in question, which were now useless.

TRAPPIST BEERS

The denomination "Trappist" applies exclusively to products made within monasteries belonging to the Strict Order of Cistercians. And this applies as much to the beer. However this did not prevent the misuse of the name over past decades. And despite judicial decisions reinforcing the strictness of the denomination, the debate does not seem to be any the less.

However that may be, five abbeys today make Trappist beers in Belgium. It should be noted that a sixth Trappist brewery existed until the First World War, that of the abbey at Achel, to the North of Limburg, on the Dutch border. Trappists are top-fermented beers of Category S, that is to say with a gravity equal to or more than 6.2°. Beer production varies a great deal according to the abbey. At the present time Westmalle comes top, followed by Chimay.

The Abbey of Notre Dame de Scourmont at Chimay

Its foundation dates back to the middle of the 19th century. In fact on 25th July 1850, on the initiative of Abbot Jourdain, priest of a neighbouring village, seventeen Cistercians from the abbey at Westvleteren, began to clear a piece of land in the heart of the forest which they had been given by the Prince of Chimay, to build a monastery. This was completed in 1864. The brewery was first finished in 1862 and the first beers were produced in 1863. However it was not until 1885 that the bottling plant was operational, and in 1920 that the products began to be sold commercially. In 1925, Prior Emmanuel Le Bail registered the trade mark of his beer, comprising the coat of arms of the abbey and the seal ADS ("Abbaye De Scourmont"). Between the wars, Chimay sold beer with a strength of 4° to 4.5°, in large bottles.

After the occupation of the abbey by the Germans during the Second World War, the monks had to renovate the monastery buildings. The brewery was then carefully "rethought", with the enlightened advice of Professor J. De Clerck, from Leuven *(see page 188)*. As a sign of recognition, on his death, he would be buried in the monks' cemetery. Father Théodore made the "prototype" brew for the Easter celebrations in 1948. *Chimay* owes its success to this monk, who led its manufacture until the beginning of the Nineties. In 1949, the better to control the product, the brewery

A Trappist at the Scourmont Abbey, in Chimay.

made a "pure culture" of the yeast which it has maintained since in its microbiological laboratory. This was joined in 1960 by a second. The brewing hall was renewed in 1954, and again in 1989. Fermentation and maturation installations were modernised in 1991.

From 41,760 hectolitres in 1973, annual production reached 84,002 hectolitres in 1983, and 105,000 hectolitres in 1993. Around one third is exported abroad, as far as the United States and Japan. Since 1978 racking has not been carried out in the abbey but in the industrial complex of Baileux, twelve kilometres away. This sector of manufacture, like commercial activity and administration, is placed under the responsibility of a non-monastic company.

Chimay is available in three versions:

• red capsule, 7 % vol. alcohol. This is the abbey's premier beer. Today it represents 35 per cent of production. In corked Bordeaux bottles, it is named "Première";

• white capsule, 8 % vol. alcohol. This beer is characterised by a hopping three to four times more than that of the other capsules. Put on the market in 1960, it represents 10 per cent of production. In corked Bordeaux bottles, it has been called "Cinq Cents" since 1986, the year of the five hundredth anniversary of the Principality of Chimay;

• blue capsule, 9 % vol. alcohol. Created when the brewery commenced, it represents 55 per cent of production. In corked Bordeaux bottles, it has the name "Grande Réserve".

These beers are mainly all consumed in Wallonia and France.

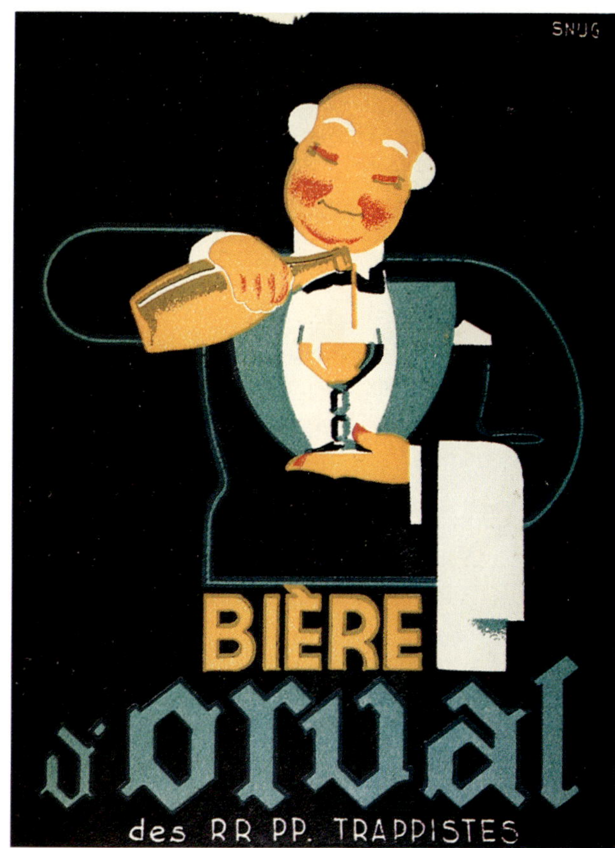

The special shape of the Orval bottle allows the pourer, when dispensing the contents, to keep an eye on the deposit of yeast at the bottom of the bottle.

The Abbey of Notre Dame d'Orval, at Villers-devant-Orval

In 1070, the Benedictines, from Calabria, settled in this lonely valley, ideally suited for prayer, on land offered to them by Count Arnould de Chiny. Forty years later the monks gave place to a small community of canons who continued building works and who, confronted by economic difficulties, asked for incorporation into the Order of Cîteaux, which was granted by Saint Bernard. Also, in 1132, Cistercians belonging to the Abbaye des Trois Fontaines, near Châlons-sur-Marne in Champagne, joined them. They adapted the monastery buildings for Cistercian requirements and began to cultivate the land.

The abbey was not spared by successive wars. Sacked in the 17th century, it was then destroyed under the Revolution. It was not until 1926 that it was reborn, on the initiative of Dom Marie-Albert van der Cruyssen, from Ghent, a monk in the Abbaye de La Trappe, in the Orne. The community was composed of monks from the Abbaye de Sept-Fons, in the Allier, an abbey which furthermore possessed a brewery. The monastery of Orval was rebuilt to plans by the architect Henri Vaes, a great admirer of Cistercian architecture, and who found his inspiration in the ruins of the abbey at Villers-la-Ville. In 1931 a brewery was created in the new abbey. The first brew was made in the following year. From the Fifties, the installation underwent a number of important transformations.

From the beginning, the brewery had the status of a limited company, in which the shares were subscribed to by the friends of the abbey, concerned to give the community the means of reconstructing and maintaining the buildings. These share-holdings were afterwards transferred to the monastic community by their owners. At the present time, the profits of the brewery are augmented by donations.

The water from a spring is located on the abbey's premises, a selection of barleys from France, Holland, and Germany, a blend of aromatic hops grown in Slovenia *(Styrian Golding)* and in the Munich region *(Hallertau Herzbrücker)*, some white candy sugar … these are the ingredients of *Orval*, characterised by a strength of 6.2 % volume alcohol. An important detail in its manufacture is that maturation is not at 0°C, as is the norm, but at a higher temperature, in accordance with the practice in making English top-fermented beers, allowing the enrichment of the beer in composites contributing to its taste and aroma. But the originality of *Orval* is above all in the cold hopping in the maturation tanks, as is the English way. This supplementary addition of hops helps to modify the aroma at the end of maturation, thanks to the slow dissolution of the aromatic composites present in the hops.

Current production at the brewery is 38,000 hectolitres a year, of which 10 per cent is exported abroad. The packaging - a 33cl skittle-shaped bottle - contributes to the "personality" of this amber beer, just as the famous lozenge-shaped label bearing the Orval legend, which was registered in 1934. As for the glass, designed in 1932 by Henri Vaes, it follows the "golden section", to aid perfect tasting.

THE CHARMING LEGEND OF ORVAL

The brand image of *Orval* represents a fish emerging from the surface of the water and clasping in its jaws a ring of gold. Thereby is evoked the legend of the Mathilde Spring. It is said, indeed, that in the 11th century, the suzerain of the area, the Countess Mathilde, Duchess of Tuscany, wanting to see the pioneer monks who had come from the South of Italy, sat at the edge of the spring. While doing so she ill-advisedly dropped her wedding ring. Desperate at having lost this precious jewel, a memento of her late husband, the Countess devoted herself to the Virgin with immense fervour. And... a trout came out of the water and returned her possession. In the face of this marvel, the Countess exclaimed, "Truly, this is a golden valley!"

The Abbey of Notre Dame de Saint Remy at Rochefort

Founded in 1230 by Gilles de Walcourt, Count of Rochefort, this abbey was first of all intended for nuns. But they suffered from the hardness of the climate and the poverty of the soil, and were replaced by monks, in 1464. Arnould from the Maison Neuve was the first Abbot of this new community. The abbey was for a long time involved in the quarrying of red marble. On the other hand, documents dating from 1595 bear witness to a brewing activity, which was then for the exclusive use of the community.

Then the French Revolution happened. The monks had to be resigned to abandon the abbey in 1794. It became a country property and sank into oblivion. It was only in 1887 that the Trappists from the abbey at Achel decided to breathe life back into a number of places. They restored the rule of their Order. Constructed in 1899, the brewery really began operating again in the first years of the 20th century. It was modernised in the Fifties, and the present brewing hall dates from 1960. The racking equipment was renewed in 1974. A dozen people, most of them belonging to the monastic community, work in the brewery.

Foreign barley, and hops from Yugoslavia and Bavaria are used in the manufacture of the beer. Production is, today, some 300 hectolitres a week. *Rochefort* exists in three versions:

- red capsule, 7.5 % vol. alcohol;
- white capsule, 9.5 % vol. alcohol;
- blue capsule, 11.3 % vol. alcohol - this *Rochefort* was formerly called "La Merveille" ("The Marvel").

The Abbey of Notre Dame du Sacré-Coeur at Westmalle

Paradoxically, this abbey was founded during the Revolution period. In 1793, three monks from La

Trappe, in the Orne (France) were refugees in Switzerland - Father Jean-Baptiste Desnoyers, Father Eugène Bonhomme de la Prade, and Brother Jean-Marie Debruyne. They decided to go to Amsterdam, and thence embark for Canada. But because of the war being fought between the Netherlands and the troops of the French Revolution, maritime links with America were both irregular and uncertain. Now it happened that the Bishop of Antwerp wanted to establish a monastery in the region. In 1794 a property, "Nooit Rust", situated in Westmalle, was therefore purchased, with its farm, to house a religious community. Other Trappists joined the three "pioneers" and by June of that year they were twelve, among whom four chose to depart for Canada. Unfortunately the eight who were settled in Westmalle had to flee, on 26th June, before the Revolutionary army. They reached Marienfeld, in Germany.

A short existence for the abbey.... they only returned there in 1804. And in 1836 a brewery was created and placed under the authority of Father Albericus Kemps from St. Œdenrode, a former journeyman-brewer. The first brew was made on 10th December of the same year. In 1865 Father brewer Ignatius Van Ham, of Prussian origin, undertook to develop the capacity of the brewery, and therefore to increase the installations, in order to finance the establishment of the Order in the Congo. The brewery having achieved its maximum output at the beginning of the Twenties, a further enlargement was necessary. Finally in 1934 work was started on building the brewery which we know today, to the plans of architect Wilfried Van der Aa of Wilrijk.

In 1932 the Prior Edmond Ooms registered the appellation "trappistenbier" for the beer from the abbey. In the following year the word was once again registered by the ASBL (non-profit-making company) of Abbaye de Westmalle. In 1935 the beer was given its present bottle.

Annual production today reaches 130,000 hectolitres. The *Trappiste de Westmalle* is available in two forms:

• the *Double* (red capsule, 6.5 % vol. alcohol), in the composition of which is brown candy sugar. and which is filtered by kieselghur. It is the only Belgian Trappist beer sold in 50 litre casks (2 % of the total production of the abbey);

• and the *Triple* (white capsule, 9 % vol. alcohol), in the composition of which is white candy sugar, and which is filtered by centrifuge.

Like Orval, the Abbey of Westmalle has its own network of sellers, which even provides for the control of exports. These beers are much appreciated in Flanders and in Holland.

The Abbey of Saint Sixtus at Westvleteren

The Cistercian monks who, in 1831, founded a religious establishment in Westvleteren, near Ypres, came from France, more precisely from the Abbey of Notre Dame du Gard, which was answerable to the Mont-des-Cats. The latter monastery housed a brewery (it was operative until the Great War), and without doubt that explains why, from 1838, the small community of the Abbey of Saint Sixtus (it was not actually accorded the status of abbey until 1871) was equipped with brewing apparatus. The following year, the first brew was made. Tradition was founded.

At the end of the Twenties, on the initiative of Dom Bonaventure De Groote, the abbey underwent major restoration and the brewery was renovated. But the extension of brewing activity seemed to some as incompatible with the monastic spirit. And at the end of the Second World War, Father Gerardus took extremely strict measures. In the first place an agreement was concluded in 1946 with the St. Bernardus Brewery (Watou), according to which this enterprise would make a beer by the Trappist method and sell it. This agreement ended in 1992. Furthermore it was decided that the production of beer by the abbey would be limited to the needs of the community, that is to say 3,500 hectolitres, divided into 420 hectolitres of a beer at 6°, 1,330 hectolitres of a beer at 8°, 70 hectolitres of *Dubbel* at 4° (reserved only for monks), and the rest of a beer at 12°. Finally, cafés and inns which belonged to the abbey were sold. The only one to remain is the Café De Vrede, opposite the monastery.

This strictness was perpetuated. Today, 5 monks work permanently in the abbey brewery. The "team" only increases in size on racking, every fifteen days. Production remains at 3,500 hectolitres, and the sale of *Abdij St. Sixtus* beers takes place only in a small shop built in the abbey walls.

The three beers produced are: the *Spéciale* (red capsule, 6 % vol. alcohol), the *Extra* (blue capsule, 8 % vol. alcohol), and the *Abt* (yellow capsule, 11 % vol. Alcohol). All the beers are made with Belgian barley, a variety of hops from Poperinge, and water from a 100 metres deep well.

From 1954, the Renaux Brewery, in Grandrieu, produced a beer called *Trappistine Beaumont*, a name which the brewer explained thus: "We have definitely rejected the possibility of taking the name *Trappist*, having regard to the increasing difficulties which this name has brought us. We thought it right to mention the gravity in order that, contrary to what the public has a tendency to believe, one can realise that instead of being a small Trappist, it is rather a real speciality of high gravity! Besides, in the logic of the word, *Trappistine* is effectively the feminine of *Trappist*, and not its diminutive."

The Trappist *B.M.S.*, from the Mynsbruggen Brewery, in Silly, was produced playing on the letters ADS (Abbaye De Scourmont). In 1960, after the De Veltem case *(see page 128)*, production was stopped.

The beer with a monastic sound, Moinette, was the first, in 1990, to have a biological sister in Belgium.

IN THE CISTERCIAN TRADITION

Cistercian monks lived with respect for the rule of Saint Benoît of Nursie, to whom the founders of the Order restored its original austerity, in Cîteaux, in Burgundy, at the turn of the 11th and 12th centuries. From Cîteaux the Order was widened by the founding of very many abbeys, and this growth owed much to the powerful personality of Saint Bernard, Abbot of Clairvaux during the second quarter of the 12th century.

Nevertheless, at the end of the Middle Ages and during the Renaissance, the Order lost its aura and, as a reaction to this decadence, a reform based on "strict observance" began in Clairvaux in 1602. It was not greeted with unanimity. Only ten or so abbeys submitted to it. In 1664 the Abbot Armand de Rancé imposed upon his Cistercian monastery of Notre Dame de la Trappe, in the Orne (France) an even more strict regime. The Cistercians of Strict Observance followed it and took the name of "Trappists".

Belgium today has six monasteries (Achel, Chimay, Orval, Rochefort, Westmalle, and Westvleteren) and six convents (Brialmont, Chimay, Clairefontaine, Klaarland, Nazareth, and Soleilmont).

According to the rule of Saint Benoît, the monks work both to provide for their own needs and to aid those who are in difficulty. Each monastery therefore cultivates its own agricultural or forest estate. Agriculture, breeding, these activities were formerly indispensable to them in providing on the one hand the raw materials necessary for making beer (barley, hops) and on the other for making cheese, a perfect accompaniment to beer. This production survives today in Chimay, Orval, and Rochefort.

CHILLING AND ITS ADVANTAGES

At the time of the growth of bottom-fermented beers, of the *Bock* and *Bavarian* style, rural Belgian brewers suffered more than their town-dwelling counterparts from this new competition. Taking account of the costs of these beers, not only for their transport, only very low profits ensued, especially as assessment of the number of consumers was uncertain. However, after the Great War, Belgian breweries adopted the motor lorry and the situation changed. Competition between large and small breweries, between the town and the country, became a reality. Celebrated in 1905 by Harold Johnson in *Le Petit Journal du Brasseur*, the *chilling process* was then practised often, principally in the Twenties.

This English process, which was used in the manufacture of top-fermented beers of a *pale ale* type, was to obtain a *chilled* product. In chilling the beer, nitrogenous materials were coagulated and eliminated after filtration. By this process, carbon dioxide diluted best, cold. Other advantages of *chilling* were on the one hand an agreeable aroma which it bestowed upon the beer, and on the other a brilliance which was like that of a bottom-fermented beer.

The method was in fact very simple. The brewing process suffered no change, either in the main or the secondary fermentation. After two or three weeks at rest, when the beer was finished, came the *chilling*. The best results were obtained if it was "rapid intermittent", or "slow". The *chilling* known as "rapid continuous" lacked in efficacy. To pick up the explanation given by Albert Mertens, of the École Supérieure de Brasserie in Leuven, in 1924, before the Association Belge du Froid, *rapid intermittent chilling* is practised "in two or more tin-plated copper cylinders, of low capacity, strongly refrigerated. The cylinders are partially filled with beer which an agitator stirs in an atmosphere of carbon dioxide under pressure. The cold stirring, under pressure, provides for saturation, and more [...] improves flocculation when its intensity is well regulated." As for *slow chilling*, as the Professor also indicated, "it is done in vats. The beer stays there for several days during which it is saturated and slowly cooled, either by the air in the cellar, or by direct cooling in the vat, which is cheaper." Although it requires a more expensive installation, the slow method proves to be superior to the other." The beers break down and saturate best, preserving more body.", concludes Albert Mertens.

Of course *chilling*, which was as it were a "grooming" of the beer, did not have the power to mask possible faults in manufacture. And specialists agreed to reserve this method for beers in bottles for rapid consumption.

Today the process is found once more, either partially or completely, in the production of *ice beers*.

FALSE "BOTTOM"

In 1899, the company of F. Kendall and Sons, of Stratford-upon-Avon, in England, traded in brewery products and was equipped with an analytical laboratory. The Kendall family chose to settle in France, in Lille, and perfected a system similar to *chilling*, for transforming top-fermented beer into beer with the taste of bottom-fermentation. Thus was born the *Kendall system*, which had as a publicity motto, "Kendalise your brewery against the bottom." It was to this end that a number of small Belgian breweries bought the equipment in the Thirties.

WHITE BEER

The Middle Ages already enjoyed this type of beer. Its success was constant, until at the turn of the 20th century blond beers, of the pils type, attracted the consumer's taste. Pushed into the shade, the "white" was reintroduced in the Sixties, in Hœgaarden, and since then it has recovered some of its former favour. In 1993 the total production of white beers was approximately 650,000 hectolitres by the Hœgaarden Brewery alone.

A time-honoured process

White beer was formerly made from malt (50 per cent), wheat (40 per cent), and oats (10 per cent), orange peel, and coriander. The method of brewing was long and complex. It was necessary to wash the draff three or four times. The cooking in the boiler lasted four to five hours, and sometimes more. At this stage came the hops, which had to be as old as possible. After that, the wort had to be left at rest in the cooling vessel until the next day. Thus placed in contact with the air, it underwent, or not, a fermentation. If fermentation did not occur, the tank had to be heated to a temperature nearing 40°C. The yeasts activated then and a froth, more or less white and loaded with impurities, emerged from the bung. Fermentation therefore resulted from the symbiosis between the top and bottom yeasts and a good quantity of lactic bacilli.

The beer was not consumed thus. It had to be racked into earthenware jugs. There one added, according to acidity, a more or less significant quantity of sugar, provoking a new fermentation. The beer was only fit to be drunk when the head was abundant and the presence of carbon dioxide expressed itself in a sparkle.

The capital of white beer

Hœgaarden was pre-eminent in beer for centuries. Traces of a brewery were found there from 1318. But it was in the middle of the 15th century that monks settled in the village and set to making wine and beer. Soon, the farmers imitated them. The Premonstratensians were also competition to them. Twelve breweries in 1709, twenty in 1745!

From the end of the 13th century to the end of the 18th century, Hœgaarden did not cease to be a source of discord between Brabant and the principality of Liège. It skilfully exploited this situation and, according to its interests, sometimes took one side, then the other. Thus it benefited for a long time from the status of a tax-free zone which it had been granted by the Prince-Bishops of Liège. The absence of tax on its beers contributed to their success, since, transported to Brussels, Charleroi, Namur, and Liège, they were sold at a more advantageous price.

If the very beginning of the 19th century saw the peak of brewing activity in Hœgaarden - thirty five breweries for 2,000 inhabitants, and one tavern for every 10 inhabitants - a slow decline followed, of which the causes were multiple. The French Revolution struck a blow to the industry. Competition became formidable and Leuven proved a serious rival. The brewers could not face up to the taxes imposed by Tirlemont. Finally, in the 1860's, a cholera epidemic was declared and, mistakenly, the doctors attributed its origins to the unhealthy state of the water which was used for the manufacture of beer. The brewers were for this reason forced to use water from wells and, by unfortunate coincidence, the beer suffered from it. Beside this loss of quality, rumours which the epidemic generated had led to consumers neglecting the beers of Hœgaarden.

At the beginning of the 20th century, the town counted no more than thirteen brewers. The two wars brought further decline. In the Fifties, two breweries had successfully survived. The most important, the Loriers Brewery, had put an end to its production of white beer before the Second World War. It still brewed Dortor, Hirsch, and Das (now brewed again, since 1996, by the De Kluis Brewery), until its take over, in 1960, by the Artois Brewery of Leuven. Its activities ended in 1972. Only the artisanal brewery of Tomsin therefore made white beer, and this until its disappearance in 1957.

The idea of "rediscovering" the white beer of Hœgaarden was in 1965 attributed to Pierre Celis, a dairyman who became a brewer and who had worked at Tomsin. He first constructed a small brewery in his stables. The brewing equipment was to say the least artisanal: a wine vat which, sawed in two, gave a fermentation tank and a mash tun; wooden pipes; a copper cauldron for boiling. And with the collaboration of the old brewer Louis Tomsin (1881-1967), the dream came true. The following year, Celis opened a real brewery. His first production was 350 hectolitres. The growth of the business allowed Celis to transform an old lemonade factory into a brewery. He called it De Kluis ("The Hermitage") and it operated from 1979. Its production

Porcelain mugs, from the different Hœgaarden breweries.

continued to expand, reaching 12,300 hectolitres in 1981 and 62,000 in 1984. But in 1985 a fire took the wind out of its sails and, when reconstruction could not be carried out, Celis left the country for the United States (see page 153). The takeover by Artois was rapid and so too its activity: 250,000 hl in 1989, 450,000 in 1991.

Characterised by a very pale colour, a light cloud, and a sweet-sour flavour, Hœgaarden's white beer has 5 % vol. alcohol. It is brewed from pale malts and wheat, and aromatised with hops, coriander, and curaçao. There is no filtration after fermentation. It is a beer "sur lie", since yeast is added during conditioning.

The white beer of Leuven

At one time this beer was very much enjoyed throughout Belgium. Its attractive price was certainly a reason. But it went down so much that quality was affected and the beer's reputation suffered. Brewing utilised 50 per cent malted barley, 40 per cent wheat, and 10 per cent oats, as well as per hectolitre, 80g of old-fashioned hops, 50g of coriander, and 50g of orange peel. The malt (with rootlets) was dried in the wind in huge well-ventilated lofts. The beer was only subject to one hour's boiling.

With a gravity of 3.5° Belgian, the Leuven beer presented a very pale colour, a slightly cloudy appearance, and a sweet-sour taste. The last brewery to make it was the house of De Eendracht, in Leuven, which was razed after its take-over by Stella Artois, in 1975.

Outside the famous white beer produced by Hœgaarden in the Brabant, mention should be made, in particular, of the *Riva Blanche (Dentergems Wit)*, made by the Riva Brewery (Dentergem) and which has seen good growth since 1980, as well as the *Brugse Tarwebier* (Bruges), and the *Haacht Wirbier* produced by the Haacht Brewery (Boortmeerbeek).

It is also necessary to mention:

• in Wallonia: *Titje* by Silly (Silly Brewery), *Blanche de Namur* (Bocq Brewery), *Blanche des Honnelles* (Abbaye des Rocs Brewery) ;

• in Flanders: *Bavik Witbier* (Bavik Brewery), *Oudenaards Wit Tarwebier* (Clarijse Brewery), *Mater Blanche* (Roman Brewery), *Steendonck Witbier* (Moorgat and Palm Brewery), *Limburgse Witbier* (Sint-Josef Brewery).

In addition, two rather special varieties of white beer have recently appeared. On the one hand, *white lambic*, made by the Timmermans Brewery, which is in fact a white beer blended with lambic. On the other hand, a white beer with fruit, *Florisgaarden*, brewed by the Huyghe Brewery, in Melle. To the white beer is added an aroma of fruit: passion fruit *(Florisgaarden Passion)*, strawberries *(Florisgaarden Fraise)*, and mangos with apricots *(Florisgaarden Ninkeberry)*. These beers have only 3 % vol. alcohol.

OTHER TYPES OF BEERS

ANTWERP BARLEY BEER. Despite its name, this beer of long tradition does not contain barley alone. To the malt is often added 5 % to 8 % oats and 4 % to 5 % wheat. The wort is boiled for a long time (three and a half to four hours), which colours it rather strongly. The simple has 1.5° Belgian, and the double 3° Belgian.

WEST FLANDERS BROWN. This "old" beer, with a gravity of around 5° Belgian, presents a brown colour and a taste of Munich caramel, just a little sour. It is brewed with a coloured malt and water which is rich in carbonates. They incorporate around 3 per cent (formerly 5 per cent) of beers matured in casks with eighteen to thirty six months of ageing.

The beers *Rodenbach* (Rodenbach Brewery), *Zulte* (Alken-Maes Brewery), and *Petrus* (Bavik Brewery) are examples.

Above: Rodenbach poster from the beginning of the Forties.

CAVES. This beer from Lier, near Mechelen, with a gravity of 5.3° Belgian, is characterised by an amber colour and a slightly acid taste of "old" beer. Malt, wheat, oats, and hops (in low quantity) are its ingredients. Boiling lasts five to six hours. Each brew was formerly split in two, giving on one hand *caves*, and on the other a lightly blended beer which had the name of *knol* or *cnol*. In the 15th century, it already had a radius outside the town of its production. In the Renaissance, the town possessed its guild of brewers. This long brewing tradition was expanded in Lier in 1967. The last brewery to make caves was that of Alfons Cuykens. When favour fell towards *ales*, he took to brewing *Sheep Ale*, named after the Flemish word for the inhabitants of Lier, *schapen*.

Today the Verhæghe Brewery, in Vichte, produces caves.

BIÈRE DARBYSTE. The name goes back to the English pastor John Darby, who in the 19th century developed a Protestant doctrine of fundamentalist strictness. This theologian had charged certain of his adherents to spread in Borinage a recipe for beer which was hardly alcoholic, in order to turn the inhabitants away from the religion of alcoholism. The beer was made in stoneware pitchers, filled with barley, figs, and sugar, which were placed behind the stove. Some of it was produced for sale, and in 1897 following complaints from the brewers of Borinage, the sale of Bière Darbyste was banned to persons not licensed.

Today the Blaugies Brewery is the only one to make it.

DIEST BEER. This beer, with a gravity of 5° Belgian, is very dark in colour, almost black. In Diest, barley (winter barley malt and 30 per cent brown malt) and wheat are used in equal quantities, as in Brussels. A few oats are also added. The grain is milled together. Hops are only put in at a rate of a little more than one eighth of a kilogram per tonne. Fermentation is stopped by the addition of a half kilogram of lime, which gives a low alcohol beer. This is only drunk five to six weeks after manufacture.

This soft beer was very fashionable in Brussels before the growth of railways. It was recommended to children's nurses. Since 1966 a Royal Decree has regulated its manufacture.

DUIVELS BIER or **LA BIÈRE DU DIABLE** (THE BEER OF THE DEVIL). This beer, with a gravity of 5° Belgian, is of cognac colour, with a soft acid taste. It is a blend of lambic and top-fermented beer, a sort of faro but a little stronger. The only brewery to make it at the present time is the Vander Linden Brewery, located in Halle.

It is the only beer with its name in two languages, French and Flemish. The name came to it, in fact, on the occa-

The Flemish word *Duivel* ("Devil") has inspired beer names, like *Duvel* (Moortgat Brewery), from 1924, and later *Satan* (De Block Brewery) and *Lucifer* (Riva Brewery).

sion of the traditional procession of the Virgin of Halle, in which a number of Walloons took part. One day, the café called "Le Vieux Mannekin-Pis" added a larger quantity of candy sugar to a cask of lambic. It refermented and produced a stronger beer. Pilgrims proclaimed, "But it is truly a beer from the Devil!" Following this, the café-owner put up a sign in his front window, with the words *Diable / Duivel*, indicating that he sold this special beer.

GILDENBIER. In medieval times, Diest was already a prosperous commercial centre, thanks to its textile industry. Various guilds were established there. Each year a festival was dedicated to them, on the occasion of which the *gildenbier* was served graciously to members of the guilds. This top-fermented beer then had a gravity which could be as much as 14° Belgian.

Today the Haacht Brewery, which took over the last Diest brewery (Cerckel Brewery), includes a gildenbier in its range of products. This brown beer has a gravity of 6.65° Belgian.

GRISETTE. This is the name of a beer from Hainaut. Its manufacture uses malted March barley, and no winter barley, as well as malted wheat, in low quantities (1/10 at least and 1/7 at most). The proportion is approximately 65 pounds of malted barley and 8 to 9 pounds of wheat for each cask of 170 litres. The wort measures 6.5° to 7° Belgian, on an ordinary brewer's beer gauge. Long boiling gives the beer its amber colour.

The best known was the *Grisette de Thieusies*, of which production came to an end in 1941.

MECHELEN BEER. The brown beer from Mechelen had a renown from the 16th century which was largely justified. It was only around 1810 that its production declined considerably. As with other Brabant beers, its manufacture used non germinated wheat.

Gouden Carolus extends this tradition today. It is made by the Het Anker (the Anchor) Brewery, set up in Mechelen from the Middle Ages. The beer was much enjoyed by the Emperor Charles V, who had been educated in Mechelen with his aunt, the Regent Marguerite of Austria, and who after his abdication had some taken to the Spanish monastery of San Yuste.

MATER BEER. This beer produced in the village of Mater, near Oudenaarde, assumes a beautiful deep red colour. Its gravity is 4.5° Belgian. Among its ingredients are Munich malt and caramel malt, as well as 10 per cent sugar candy, and Saaz and Hallertau hops. It is refermented in the bottle.

The Roman Brewery, in Mater, is the only one to make it at the present time.

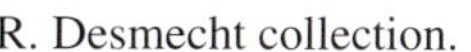
R. Desmecht collection.

OUDENAARDE BEER. With a gravity of around 5° Belgian, this beer is deep red and has a taste of sourish caramel. Its ingredients are winter barley, caramel malt, roasted malt, and Aalst hops. It undergoes a night of boiling. It is racked into champagne bottles and refermented in the cellar.

In 1939 eight breweries made Oudenaarde beer. Today there are only two: Liefmans Brewery and Clarysse Brewery (Félix).

SAISON. This Walloon beer is characterised by a gravity of 4° Belgian, an amber colour, and a slightly acid taste. It is in fact a blend of an old acid beer (formerly matured in wooden casks) and top-fermented beers brewed in April and May.

The best known beers of this type are: *Saison Régal* (Bocq Brewery), *Saison Dupont* (Dupont Brewery), *Saison de Silly* (Silly Brewery), *Saison de Pipaix* (Pipaix Brewery), and *Saison de Blaugies* (Blaugies Brewery).

UYTZET. According to Doctor Wauters (*Dissertation on the manner of making Uytzet*, 1798) this beer, made in Ghent, Bruges, and around, was created by a brewer-innkeeper in Wetteren, around 1730. During the epidemics of 1791 in Dendermonde and 1794 in Wetteren, those who had drunk it were saved from death. It was extremely popular throughout the 19th century, and was largely exported. Even faro and lambic in Brussels suffered from its success. There were three versions: ordinary, double, and triple. Its ingredients were barley, wheat, and oats.

The word *uytzet* came from the Flemish *zet uit*, "put outside", since its inventor removed some of the beer from the boiler, after a boiling of five to six hours (in place of the thirty to forty hours which was the usage of the time), and had it ferment with an old yeast, before putting it in casks.

ZOTTEGEM. The characteristics of this beer are a gravity of around 6° Belgian, an amber colour, a strong perfume, and a taste of top yeast, slightly acid. Its flavour is no longer as sour as before. For its manufacture hard water is used, together with caramel malt, pale malt, and hops from the region. Lactic fermentation takes place in casks and vats. There is no filtration. The beer is racked into champagne bottles and refermented in the cellar.

In 1939 seven breweries made Zottegem, for a population of 6,000. Today only one survives, the Crombé Brewery.

WHAT IS MEANT BY ...?

Ale. This is the name given to all top-fermented beer in England.

Blended beer. It happens that, for one reason or another, beer is blended either with other beers of different gravity, acidity, or age, or with products with a generally acid character (vinegar for example). This operation, which is called "blending", is frequently carried out for the manufacture of lambic and saison.

The most widely distributed blended beer in Belgium is *Jack Op*, from the Van Roost Brewery in Werchter, today brewed by the Brasserie Belle-Vue.

Household beer. This is a weaker beer than that which is served in drinks outlets. It is like table beer*.

Table beer. This is the name either for a light and digestible beer with a lightly acidulous taste, or a strong beer blend which is consumed with a meal. More officially, a Royal Decree dated 31st March 1993, reserves this appellation for beers with an original gravity between 1° and 4° Belgian.

Alcohol-free beer. This is either a beer which has been fermented, but then de-alcoholised by inverse osmosis or special filtration, or a beer where fermentation has been stopped. Throughout Benelux an alcohol-free beer must contain no more than 0.5 % of alcohol in volume, while in Germany, this percentage is 0.00 %.

A beer known as *low-alcohol* has a low alcohol content. In Benelux such a beer may contain between 0.5 % and 1.2 % of alcohol by volume. In comparison, the proportions are for example 0.5 % to 1.2 % for Great Britain, and 0.7 % to 1.5 % in Greece.

Double. This word, very old but disappearing in the 18th century, came back into fashion at the beginning of the 20th century. It indicates a beer for the manufacture of which double the materials are used, giving it its double gravity. Generally it is a brown beer with an alcohol content of around 8°.

Milk stout. This beer of stout* type was perfected from 1912. Lactose is added to the wort or to the beer, in the proportion of 4 kilogram for 165 litres. Some incorporate in this blend some 280 grams of powdered milk per hectolitre.

Pale ale. Less heady than ale*, this beer is amber in colour, and characterised by a very agreeable bitterness. Formerly the vats in which it was contained held a bag of hops, Grains of Paradise and other aromatics.

Scotch ale. It is the ale of Scotland, widely represented on the continent. It is like London ale, but with less colour and more alcohol.

Several factors influenced the significant position taken by English beers on the Belgian market: the decline in the manufacture of "indigenous" beers, following taxation on the capacity of the mash-tun; the arrival in Belgium of numerous English engineers at the end of the 19th century, in the context of the industrial growth of the country; and lastly the influence exercised by the English soldiers in the Great War. To face up to this competition, brewers decided to manufacture their own Scotch.

The *Scotch* from the Silly Brewery is today one of the last existing Belgian Scotches.

Stout. This black beer is extremely nourishing and dethroned porter, of which it is a variant. Taking account of the success of English beers in Belgium, in the 19th century, Belgian brewers undertook to make them. In Wallonia, the *Stout Barmy*, from the Union Brewery, in Jumet, and the Stout from the Impérial Brewery in Brussels, were the best known.

Today the Brasserie Bios, in Ertevelde, and the Brasserie Facon, in Bellegem, produce it.

Triple. This term qualifies a strong beer, denser than a double. Nevertheless it does not have triple gravity, and therefore does not require triple quantities of raw materials, because brewing would be impossible! Triple nears 9° of alcohol. It is generally of a blond colour.

FAMOUS BEERS OF YESTERYEAR

• *Aarschots Bruin* was a beer with a gravity of 4.5° Belgian, and a reddish colour. Its taste was slightly sour and its bouquet that of an "old" beer. Among its ingredients were 30 per cent of aromatic malt, 20 per cent wheat, and a little hops.

The breweries of Valvekens and Tielemans were the last to make it, in Aarschot. Today the Huyghe Brewery, in Melle, produces one.

• *Liège Beer*, also called *Saison de Liège*, was characterised by being the weakest in the kingdom. Perhaps this low gravity was due to the fact that after having drunk a few drops of "Pécket" (the name given to the genever of Liège), workers preferred to turn to a very light beer. It was perfect for them to dilute the pécket in the beer rather than water.

The yeast used was not very attenuating: 10 % to 12 % less than others. Thus one obtained a beer presenting a fuller body than a beer of the same gravity, having been fermented from an ordinary yeast. Taking account of the slight attenuation, the secondary fermentation was important and the beer sported a strong head.

• *Peeterman* was an amber beer made in Leuven. It took its name from the nickname given to Leuvenists. It was brewed like the white beer of Leuven *(see page 135)*. The only difference was that it had four hours of boiling. The malt was used with rootlets.

The last brewery to make it was the house of Ed Eendracht, in Leuven.

• *Pittem Beer*, although amber, was a sort of white beer. It formerly had a certain reputation in East Flanders. In Bruges and in Blankenberge, it was consumed in great quantities.

• *Seef* was formerly brewed in Antwerp. Today it has disappeared, and remains unknown. All that we do know, through a brewing encyclopaedia from 1793, *Den Volmachten Bier Brouwer*, is that spices like coriander, cinnamon, and cloves, were among its ingredients.

• *Zoeg*, a beer from Tienen, had a gravity of 3.5° Belgian, a pale colour, and a flavour just a little hopped and very sugared, due to the addition of sugar (2.5 kilos per hectolitre) at the time of its expedition to the client.

"The Beer of Doctors"; such was its nickname since the most important brewery in Tienen, Pierraerts, counted a doctor among the members of its family, who recommended this beverage to all his patients. The success of Zoeg was such that it was also manufactured in the neighbouring town of Hœgaarden, where it was called *Strieep*.

SPECIALE
ZOEG
DES DOCTEURS

THE LANGUAGE OF BEER

Beer contains some eight hundred ingredients which contribute to its flavour, to which both the consumer's sense of smell and taste respond. This flavour depends, of course, on the composition of the beer, and the process of brewing. Needless to say there is no one flavour type, but a multitude.

In the Seventies, a terminology of flavour was elaborated by a group of American researchers. It was intended by means of forty-four carefully selected terms, to facilitate communication between professionals, and, thanks to seventy-eight supplementary terms, to permit the definition of various identifiable degrees of flavour.

The appearance of the beer

Cream. This is the term which should be used to indicate the head. One "judges" it through its development, his finesse, its firmness (or duration), and its consistency. It should stick to the glass. If it does not hold, despite irreproachable conditions of hygiene, the cause is a weak saturation or an infection in the beer.

It should be noted that one finds some gummy materials in barley, wheat, and hops, and these make the head on the beer, since without them the globules will not take a hold.

Creamy. This speaks of a beer with a beautiful head, fine, resembling cream and which sticks well to the glass.

Free-running. This describes a beer which flows like oil. It is flat, glutinous, viscous. The origin of this defect is a deterioration of the malt or the wort - the dextrin converts into a vegetal mucus. The best way to cure such a beer is to leave it alone and wait. It is sufficient then to rack it and so separate it from the draff. It may be used for blending with other beers.

One should know that light exercises an unfavourable influence on the flavour of beer. A bottle in brown glass protects the drink better than a transparent or green bottle. Nevertheless, alterations in taste may also arise with brown bottles, if they are subjected to prolonged exposure to sunlight (beyond three hours), to diffused daylight (beyond 32 hours), and to artificial light (beyond 112 hours).

The popular expression "liquid bread" came from the fact that for a long time beer was considered as nutritional. But today it is thought of rather as refreshment. Pleasure has taken the place of health.

Do not confuse "aroma" with "bouquet".

• When one says that a beer "has bouquet", this indicates that it exudes a smell like a bouquet of flowers. The essential oils of the barley and the hops, liberated by the release of carbon dioxide, form the bouquet of the beer. As soon as the beer is poured into the mug or glass, habit has it that one smells it to appreciate the quality of its bouquet. All well-kept beers should have this.

• Of course, the aroma is also a matter of odour. A beer which has aroma contains substances provided with a certain bouquet (or perfume). But unlike the bouquet which brings out the smell, it is the mouth which perceives if the beer contains aromatics.

The vocabulary of taste

Acid. Said of a beer with a very sharp taste, which it owes to acetic acid. This is a fault if this taste affects a pils or a top-fermented beer. But it is normal in beers of spontaneous fermentation (gueuze, in particular) or in white beer, when it is very young.

Acidulous. Said of a beer which owes its flavour to the presence of a certain quantity of lactic acid. An acidulous beer is weakly acid. It produces a refreshing sensation in the digestive tract. It is the taste which "bières de garde" assume.

Acrid. Said of a beer both hard and acid, generating a burning and irritating sensation in the digestive tract.

Astringent. Said of a beer which grabs the throat. This defect comes from the straw of the barley and the tannin in the hops.

Bitterness. Bitter materials in the hops are the origin of this peculiarity in beer. The bitter taste leaves a sensation of freshness in the mouth, and is bracing. It stimulates the digestive function. All the nuances of bitterness differ with the various types of beer.

The intensity of bitterness is calculated on the European Bitterness Unit (EBU). This European standard of bitterness is expressed by the litre. The number of units depends on the hops added to the wort. The EBU content, per litre, varies between 25 and 35 for a pils, between 10 and 15 for a white beer or a household beer, and between 30 and 40 for a strong top beer.

A bad bitterness may be attributed either to a too significant hopping, or to a defective preservation of the hops, which have not been protected from the air.

Flat. Said of a beer deprived of flavour and which has lost all its properties. It no longer contains sugar to convert into alcohol and therefore more alcohol to generate an acidity.

Full-bodied. Said of a beer which has body and tone. This quality, which characterises all good old beers, expresses itself in a certain alcoholic strength and a fleshy consistency, which is both vinous and mellow. A full-bodied beer communicates to the stomach a kindly warmth.

Hard. Said of a beer which is not so agreeable to drink, and rather indigestible. Long ago, numerous breweries burned the better sugar of the wort owing to the addition of lime in the heater. They thus obtained a coloration, at the expense of fine sugar. To the extent that this is the sugar which bestows upon the beer its softness, its vinous and sparkling character, a hard beer is devoid of head and presents neither mouth nor strength.

Mellow. Said of a beer which has mouth*.

Mouth. A beer which has mouth is agreeable to the taste, and refreshes the tongue and the palate, exciting the saliva glands.

A beer with mouth generally has body and mellowness. This quality originates in the nitrogenous materials, proteins, albuminoids, that is to say the glutinous parts, nutritives, and embryonics of the grain, aided by the alcohol, the carbon dioxide, and a good freshness.

More and more used for gastronomy, beer conferred finesse and flavour on all sorts of dishes.

Flemish beers were often compared with their great "rival", wine.

Musty. Said of a beer which does not sparkle any more, is dull and lacking in taste. A beer which remains too long in the glass becomes dull, and for that reason loses its aroma, its bouquet, and its freshness.

Soft. Said of a beer which is not acid, but glucosed, even cloying if it is too sugary. An insufficient fermentation is the origin of this characteristic.. The keeping of a soft beer is more difficult than that of a bitter or acid beer.

Sour. *See acid*

Tonic. Said of a beer which fortifies and quenches the thirst, which "gives a tone" to ones organs. A tonic beer contains nitrogenous materials. A strong beer is tonic, while a weak beer is relaxing.

Vinous. Said of a beer which is slightly acid.

Old advertisements often placed the accent on the hygienic, nutritive, and digestive virtues of beer. See page 144 for an 1897 carton panel.

To each country its taste

In a study of special Belgian beers, at the beginning of the Eighties, a Jemeppe student, D. Millecam, divided beers up according to three tastes, each of them being linked to a basic ingredient: bitterness (hops), sour (yeast), and soft (malt). And starting from there, he placed in evidence that the Walloons loved the bitter soft, that the Flemish leant towards sweet and sour, and that the Brussels folk preferred acid.

This extremely interesting analysis was taken over and deepened by G. Marinckx, of the Avouerie d'Anthisnes, who dedicated conferences and writings to it. Of course it was debated, but it had the merit of attracting the attention of brewers to the increasing importance of taste to beer enthusiasts.

In 1984, Peter Crombecq developed this approach, and analysed beer in accordance with the same criteria in his first work on the taste of Belgian beers. His idea taught lessons. In fact the same year an association was formed, *The Objective Beer Tasters*, with the aim of protecting the traditional taste of Belgian beers. Today they are very active.

Spot the reason for some major defects ...

- The beer has a disagreeable odour? It is a lack of hygiene in the maturing cellar, or an insufficiency of aeration.
- The beer releases a mouldy aroma? It has been in contact with a chlorinated product or a bad quality cork.
- The beer tastes of butter? This is due to a defect in fermentation and, more precisely, an excess of diacetyl acid.
- The beer has an oxidised taste? The beer has been in contact with the air too long. It is a taste of papier maché.
- The beer tastes of straw? Several causes are possible: bad preservation of the malt, too long a brewing, a badly cleaned filter plate.
- The beer tastes of burnt caramel? The malt has been roasted too much. On the other hand, this taste is elegant enough in some beers (e.g. stout).
- The beer tastes of old biscuits? Pasteurisation was too long and at too high a temperature, which hinders the yeast.
- The beer tastes of light? This taste comes from prolonged exposure to light, on display in the shop for example. Such a defect was common at the time of green bottles. The use of brown bottles reduced it, but it is still encountered too often in hyper-markets and other large shops.

THE TASTING RITUAL

1. LOOK AT THE BEER :

• the colour

sparkling . . . .
blond . . . .
golden . . . .
amber . . . .
brown . . . .

• the clarity

limpid . . . .
veiled . . . .
cloudy . . . .

• the head

formation of a hat . . . .
size of bubbles . . . .
colour . . . .
hold . . . .
consistency . . . .
adherence to the glass . . . .

• the saturation

(release of carbon dioxide to the eye)

abundant . . . .
weak . . . .

2. SMELL THE BEER :

(smell the top of the glass)

• the odour

agreeable . . . .
neutral . . . .
disagreeable . . . .

3. DEFINE THE AROMA :

(smell the top of the glass)

too aromatic . . . .
good . . . .
not enough aromatic . . . .

• the hops

fresh . . . .
average . . . .
aged . . . .

• the esters

(volatile materials of which the quantity is linked to conditions of fermentation and the stock of the yeast used)

fruity : excessive . . . .
sufficient . . . .
insufficient . . . .
flowery : excessive . . . .
sufficient . . . .
insufficient . . . .
success . . . .

• the sulphur

(taste of yeast)

not sulphurous . . . .
sulphurous . . . .
too sulphurous . . . .

4. DEFINE THE FLAVOUR :

(drink a mouthful slowly, "chewing" the beer)

• the taste

bitter . . . .
sugary, soft . . . .
sour . . . .

• the bitterness

strong . . . .
balanced . . . .
weak . . . .

• the mouth (or body)

mellow . . . .
thick . . . .
dry . . . .
hard . . . .

5. DEFINE THE AFTER-TASTE :

(which remained after drinking)

late bitterness . . . .
astringency . . . .
other . . . .

TITRE CRÉÉ APRÈS LE 6-10-1944

B L S C

BRASSERIE DE LÉOPOLDVILLE

BRASSERIE DE LEOPOLDVILLE
Société congolaise à responsabilité limitée

CAPITAL SOCIAL
357.500.000
FRANCS CONGOLAIS

SOCIÉTÉ CONGOLAISE A RESPONSABILITÉ LIMITÉE

constituée par acte de Me André TAYMANS, notaire de résidence à Bruxelles, le 23 octobre 1923, publié aux annexes du « Moniteur Belge » du 16 novembre 1923, acte n° 11656, et au « Bulletin Officiel du Congo Belge » du 15 janvier 1924, et modifié suivant actes
du 24- 7-1925 - Ann. M.B. des 10/11- 8-1925 n° 9823; Ann. au B.O. du C.B. du 15- 9-1925
du 5-10-1926 - » du 23-10-1926 n° 11425; » » du 15-12-1926
du 3- 4-1929 - » du 26- 4-1929 n° 6343; » » du 15- 6-1929
du 27- 7-1937 - » du 12- 8-1937 n° 12336; » » du 15- 9-1937
du 2- 5-1939 - » des 22/23- 5-1939 n° 8232; » » du 15- 5-1940
du 26- 5-1948 - » des 2/ 3- 8-1948 n° 16541; » » du 15- 8-1948
du 23- 5-1951 - » du 19- 6-1951 n° 17053; » » du 15- 7-1951
du 20- 7-1951 - » du 29- 7-1951 n° 17834; » » du 15- 9-1951
du 14-12-1955 - » des 26/27/28-12-1955 n° 30196; » » du 1- 2-1956
du 15- 5-1956 - » du 9- 6-1956 n° 15591; » » du 1- 7-1956

Siège social : **LÉOPOLDVILLE (Congo Belge)**
Siège administratif : **BRUXELLES**
Registre de Commerce : Bruxelles n° 450

Capital social : **357.500.000 francs congolais**
représenté par 618.750 parts sociales sans désignation de valeur représentant chacune 1/618750[e] de l'avoir social.

PART SOCIALE

sans désignation de valeur, au porteur

N°

Bruxelles, le 15 juillet 1956.

Un Administrateur, **Un Administrateur,**

Les coupons sont payés aux endroits et aux époques déterminés par le Conseil d'administration
TITRE CRÉÉ APRÈS LE 6 OCTOBRE 1944

Geo

Imprimerie Industrielle et Financière, 47, rue du Houblon, Bruxelles.

AT THE TIME OF THE BELGIAN CONGO...

From 1878, the Welsh explorer Henry Morton Stanley worked for the International African Association (A.I.A.) and started out to penetrate the Congolese territory. This association was founded, in 1876, under King Léopold II of Belgium who directed his politics in the shadows. Following the Berlin Conference (1884-1885) during which the division of Black Africa took place, the independent state of the Congo was recognised and Léopold II became ruler, after having been thus authorised by the Belgian Parliament in April 1885. Belgium had no rights over this African state and all relations went through the King. However, his help was considerable and the financial loans which were given to the young Congolese state made it the heir of Léopold II. Hence the King decided, through his testament which he made public in 1980, to leave the Congo to Belgium. In 1908, the annexation was voted by the Parliament. From then on, the Belgian state managed the country, eighty times larger than its own, and undertook to enhance it.

Spread out in a multitude of tribes, the Congolese population only knew, in the second half of the 19th century, an economy of self-sufficiency. It was from its food crops that it produced its "beers" in the most non-industrialised fashion. This is a tradition which remains today, as certain natives continue to manufacture Mubisi, a drink with a banana base and of a reddish colour. Not very strong and of a pleasant taste if consumed straight away, it becomes very intoxicating if kept. The fermentation which occurs, transforms the drink into a bitter and refreshing liquid, not without danger. Another local fermented drink, but this time made of maize and sorgho, Kibuku is slightly fizzy; its alcohol content is 5 %.

Together with these ancestral beers, the Congo was soon to discover European-style beers. This was due to the development of communications. In 1889, the Congo Railway Company was founded in Brussels; and with it came the arrival of numerous missionaries and the utilisation of mining resources. It is thus through religion that a real brewing activity was started. The first brewery was founded in 1899 in Kimuenza, by Brother Van de Straeten. The equipment was supplied by Struyf Coppens of Antwerp. The fermentation tank was built on the water so that, in spite of the climate, the temperature was always a constant 18 to 20°C. The main ingredient was the sorghum and very few hops were used. The second brewery was at the Jesuit mission of Kisantu. In 1900, Brother Gillet ordered the brewing hall from the workshops of Vervoort in Hautrage. Fermentation was spontaneous and the drink thus obtained, brown and acid, was reminiscent of faro.

Colonial policy in the Congo influenced graphic artists in Belgium.

The economy of the country benefited, at the time, from large amounts of Belgian capital and it was not until 1910 that these investments started to become profitable. During these years of growth, a study was made for the creation of a brewery in Elisabethville (today called Lubumbashi), in the Southern Province of Katanga. This rich mining region, with a healthy climate due to its altitude, seemed to be ideal for this type of establishment. Water and infection problems could be forgotten. It had been planned to import concentrated hop wort and to let it ferment on site. The solution arrived with the invention of the "Nathan" fermentation system in conical-cylindrical vats.

But this was not totally satisfactory since the aluminium used was not pure enough and oxidised

This fermentation hall in the Elisabethville Brewery (Katanga) shows the degree of hygiene in tropical countries provided by the Nathan system *(see page 65)*.

easily. It was not until the 1920's that the quality of aluminium improved and the project could be defined. The brewery of Katanga was founded in 1923. This was shortly followed by the creation of the Léopoldville Brewery, which, as its name indicates, was set up in the capital of the colony, Léopoldville (today Kinshasa). It is true that the context had become more favourable in view of the increase in the European population, which provided prospective customers. The Congo "absorbed" some 35,000 hectolitres of beer at this time.

The breweries took advantage of this demand and grew rapidly. However, the crisis in the Thirties was already looming. Anxious to safeguard their assets and reduce the risks, a number of Katanga Brewery shareholders set up Interbra. This company possessed shares, in Belgium, in the Zeeberg (Aalst) and Labor (Mons) breweries, in France in the Union Messine (Metz) and Saint-Eloi (Tours) breweries, and on the

Above: label from the De Blieck Brewery in Aalst, intended for export to the Congo.

Below: label inspired by Congolese fauna. Puma Pils was not exported to the Congo.

African Continent in the Léopoldville (Congo) as well as in the NV Koloniale Brouweryen (Soerabaya, Indonesia) breweries. It should be noted that by purchasing the latter in 1937, Heineken began its extension outside Holland.

Then the war broke out. In spite of its inevitable problems, unlike its neighbours, the Congo was lucky not to suffer any major restrictions during the long period of unrest which followed. The post-war years were the beginning of a phase of calm and economic expansion for the colony. Crowned by an excellent reputation, Simba beer saw its production continuously increase. So much that a new manufacturing unit was set up on 12th July 1951 in Luluabourg (today Kananga), in the province of Western Kasai. The natives were as much involved as the Europeans in this increasing consumption. This led to a debate in 1954 in the Chamber of Representatives on the possible replacement of family benefits granted to the Congolese population by food supplements to be given to women and children, since the present benefits were disappearing into drink! But in order to satisfy beer drinkers, breweries opened in Stanleyville (today Kisangani) in 1957 and Boma in 1958.

From 1956, the Congolese question had arisen. The radicalisation of the nationalist movement in 1958 precipitated the emancipation process. The Congo's independence was declared on 30th June 1960. This led to serious disturbances and the province of Katanga seceded. Due to this, the brewery of Katanga lost several customers, whilst the progressive integration of Africans led to a reduction in white personnel (46 per cent in 1961). The situation was no easier for the Stanleyville Brewery which had to import its raw materials via Uganda. However, for all brewery companies the main problem was the maintenance of equipment.

Relations between Belgium and the Congo - which became Zaire in 1971 - were certainly unstable, with periods of crises and respite. The "Zairianisation" of the economy which expressed itself in the nationalisation of Belgian companies, made co-operation a complex matter. In 1991, faced with disturbances which were multiplying in the country, the Belgian Government refused, to support Kinshasa's regime, feeling that immediate democratic reforms were needed. In this climate of economic and social difficulty for the Congolese population, the consumption of beer considerably declined, from 4 million hectolitres in 1990 to 1.3 million in 1993. This, together with regulatory problems, represented a crucial obstacle to the profitability of breweries.

At the present time, three groups share the beer market in Zaire:

• Bralima - CIB, a subsidiary of Heineken. Its five breweries are located at Kinshasa, Boma, Mbandaka and Kisangani. It produces a lager called Primus;

• Brasimba, four breweries which are situated at Lubumbashi, Likasi, Kamina, Kolwezi and Manono and which produce lagers called Tembo and Simba. These breweries belonged to Interbrew until 1994, when the group passed them on to Sopagem, a subsidiary of the French group Castel, in exchange for a share-holding of 10 per cent in Sopagem;

• Unibra was founded by the groups Empain, Sarma and the Wielemans-Ceuppens brewery. Later on, Alfred Van Der Kelen and Michel Relecom were also involved. Its four breweries are located at Kinshasa, Kanaga, Isiro and Kisangani. The production has been Skol pils since 1966. In January 1996, Unibra sold its breweries to the Castel group.

A THERAPEUTIC BEER...

Only just settled in the Congo, the Europeans found themselves faced with disease and endemic epidemics. Thus, from 1888 to 1914, some three hundred missionaries died, among which some one hundred and fourteen were under forty years of age and eighty-five under thirty years. Another striking figure was that 1,205 died during the building of the Lower Congo railway.

In this unfavourable context, beer was found to have anti-infection properties. Hence the interest shown by the missionaries and their endeavour to brew it themselves. It would appear that this was effective as, on the eve of the Second World War, thanks to this healthy drink, the European death rate was reduced to 7 per cent as opposed to 12.33 per cent in 1929!

IMPORTS OF BEER INTO THE CONGO

- **1920:** Belgian beers were mainly produced by the Tivoli brewery in Antwerp (which ceased production in 1949). Each week a ship transported crates of beer on its bridge to the colony where, without appropriate refrigeration, it was drunk at 25°C.
- **1938:** beers arriving from Germany represented 82 per cent of imports and those from Belgium 6.5 per cent.
- **From 1945:** the hostilities of the Second World War having ended, the Belgian Government imposed export licences on cargoes shipped to the Congo, thus reducing the import of Belgian beer in the colony.
- **1949:** German beers represented 37.8 per cent of imports and Belgian beers only 19.5 per cent.

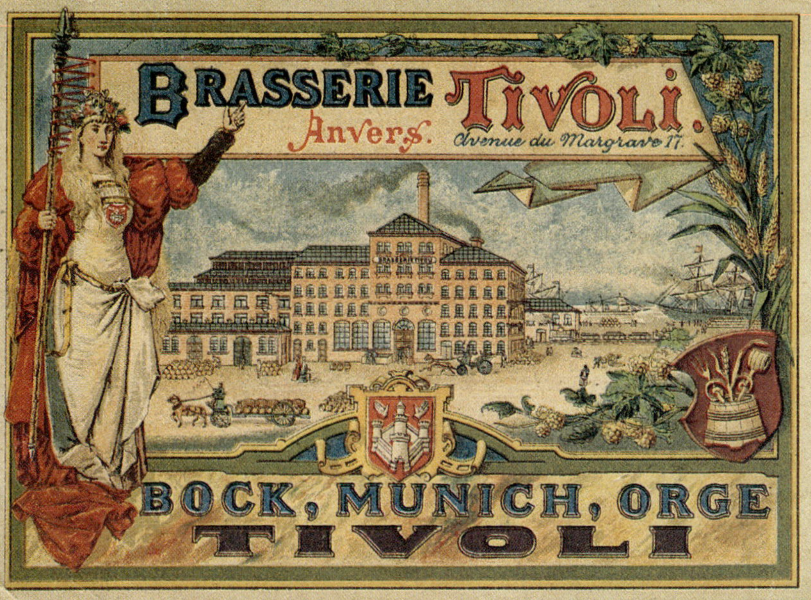

Above: a label from the Tivoli Brewery.

Opposite: a visiting card from the same brewery.

THE BREWERY OF KATANGA (ELISABETHVILLE)

• **Formation:** 8 December 1923

• **Financial conreoller:** M. Chaidron, of Haine Saint Pierre (Hainaut).

• **Principal Shareholders:** La Mutualité Coloniale (2,270 shares); Wielemans Breweries (100 shares); Pierre Walkiers of the Koekelberg Brewery (50 shares); Maurice Lippens, Honorary Governor of the Congo (40 shares).

• **History:** at the beginning, progress was rapid. From 40,000 bottles per month in 1924, production rose to 100,000 in 1927. In 1931, a production unit was set up in Jadotville (today Likasi), but the crisis led to a decline in sales and it closed in 1932.

The situation improved after the war and the growth of the Katanga brewery was as follows:

1949	299,338 hl
1950	369,119 hl
1951	478,501 hl
1952	646,203 hl
1955	over one million hectolitres

However, the time following Independence was tumultuous and supplies were difficult. An article which appeared in the *New York Times*, on 8th October 1960 indicated that Congolese soldiers were threatening to rebel if the delivery of beer were stopped. Katangese soldiers celebrated the cease-fire by throwing *Simba* bottles in the air. Transports to the Katangese army carried as many bottles of beer as arms. United Nations troops consumed approximately 1,500 cases per week and, when the brewery refused to guarantee delivery, supplies had to arrive from Leopoldville by plane.

• **Beer:** *Simba* pils

THE BREWERY OF LEOPOLDVILLE

• **Formation:** 23 October 1923

• **Principal Shareholders:** Compagnie Générale du Congo (1,100 shares); Valère Ségard of the Labor Brewery in Mons (400 shares); André Goffaerts, seminarist at the Park Abbaye in Heverlee (Leuven) (400 shares).

• **History:** merged with the Ruanda-Burundi Brewery in 1957 to become *Bralima* (Brasseries, Limonadiers, Malteries Africaines brewers, lemonade manufacturers and African malt-houses). It was later taken over by Heineken.

• **Beer:** *Primus* pils

At the centre of this pre-war beermat, a portrait of the famous Antwerp painter Peter-Paul Rubens (1577-1640). The Nice Brewery (France) had its registered office in Antwerp.

BELGIAN BREWERIES AROUND THE WORLD

Possessing several brewery schools *(see p.187)*, Belgium, being a small country, only provided a very limited scope of activity for those who trained there and wished to work in the field of beer. Hence the need to "export" themselves and look for work elsewhere. This is not a new situation. Already in 1914, a German study showed that 6,000 workers in France were employed by breweries, and that 210 were Belgian and only 20 German.

Belgian brewers are found in every region. African countries, Eastern countries, the United States ... even Brazil where, around 1910, a Paul Huart taught brewing at the Bahia agricultural school in San Benito dos Lages. Closer to home, one of the greatest travellers was Marcel Gocar. After the Kœkelberg and Mater Breweries in Belgium, he organised brewing production in Fort-de-France (Martinique), Beira (Mozambique), Managua (Nicaragua), Belo Horizonte (Brazil), Teheran (Iran) and Bagdad (Iraq).

Although the know-how of Belgian brewers has always been renowned throughout the world, today foreign market penetration mostly takes place through Interbrew. Following numerous acquisitions and shareholdings, the top Belgian brewery group became, in 1995, the fourth world-wide.

ON THE AFRICAN CONTINENT

• In Algeria, the **S.A. Brasserie d'Alger** was created on the 5th November 1906, at the initiative of Léon Verhelst, Professor at the École Supérieure de Brasserie in Leuven. At the side of the latter were: Jean Lannoy, brewer in Ixelles; Edgar Brissonnet, Belgian Consul in Algiers, Emile Tielemans, brewer in Aarschot; Emile Van Dromme, brewer in Menin; Emile Van den Heuvel, brewer in Molenbeek; and Léon Vuylsteke, brewer in Menin.

In 1975, the capacity was of 250,000 hectolitres and the beer was called *Panter Pils*.

• In the Central African Empire, at Bangui, the **MOCAF Brewery** dates back to the 1950's. Following a study trip to Africa, in 1950, the leaders of Motte Cordonnier decided to set up a brewery in Bangui. The following year they founded a limited company, MOCAF (Motte Cordonnier Afrique). Production growth was rapid: from 10,000 hectolitres per year at first, then 120,000 hectolitres in 1975, it reached 250,000 hectolitres in 1993. Its products are: *Mocaf Blonde* and *Super Mocaf*.

The brewery joined Interbrew in 1981 when Motte Cordonnier was taken over by the group. It was then sold to Sopagem, a subsidiary of the French group Castel.

• In the Congo, the **Brazzaville Brewery** was founded in 1950 by the group Interbra of which the Belgian group Lambert and Heineken were shareholders. Its capacity was 150,000 hectolitres. When Heineken took over the Lambert group shares, the brewery lost its Belgian interest.

• On the Ivory Coast, the **Solibra Brewery** (Société de Limonaderie et Brasserie d'Afrique) was created in 1955 with a capital of 800 million CFA francs. Its annual capacity, initially 100,000 hectolitres, is presently 1.3 million hectolitres. It produces three beers: a *Bock*, a *Brune* (Stout) and the *Mamba*, which is exported to the United States.

Interbrew, which had purchased this brewery, sold it, in 1994, to Sopagem, a subsidiary of the French group Castel.

• In Egypt, it was the **Crown Brewery Company**. Founded in 1898 by Albert Heyndrickx, this brewery was the first on the African continent to use ammoniac compressors. It took the name of Brasserie des Pyramides in 1901. It owned two factories, one in Cairo and one in Alexandria. Upon the death of Albert Heyndrickx, it changed hands.

ASIA

In June 1994, the Interbrew group signed a joint-venture agreement with the **Chinese brewery Zhu Jiang**, established in Guangzhou (Canton), in the province of Guangdong and with the Belgo-Chinese commercial company Hamdex. The distribution of shares of the new company was as follows: 45 percent for Interbrew, 45 percent for Zhu Jiang and 10 percent for Hamdex. Set up at the beginning of the 1980's, with the technical support of the ex-Artois group and operational since 1983, the Zhu Jiang brewery is the largest in the South of the country and the third in China. Its main product is a pils of the same name.

Following the Interbrew share take-over, it took on production and marketing of *Stella Artois* in China, Hong-Kong and Macao. Furthermore, Interbrew guaranteed its immediate technical assistance to increase capacity from 1.7 million hectolitres in 1993 to 2.2 million hectolitres, by the installation of Meura 20001 wort filters and the building of a water purification station. This was a simple step, it would seem, in view of the strong industrial growth which has marked the Guangdong province since the 1980's. Zhu Jiang undertook, at the same time, to build a new brewery which could produce 4 million hectolitres per year and to increase the annual capacity of its malt-house from 16,000 tons to 180,000 tons.

IN THE UNITED STATES

• A native of Binche, Mr. Brogniez was first brewer in Lichtervelde with Theophiel Labens. He perfected the *Blonde Extra de Lichtervelde* or *Blonde des Flandres* which met with immense success and was even sold in Brussels. Having left this brewery in 1904 he took up residence in the United States, at Terre Haute in Indiana and in 1905 created a co-operative brewery, **The People Brewing Company**. Half his clientele were innkeeper shareholders or, at least, had monetary obligations towards the brewery.

The brewery produced, in 1912, 30,000 barrels of beer, i.e. some 35,190 hectolitres. Two beers were made. One, ordinary, was at 12.5° Balling; in its composition was 40% of refined grits and hops from Oregon. The other, special, was at 13.5° Balling and was brewed with 40 per cent rice and German hops. Malt came from the Schwill malt-house of Chicago, considered the largest in America at the time. The brewery always used the same yeast in spite of the high dosage of raw grain which was used and the degeneration of yeast which was attributed to it.

The brewery closed down in 1918 due to prohibition.

• More recently, in June 1991, after several trips to Belgium, Jeff Lebesh and Kim Jordan decided to brew Belgian beers in the cellars of their house at Fort Collins, in Colorado. They started with a production of 8.5 *barrels*, i.e. 997 litres. Success followed. From May 1992

they set out to find larger premises and a disused railway station became their brewery. In September of the next year, a Belgian engineer joined them and annual production reached 15,000 *barrels*, i.e. 17,595 hectolitres.

The **New Belgium Brewing Company** manufactures six beers, among them *Abbey* which won a gold medal at the Great American Beer Festival in Denver, in 1993.

• The **Celis Brewery**, in Austin, Texas, was mainly created out of a failure. Pierre Celis relaunched the traditional Hoegaarden white beer of the Sixties which was a success *(see p. 134)*. Unfortunately, in 1985 a fire destroyed most of the buildings. In order to rebuild, partners had to be found. Artois took 50 per cent of the capital with an option on the rest. The Artois-Piedboeuf merger prompted Celis' decision to sell his shares and attempt the American adventure in 1990.

The following year, Celis Brewery saw the light of day. Investment was 12 million dollars, 55 per cent by the Celis family and 45 per cent was divided between the Belgian holding company Suronger and the financial group Lecocq, with Christine Celis, daughter of Pierre Celis, as President. Success was quick to come and production soon exceeded the forecast 12,000 hectolitres. Today, the Celis Brewery brews four beers: a white beer *(Celis White)*, an amber top-fermented beer *(Celis Pale Bock)*, a pils *(Celis Golden)*, and a high alcohol beer *(Celis Grand Cru)*. The brewery holds the forty-sixth place among 200 American breweries.

At the beginning of 1994, Pierre Celis returned to Europe through his *Celis White* and *Celis Pale Bock* beers, which avoid the 40 per cent tax set by the European Union on imported beer, by being brewed under licence in Belgium by the De Smedt Brewery in Opwijk, and marketed by Celis Europa!

In July 1995, the Interbrew Group "set foot" in North America by purchasing the entire capital of the Canadian group **Labatt**. Second brewer in Canada, this group controls nine breweries in Canada and the **Latrobe** Brewery in the United States. Furthermore, it holds 22 percent of the Mexican Femsa Cerveza and 100 per cent of the group **Moretti** which, with three breweries, represents 10 per cent of beer in Italy. This absorption means 18.6 million hectolitres per year added to a production of the same amount!

The brewing hall in the **Celis Brewery,** established in Texas since 1991, comes from the Dendria Brewery in Onkerzele, where *Whitbread Pale Ale* was brewed for the Belgian market. At the centre, Pierre Celis, the founder.

ON THE FRENCH COAST

• On the boulevard Riquier in Nice, stands the **Brasserie de Nice**, first brewery to set up on the Côte-d'Azur. It was founded in 1897 by Albert Heyndrickx who was its majority shareholder. The Antwerp head-office was moved to Brussels upon the death of Albert Heyndrickx. The Belgian engineer J. Montulet-Piedboeuf worked at the Brasserie de Nice until December 1901 when Léon Verhelst, teacher at the École de Brasserie in Leuven, replaced him until his death in 1955.

At its peak, the brewery produced 80,000 hectolitres per year. Its malt-house operated until the Second World War and was closed due to its production being of insufficient quality.

On the death of Raymond Heyndrickx in 1947, the brewery went to Artois Leuven. However, its town location in the middle of Nice and its low production led to its disappearance in 1966.

• It was in 1899 that Albert Heyndrickx created the **S.A. de Brasserie et Malterie du Croissant**, set up at 35 avenue de la Défense in Puteaux. This was taken over in 1911 by Hanus, a brewer from Charmes and Proudhon, a beer warehouseman in Paris. They traded under the name of Brasserie de la Ville de Paris. The brewery closed its doors in the 1930's.

A PRECIOUS DOCUMENT

Unfortunately very little information has reached us on the brewery set up in Ajaccio, **Poggi, Carabelli et De Braux Brasseurs**, which produced the first beer in Corsica in 1902. However, a letter addressed by the Belgian master-brewer J. Montulet-Piedboeuf to the paper *Le Petit Journal du Brasseur*, on 28th June of that year, contains information on this unexpected insular produce:

" [...]Called twice to Corsica, I arrived, with reduced tools for the time being, to produce a good local beer of 12 per cent Balling of mixed fermentation at a temperature regulated in the tank.

"This first beer was tasted today and found to be excellent and very much appreciated for the country where, despite several trials over ten months, one was not able to produce beer.

"A small brewery would be profitable here. The price of beer, sold to retailers, is Fr.76 per hectolitre for the Spatenbräu, and even then there is a considerable amount of wastage. Prices are also very high for the Tourtel, the Meuse, the Velten, the Gruber de Melun beers, etc. and for all beers which naturally suffer from transport by sea and without ice.

"Ajaccio water is soft and very pure. In this region there is always a cool temperature during the night and in the shade; the suns rays are tempered by the cool sea breeze or by the mountain winds [...].

"Yearly sales do not reach 10,000 hectolitres due to the excessive sale price of beer. However, judging by the number of requests, the products obtained and the lower prices which can be made for local beer, it becomes more conceivable.

"Corsica has 290,168 inhabitants of which Ajaccio, Bastia, Sartène and Corté are the main centres. These are linked by a picturesque and bold railway built by a company of Belgian engineers [..].

It should be noted that it is also J. Montulet-Piedboeuf, ex-director of the Grandes Brasserie et Malterie de la Meuse at Oupeye which, with the contribution of his brother, produced the first beer on the Côte-d'Azur.

THE OMNIPRESENT HEYNDRICKX FAMILY

When looking at the first breweries set up with Belgian capital outside Belgium, the Heyndrickx family name often appears. This notoriety is due to Albert Heyndrickx who, at the turn of the 20th century, was the first Belgian brewer to set up multiple breweries abroad. These were: in 1897 the Brasserie de Nice (Rubens); in 1898 the Crown Brewery in Egypt; in 1899 the Brasserie du Croissant in Puteaux, near Paris, and in 1902 the Brasserie et Malterie de Lyon in France. Without forgetting that, from 1905, this knight of the brewery even operated a brewery himself as deputy director of the Masséna Brewery which was founded that year in Nice, on the Place Tende.

In his own country, Albert Heyndrickx acquired the Delloye Masson Brewery which was situated at 73, rue Henry, in Brussels, where the head-office of the Royal de Laeken Brewery was also established. It was, with the latter, the first to introduce bottom-fermentation in Belgium, leading this new production with the brewing of lambic, upon which the reputation of the Royal Laeken Brewery was founded.

Moreover, the invention of the double envelope tank, which allows the wort to be heated through the sides of the boiler, is attributed to his father. At a time when a tax was imposed on mash-tuns (the Law of 1822), this new equipment had the advantage of holding more raw materials.

Albert Heyndrickx's eldest son, Guy, did not follow in his father's footsteps. He became a diplomat and was appointed plenipotentiary minister and special envoy at the Belgian Embassy in Moscow. He died in America during the war. However, his second son, Raymond, learnt the profession of brewer at the Brasserie de Puteaux and the Brasserie de Vaix in Lyon, before managing the Brussels brewery. However, he remained a bachelor and had no children and everything that Albert Heyndrickx had "built" was dismantled at his death in 1947.

Albert Heyndrickx's brother, Théophile, managed the Théophile Heyndrickx brewery and malt-house in Lodelinsart, which was to become, in 1941, the Montplaisir Brewery and malt-house and which was taken over in 1953 by the Brasserie de l'Union at Jumet.

• In 1971, taking into account the success on the French market of its subsidiaries Chevalier Marin in Mechelen and Léopold in Brussels, the Artois Brewery launched a take-over bid for the Grande Brasserie Ardennaise and the Union Lorraine de Brasserie, the latter being formed by the Saint-Nicolas-de-Port and the Baccarat Breweries where the French Brewery Museum is presently situated.

The Motte-Cordonnier Brewery, of Armentières, then joined the group. In 1981 the activities of Artois in France took the name of **Sébastien Artois**. This subsidiary produced 1.9 million hectolitres of pils, and distributed 130 hectolitres of *Blanche de Hoegaarden* and *Leffe*. Production ceased in 1991.

Other Belgian breweries emigrated. The Van Engelandt Brewery, situated in Fresnoy-le-Grand, in the Aisne (France), was a perfect example of this. The business closed down in 1940.

IN THE REST OF EUROPE

• The Bulgarian market opened to Interbrew in 1995, with a share-holding of 70 per cent in the **Kamenitza** Brewery in Plovdiv, which annually produces 300,000 hectolitres of *Kamenitza* pils. A malt-house and a warehouse also went with the acquisition.

• In Croatia, the Interbrew group acquired, in May 1994, 23.7 per cent of the shares in the largest Croatian brewery, the **Zagrebacka Pivovara**, and thus became the major foreign investor in the country. With its production of 760,000 hectolitres, this company covers 28 per cent of the Croatian beer market, the rest distributed between the other remaining breweries.

• In Spain, the **Cerveza Barcelona Lamot** Brewery, situated in Pareto del Valles, was built by the Lamot Brewery of Mechelen, following a merger with the Moritz Brewery in 1966. Its capacity was then 360,000 hectolitres. The Bass group, which took over the Lamot brewery in 1970, sold it.

• Set up at Bocs, near Misckole, in the North-East of Hungary, the **Borsodi Sorgyar Brewery** entered the Interbrew group in 1991. Its growth was rapid. From 1,200,000 at its start in 1978, its production almost tripled to 3,000,000 hectolitres. It produces nine bottom-fermented beers, amongst which the pils *Vilagos* and the *Spaten* (under licence). Since 1978 this brewery has produced the only alcohol-free beer in Hungary, the *Polo*. Some of its beers are exported to Italy and Sweden.

• In Italy, the Interbrew group took over, in 1985, the **Von Wunster** Brewery, created in 1879 and situated at Comun Nuovo, in the province of Bergamo. At the centre of its production is the *Classica von Wunster* (600,000 hectolitres in 1991). It also brews *Stella Artois*.

Together with this acquisition, Interbrew set up a distribution company in North Italy. However, the Italian market was difficult due to the low consumption of beer and the competition. The Belgian group therefore chose, in 1995, to sell its Italian subsidiaries to Heineken, the Dutch group who undertook to brew *Stella Artois* under licence and to distribute *Loburg*, *Leffe*, *Hoegaarden* and *Belle-Vue* in Italy.

• In the Netherlands, the **Dommelsch** Brewery belongs to Interbrew. This company, situated in Dommelen, in the Brabant Campine in the South of the country, goes back a long time. It was founded in 1744 by Willem Snieders. It remained in the same family until 1968 when it was sold to Artois Leuven.

The brewery produced *Dommelsch Pils* (over 600,000 hectolitres per year) and an alcohol-free pils *Dommelsch NA*. Furthermore, Interbrew, through its cafés, distributes *Hoegaarden*, *Vieux Temps*, *Belle-Vue* and the *Leffe*.

More recently, in 1994, the Interbrew group purchased **Allied Breweries Nederland**, subsidiary of the British Allied Domecq plc, which, in the North of Dutch

On its arrival on the Dutch market, Stella Artois took over the Dommelsch Brewery and concluded an agreement with the only Trappist monastery in Holland, in Tilbourg. This agreement was later cancelled.

Limburg manages the Oranjeboom Bierbrouwerij in Breda and the Arcense Bierbrouwerij in Aken. The purpose of this acquisition was to strengthen Interbrew's penetration of the Netherlands, realm of the giant Heineken, thus taking second place on the Dutch market.

• Before the First World War, the Eastern countries were already attracting investors. In Rumania things were not always easy. To prove this, the circular letter addressed by a brewer called Basilescu to all the teachers in the country, in 1907 said "[...] I ask you with all my heart to insist that the distributors of alcoholic drinks in your commune introduce beer to their fellow-citizens and to request them to obtain the beer which they need from my factory in New Bucharest.

"By doing this [...] you encourage the efforts of a colleague who [...] teaches the Rumanian youth to like and respect economic work [...] which alone brings us to take over from foreign hands our sources of National riches and will allow us economical and political emancipation. [...].

"[...] I will place at your personal disposal one franc for each hectolitre of beer or for each 50 bottle crate to be sold thanks to your help in your commune."

Despite this prejudice the brewer ended up collaborating with foreign "invaders". In 1910, he contributed his New Bucharest brewery to form a Belgian company, **Les Grandes Brasseries de Bucarest**, the head office of which was in Brussels. From 1911, the Grandes Brasseries de l'Etoile took over management and technical aid. This ended in an enormous fiasco which led to their bankruptcy.

Today, Belgian penetration of Rumania is significant. 1994 was fruitful. In June, the Interbrew group signed a joint-venture agreement with the new Rumanian brewery, **Bianca**, at Blaj, in Transylvania. This collaboration produced, in the first instance, the finishing of the construction of the brewery with a yearly capacity of 500,000 hectolitres in its conical-cylindrical vats which were a novelty in that country. The Bianca Brewery produced Aalst's Bergenbier pils under licence, which it marketed in Rumania.

LES GRANDES BRASSERIES DE BUCAREST
BUCAREST-NOUVEAU
(SOCIÉTE ANONYME BELGE)
Constituée par acte passé devant Me Albert RICHIR, notaire à Bruxelles le 13 Août 1910 et publié aux annexes du MONITEUR BELGE du 26 Août 1910, acte numéro 5180
Siège social : BRUXELLES
CAPITAL SOCIAL : 4,000,000 DE FRANCS
Représenté par 20,000 Actions de Capital de 200 Francs chacune
IL EST CRÉÉ, EN OUTRE, 2000 PARTS DE FONDATEUR SANS DESIGNATION DE VALEUR
ACTION DE CAPITAL DE 200 FRANCS
N° 09115
Un Administrateur, AU PORTEUR ET ENTIÈREMENT LIBÉRÉE Un Administrateur,

Share certificate issued in Brussels, in 1910, for Les Grandes Brasseries de Bucarest.

The Bianca Brewery produced the pils *Bergenbier*, from Aalst, under licence, for sale on the Rumanian market.

On the other hand, in August of the same year, the Interbrew group acquired a 51 per cent shareholding in the **Probercq Brewery** which had a 150,000 hectolitre annual capacity. This young Rumanian company - operational since Spring 1993 - produces, under licence, a pils beer from the Austrian brewery of Eggenberger, the *Hopfenkönig*, which is the only pils marketed in the country.

This acquisition by Interbrew led to an increase in the production capacity of Probercq, which rapidly reached 450,000 hectolitres.

A BELGIAN BREWERY IN SWEDEN

Behind this faraway development hides the silhouette of a person very much out of the ordinary: Louis de Geer (1587-1682). A renowned financier, he started his career in Liège, continued in Dordrecht, then Amsterdam, before becoming King Gustave-Adolphe of Sweden's banker. It is thanks to him that up-to-date techniques used in Liège's metal industry were introduced into Sweden.

He became the main supplier of military equipment and artillery for the Swedish army and took advantage of the terrible Thirty Years War (1618-1648) to assert this position. This was done in collaboration with compatriots of Louis de Geer, the Bêche brothers who had been metallurgists in Sweden since 1595.

Naturalised Swedish in 1627, this talented business man did not forget his country of birth and his taste for beer. Even more so as Walloon metallurgists worked for him in Sweden, and thus the Lövstabruk brewery was born. It was only in 1916 that the malt-house ceased activity and the last brewing took place in 1971! Today it is a museum, whose president is a descendant of Louis de Geer.

The study of a 17th century Walloon brewery led inevitably to Sweden, to Lövstabruk. As is shown by the exterior (above) and the interior (opposite), this ancient brewery is in a rare state of preservation.

BELGIAN BEERS ABROAD

Taking into account the importance of its brewing industry, it is rather surprising that Belgium only became interested in the export market somewhat belatedly, and that it was not really until the Fifties that sales of beer abroad began to grow. One may without doubt attribute this tardiness to the fact that only beers of a superior category, and among them beers with a sufficiently widespread brand image, were suitable even to be considered for export.

In 1950 the amount of exports had risen to a mere 5,240 hectolitres, which represented 0.05 per cent of Belgian production. The principal purchasing countries were then Italy, Great Britain, the Belgian Congo, Ruanda-Urundi, and Haiti. This was above all thanks to the Common Market, which had come into being. At first sight, there was an increase. In 1964, for examplc, exports attained 6.30 per cent of national production. This expansion continued through the Seventies, the "Europeanisation" of products accelerating the process, and allowing exports to account for some 15 per cent of production.

It is true that to develop the consumption of beer in countries where wine was the traditional drink, was not an easy matter. In France, barley having been rationed for many years after the Second World War, the quality of their beers was inferior to that of Belgian beers. And the penetration of the foreign market began with pils. Anxious to distinguish itself from the sales policy of the Danes, who offered luxury beers at a higher cost than French beers, they opted for a "popular" product simply to rival the Alsatian beers in particular, and which would first of all be known in all the cafés. Belgian brewers were therefore constrained to impose prices without any comparison to cost price. The breweries of Wielemans, Léopold, and Lamot found success. Between 1955 and 1964 sales on the French market were multiplied by forty times!

Encouraged by the progress of its subsidiaries, Léopold and Meiressonne, the Artois brewery began exporting in 1958. The success of *Stella* was convincing. In 1978 nearly 15,000 French cafés sold it. This aroused the ambition in the Belgian company to take third place in France, after the BSN group (Kronenbourg, Kanterbrau) and the Société Européenne de Brasseries (33 and Slavia), which had taken over Mutzig. The results were also very satisfying for *Jupiler*. At the end of the Seventies, Piedbœuf exported more than 10 per cent of its production. Certain regions were, of course, more favourably disposed towards pils, Picardy more than any, and Haute-Normandy for draught beer.

Otherwise, in the Seventies some Paris cafés began to offer their customers special beers from Belgium. Taking an interest in the beers of the North, and going to this region for supplies, they discovered these products in the neighbourhood of the Jenlain brewery, at thc first existing importer, the *Panaville* establishments.

In other countries, Belgian beers had a mixed reception. Faithful to its Law of 1516, Germany showed great reticence, which weakened from 1963. Great Britain proved a difficult market, and it remained so. On the other hand, the Netherlands showed a neighbourly interest in Belgian production. Around one fifth of Artois exports was soon destined for them, and Piedbœuf forwarded several dozen thousands of hectolitres there. The greatest exports of special beers were provided by the breweries of Palm, de Steenhuffel, and De Koninck, of Antwerp.

As for distant countries (like the United States, or the countries of continental Africa), their success was linked to the establishment of Belgian breweries around the world *(see page 151)*.

Today, exports of Belgian beers represent almost 25 per cent of total production, which is well above the average for European exports. France is the principal outlet, followed by the Netherlands, Italy, and Spain. Between 1990 and 1992, this external market registered a 10 per cent increase. The Belgian brewery can look forward to a bright future...

A PERSONALITY IN BELGIAN BREWING

Chairman of Unibex from its creation until 1994, Jean Van Damme (1924 - 1994) left his mark on the history of Belgian brewing in the 20th century. He was one of the last "men of practical experience" to accede to such high responsibility.

His career began in 1934, in Liège, in the café sales department, and he was already characterised by a deep care for quality so far as beer at point of sale was concerned. It was due to him that *Extra-Pils* was established in the Ghent region, then in the immediate after-war years the development of taking over small brewers by Piedbœuf, and bringing the brewery to its peak. Appointed Chairman in 1987, the following year he signed the merger with Stella-Artois, from which came Interbrew. He was Vice-Chairman of the Board of Directors of the group until 1993.

It was in 1947 that the *Union des Brasseries d'Exportation* (or *Unibex*) was created, with its head office in Brussels and which had as its object the study, the protection, and the development of the professional interests of its members. Today, this Union centralises studies concerning customs and administrative regulations in brewing matters. It is likewise preoccupied with limiting competition between Belgian breweries, and establishing a pricing framework.

The development of the tourist industry allowed the name of Belgian beers to be carried far and wide, and brewers took this into account in their advertising campaigns.

AFFICHE DE BERCHMANS

BELGIQUE

BOCK de KOEKELBERG

WILLIAM'S SCOTCH ALE

STOUT BASS & Co.'S PALE ALE

8. Rue Simonon (Guillemins)

A. BÉNARD LIÉGE.

LES AFFICHES ÉTRANGÈRES

G. BOUDET, ÉDITEUR

IMPRIMERIE CHAIX

Famous poster by Émile Berchmans (1896), attesting to the wealth of importers of English beers in Belgium.

FOREIGN BEERS IN BELGIUM

The introduction, in 1822, of a tax on the capacity of the mash-tun, struck a blow against the brewing industry and greatly benefited the influx of foreign beers into Belgium. So in the 1860's, some cafés in Brussels were serving foreign beers. Their number rose to twenty five in 1883. These beers were mainly imported in barrels.

At first, German beers occupied pride of place. Belgium was the principal export market for Germany. For instance, the amount of imports coming from Germany was almost 125,000 hectolitres in 1910, and a little more than 131,000 in 1911. The two World Wars had the effect of changing this situation. At the beginning of the Fifties, Germany only forwarded minimal quantities to Belgium. Other sources, which came to dominate, were then Great Britain, the Netherlands, and Denmark.

Then the market evolved from 1955. Imports of German beers began to climb again with renewed vigour after the Brussels Universal Exhibition of 1958, with the favour now being shown to beers of the *dort* type. A study carried out in 1959 showed that the most enjoyed foreign beers in Belgium were those from Germany, followed closely by those from England, while a long way behind were the beers of Denmark, then the Netherlands, Czechoslovakia and France (equally), with, finally, the beers of Luxembourg. In the face of this advance of German beers, the reaction of Belgian brewers was not to wait, and imports fell.

During the Sixties consumers' taste developed in the direction of luxury beers of the Pilsen type. This explains the success then enjoyed by Danish beers, which benefited from a discerning marketing policy, given an image of great quality to justify the cost. There was great interest over the following decade, in an economic context more open to foreign products. The entirety of imports was some 8 per cent greater that internal consumption. Once again the brewers reacted, Belgian consumers became aware of their brewing heritage, and imports felt it. Account taken of the increasing success of special Belgian beers, 1978 was the key year, from which the import market has not ceased to decline.

Moreover, both to make up for more or less stagnant domestic demand and to "exploit" the homogenisation, even Europeanisation, of tastes, foreign brewers chose to set up in Belgium and to reinforce their presence.

German beers

The importation of German beers had its highs and its lows, as we have seen. The reception was sometimes mixed. An example is *Hannen Alt*. In 1975 an agreement was concluded between the Anglo-Belge Brewery and the German brewery of Hannen, in Willich, with a view to selling this top-fermented beer in Belgium. This was a failure. After four years, these imports ceased.

On the other hand, *Spatenbräu* was extremely successful. The Claenback tavern in Brussels, was the first to sell it in Belgium, in 1885. Around 1910 there was a single shadow over this success: beers of the Munich type brewed by Belgian brewers. At the present time this German beer is distributed by Haeltermann. And over a more recent period, products from the firms of Bitburger and Warsteiner sporadically occupy this "niche" for beers of the pils type in Belgium.

English beers

The British groups Watney and Bass hold 10 per cent of the Belgian market. This economic trade goes back a

This advertising panel, in cardboard, from the Bass Brewery, carries the number of the bottler: No 253 for the firm of Simon, in Saint-Gilles.

long way. In fact, Bass *Pale Ale*, which would be the oldest registered beer brand in the world (1876), was introduced in Belgium in 1865, and was the first foreign brand to be registered (1880). When it began in our land, several companies distributed it: Julien Baker (Antwerp), Édouard Libotte (Liège), Simon and Sons (Saint Gilles), and Wouters (Brussels). At the end of a two-day voyage, the Bass barrels were loaded on red carts, pulled by superbly harnessed drays. These served as the very best advertisement.

However it was only in 1970 that the most important British brewery set up in Belgium, with the purchase of Brasserie Lamot in Mechelen, the production of which represented about 4 per cent of Belgian production. The operation was to import some 200,000 hectolitres of English beer, but also to produce nearly 500,000 hectolitres in Belgium. In 1978 Bass launched its brands "Les Brasseurs de la Dyle", intended for independent merchants, and "Carling Black Label", for the international market. A new distribution centre, the Bass Distribution Centre, was opened in Mechelen.

But in 1981 Bass Belgium transferred all its Belgian interests to the Brasserie Piedbœuf. Production was maintained at the Lamot Brewery. Two companies were founded to continue the sale of Bass products: one, Bass Lamot, responsible for Bass in Belgium, France, and the Netherlands; and the other, Bass Sales Belgium, intended to supply retailers and free cafés.

As for the Watney group, its strong position in Belgium was made by the take-over of breweries: Delbruyère (90 per cent, 1966), Vandenheuvel-Ixelberg (83.5 per cent, 1968), Maes (90 per cent, 1969). In 1976 it readjusted its production and distribution policy on the Belgian market-place. Henceforward production was to be provided by Maes, in Waterloo (for pils), and in the brewery of Watney Belgium, in Châtelet (for top-fermented beers - Delbruyère for example). Two years later, Watney was integrated into the Grand Metropolitan group. Then the Kronenbourg brewery took over the Belgian interests of Watney. The licence to manufacture remains with the Union Brewery, in Jumet, which belongs to the Alken-Maes group.

Danish beers

The Carlsberg Brewery registered its brand well before the agreement signed with the Haelterman group (1964). When it commenced in Belgium, consumption of its beer did not exceed 1,000 hectolitres. In 1976 sales touched 400,000 hectolitres!

In 1989, Carlsberg International changed partners, and opted for a collaboration with Interbrew. But the European Commission objected to this "entente" since, according to it, it gave the Interbrew group an illicit monopoly over luxury beers on the Belgian market. Legal proceedings were commenced, at the end of which Interbrew is dependent upon Carlsberg Importers for the purchase of Carlsberg, while continuing to guarantee production of Tuborg, and bottling of Carlsberg. Interbrew sells and distributes Carlsberg and Tuborg beers to cafés. As for Haelterman, they are involved in distributing to wholesalers and shop chains.

Today the market in Belgium is represented by 900 tied cafés (600 Carlsberg, 300 Tuborg), where the beer is sold on draught. The two beers on their own constitute 90 per cent of the "luxury" pils sector.

French beers

Before Kronenbourg took a share-holding in the Anglo-Belge Brewery, at Zulte (1980), in the Alken Brewery, in Alken (1978), and in the Maes Brewery (1988), the 130,000 hectolitres of beer imported from France were represented for the most part by *Kronenbourg*, sold in shops. Later, this beer being produced in Belgium, French exports declined, to climb again in 1989-90 with the introduction of *Tourtel* in Belgium. But this alcohol-free beer is now brewed here, and for this reason the French share is falling again. Only amber and brown Tourtel, and some other beers such as *Météor* and *Jeanne d'Arc*, remain on sale.

Dutch beers

The sixth Trappist beer in the world, *La Trappe*, was already distributed in Belgium at the beginning of the century, by an agent established in Ixelles. Nevertheless one could not really speak of importation until 1980 when the John Martin company took on responsibility for it. As for *Heineken*, of which the market is approximately 40,000 hectolitres, its sales are restricted to the wholesale sector, to the hotel trade, SHAPE, and so on.

Since 1994 Heineken has imported *Wieckse Witte* into Belgium.

Irish beers

If, on 18th April 1888, the Guinness brand was registered in Brussels, it was not until 1912 that the beer saw any significant growth. It was, in fact, from this date that the John Martin company imported, from Dublin, the famous *stout*, with 8 % vol. alcohol. Sixty years later, its imports peaked at 34,065 hectolitres. Today its consumption in Belgium averages around 30,000 hectolitres. It should be noted that the alcohol content of Guinness is 7.5 % vol. alcohol in Belgium, 5.4 % vol. alcohol in the United States, and 4.1 % vol. alcohol in Ireland. John Martin also imports the amber Irish beer *Kilkenny*.

Another Irish *stout*, produced by Murphy's, was introduced on the Belgian market in 1994, by Heineken.

Luxembourg beers

From 1860 Luxembourg exported beers to Belgium. However, customs agreements which linked the country with Prussia checked this trade. It was only from 1922 that exports increased and became regular. The figures speak for themselves: 5,900 hectolitres in 1921, and some 100,000 hectolitres today.

Three breweries are represented on the Belgian market: Mousel, in Wallonia, and above all in Brussels; Diekirch, in Wallonia above all, but also a little throughout for its *Kaly Pils*, a beer of the Association of Beer Merchants; and lastly for some years now, the Bofferding Brewery, in the south of the country.

AN OLD ENGLISH ESTABLISHMENT

In 1904, the Whitbread Brewery set up a direct import branch in Brussels. Four years later, once the brand was registered, depots were built in Molenbeek, in the suburbs of the Belgian capital. The beer arrived from London by sea and the River Scheldt, in 500 litre casks, and some days later it was bottled at Molenbeek. *Stout* and *Pale Ale* remained three to five weeks, before being sold, for the most part in Hainaut.

This establishment rapidly expanded. Depots were built in Antwerp (1906), Liège (1910), and Ghent (1930). In 1954, the Whitbread Brewery introduced a night delivery service by tanker lorries and ferry, the new itinerary using Dover and Dunkirk. Bottling continued to be done in Belgium.

Becoming insufficient, the Brussels depot was transferred in 1964 to Mechelen. Then, taking sales into account, *Pale Ale* was produced with Ginder Ale in Merchtem (1979) and at Interbrew in Leuven (1990).

TO THE CREDIT OF MASTER KANTER...

Master Kanter is above all known for having worked at the Brasserie de Charmes (Vosges) in France, the brewery from which came the celebrated beer *Kanterbräu*. This was before, around 1920, he bought the Walsheim Brewery, established in the Saar, when he created the "Comptoir International Walsheim", a holding company with its registered office in Luxembourg. From 1931, the "Société Belge des bières Walsheim" was established in Etterbeek. It was directed by his brother Harry. Success was such that in 1933 Louis Malengreaux, a brewer in Wasmes-lez-Mons, copied the logo with his *Claeren Bier*.

The advent of Hitler and the fact that Master Kanter was of Jewish origin brought an end to the establishment in Belgium. Kanter left Germany and set up in the Vosges.

Of surrealist inspiration, the poster designed by Raymond Van Doren for the Van Roy Brewery, in Wieze, in 1954.

ART IN THE SERVICE OF BEER

Like other consumer goods, beer has used advertising from the start when still striving, at the beginning of the industrial era. Posters, lithographs, calendars, beermats and labels. Since then, there has not been a prop which could not be illustrated. It was, however, the poster which occupied the main advertising scene. During the second half of the 19th century, colour lithography was perfected, thanks to the Frenchman Jules Chéret. This was the turning point in its history of success and it earned the interest of artists who saw in it a new means of expression. No doubt industrialists, and therefore breweries, were able to see the implications of a quality iconographic language, not only for the brand image of their product, but also for the contribution to the artistic heritage that it could represent.

Printer-lithographers, such as O. De Rycker & Mendel (Brussels), J.L. Goffart, (Brussels), August Bénard (Liège) and Henri Poncelet (Liège), made it their speciality. The years 1880 - 1890 thus saw, in Belgium, a blossoming of posters, often created by well-known artists. Armand Rassenfosse and Emile Berchmans were, with Adolphe Crespin, the pioneers of this new art form which, while taking its style from the successive trends of the times (neo-impressionism, Art Nouveau, symbolism, etc.) distinguished itself from painting by its spontaneity, fluidity and strength, which enabled, and even commanded, its use in advertising.

At the beginning of the 20th century, posters became more subdued. The multiple treatment, even partitioning, of the subject and the frequent overloading of the layout gave way to a unity of image. The refined effect gained in power and efficiency. As the famous poster artist Privat-Livemont said: "The artist should seek simplicity. Instead of an ants' nest, he should draw an attractive picture which, through its position, its environment, its decoration, in a word by its entirety, should suit the object of which he must stimulate the publicity. The shape should be large and beautiful and impress by its simplicity. A poster should not only be an advertisement, but also [...] a stimulus for Art Nouveau."

The postermania which spread over Belgium at the turn of the century diminished after the Great War. But the poster continued to inspire artists and enabled commercial companies to communicate with the public. From then on, less concerned with ornamentation than with the functional, it inherited a search for formal art - Cubism and Constructivism. In the 1930's, the Bauhaus influence was felt in poster design. The work of Leo Narfurt carries the mark. This did not however stop the "decorative" style inaugurated by the previous century, from continuing in parallel. Every design had its creators and ... its adepts.

After the Second World War, the cohabitation between these two concepts of the poster, one plain and the other decorative, came to an end and emerged as "contemporary" which, through a certain austerity, reflected in some way the economical wounds provoked by the conflict. The style was not without evoking that of the 1930's and, marked by incertitude, testified that the poster was, yet again, in search of itself. The deciding factor in its evolution was the necessity to accelerate its language, by enlarging its size and by intensifying its visual message. Indeed photography, rich with thousands of new possibilities, began to rival drawing, but the latter has shown us that, to date, it is not even close to having used up its abundance of inspiration.

ÉMILE BERCHMANS

(Liège 1867-1947)

As a decorator, he painted the ceilings of the Liège and Verviers theatres, as well as the dome of the Church of St Michel in Aachen. As a painter, he executed work inspired by symbolism, where he liked to marry different techniques in order to obtain unrealistic effects.

In his work as poster artist, he created his first compositions in 1888, the year when he started his collaboration with the Liège publisher Auguste Bénard. His style rapidly became more defined, combining his interest in simplicity with a great sense of colour and light. With Auguste Domman and Armand Rassenfosse (with whom he founded the newspaper *Caprice Revue*), Emile

Berchmans was one of the first in Belgium to take poster art to the top.

In 1896, Émile Berchmans created a superb poster for Libotte-Thiriar, wholesaler and importer of beer in Liège.

Albert Chavepeyer

(Châtelet 1899-1986)

After starting as a house-painter in the family business, he studied at the Académie de Châtelet, then started a studio in 1922 with his brother Émile, a talented photographer, and specialised in portraits. In 1925, he left his home town to become drawer-retoucher at the Weidar printers in Liège. Among his first works is a poster created for the Fabrique Nationale d'Armes which won him a first prize and contributed to his fame.

His advertisements for the brewery world were for Delbruyère, in Châtelet, Bavery in Couillet and Faleau in Châtelineau.

Delamare et Clerf

Francis Delamare appeared in the poster world around 1914 with several compositions for Brussels theatres. At the beginning of the 1920's, he started, together with Cerf, one of the first Belgian advertising companies in Brussels. This company gathered together many artists,

Poster after Albert Chavepeyer.

such as the architect Obosinsky and the painter Raymond Van Doren. The works were numerous and varied: catalogues, brochures, and, of course, posters, amongst which were those for the Union-Match, Cigarettes Saint-Michel and for Stella Artois. A quarterly publication was produced, entitled Notoriété, dedicated to their work.

Very soon, Delamare and Cerf posters acquired an international audience and were hung in exhibitions throughout Europe. However, Cerf disappeared on the 1st April 1940 and Delamare alone led the business for another few years.

The brewery world also owes credit to Delamare and Cerf for the posters for Stella Artois in Leuven and for the Slaghmuylder brewery in Ninove.

Godefroid Devreese

(Courtrai 1861 - Brussels 1941)

Sculptor and medal-engraver, he created many monuments, such as that of the Battle of the Golden Spurs in Kortrijk. He produced over four hundred medals of which several were for the Brewery Association.

He was made a member of the Académie Royale de Belgique.

Jean Dratz

(Mons 1903 - Saint-Ghislain 1967)

Landscape painter, he was also a cartoonist in a style which has often been compared with that of the Frenchman Albert Dubout.

He also created a few posters, mainly during the years 1940 to 1950. Amongst these is a creation for Archiduc beers of the Duvieusart Brewery in Nivelles. (See also the postcard for lambic and faro on page 121)

Emile Dupuis

(Orléans, France 1877 - ?)

Upon his arrival in Liège in 1902, he worked for the publisher-printer Auguste Bénard and was soon given responsibility for the drawing and lithography workshop. He created numerous advertising posters and won competitions for several of these, such as his poster for the 1905 Universal Exhibition in Liège in 1903. He also produced a poster for the Longchamps Brewery in Verviers.

His eclectic style sometimes evokes the art of Mucha, sometimes that of Armand Rassenfosse.

In 1940, the artist returned to France and all trace was lost of him.

Franz Gaillard

(Brussels 1861 - 1932)

Painter of landscapes and portraits, he was also a cartoonist and collaborated with several newspapers such as the *Patriote Illustré* and the *Globe Illustré*. He produced a few posters between 1893 and 1896.

His contribution to the world of beer was through the newspaper *Le Petit Journal du Brasseur* of which he did the layout and the design of advertisement drawings. We also owe to him the logo showing a Gaul on an earthenware bottle which he produced for the René Grard Brewery of Jemmapes. (See page 180)

Jean-Jacques Gaillard

(Brussels 1890 - Saint-Gilles 1976)

Son of Franz Gaillard, he subscribed, from the beginning, to the "Brabant Fauvisme" current. He favoured landscapes, still-life and portraits. He would treat them in a symbolist or abstract style, but always poetically. His paintings and drawings combined the interpretation of a subject and the suggestion of an idea. He mixed water-colours, writing and collage in his "drawings". The game of words intermingled with drawn lines and thus created a lyrical animation from which an almost musical visual rhythm would burst.

Drawing made by Franz Gaillard for an advertisement dedicated to Quercine, a material used in the insulation of hop lofts, barrels, and cellars, etc. (In *Le Petit Journal du Brasseur*, at the beginning of the 20th century).

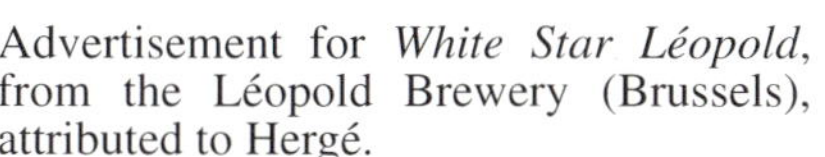
Advertisement for *White Star Léopold*, from the Léopold Brewery (Brussels), attributed to Hergé.

For the Brussels Universal Exhibition, in 1958, he created sketches of "Happy Belgium", recreating with talent the atmosphere of the café.

John Gilroy

(Newcastle-upon-Tyne 1898 - ?)

Attracted to painting and drawing early in life, he first taught art at the Royal College in London. However, his taste for posters and publicity led him to a new career in 1925, when he joined S.H. Benson Ltd. He fast became one of the most talented creators in the British advertisement world.

He created the famous Guinness advertisements of which the first was produced in 1930. In Belgium he created an advertisement for the Wielemans Ceuppens Brewery in Forest, Wiel's, and an advertisement for Ginder Ale in Merchtem.

Hergé (born Georges Remi)

(Etterbeek, near Brussels, 1907 - Brussels 1983)

Creator of the infamous Tintin et Milou in 1929, then of the series Quick et Flupke (1930) and Jo, Zette and Jocko Brussels urchins (1936), Hergé was one of the pioneers of comic strips in Belgium and in Europe. His graphic "clearline" style was to attract many followers.

Sketch of a poster by John Gilroy (in the Fifties).

As a publicity artist, he contributed to the Catholic press before the war as well as to Scout periodicals. He created commercial and political posters, together with menus and advertising blotting-paper for the Léopold Brewery.

Kris Herteleer

(Roeselare 1955)

After having studied architecture he took over, together with his brother, the Costenoble Brewery in Esen, near Dixmuide.

Drawing by Kris Herteleer, of the Dolle Brouwers ("Mad Brewers") Brewery, in Esen

"If my drawings are better than others, it is that they go to the end, they destroy everything. But they go to the end because I go there myself, and that destroys me as well." In this way the French comic artist *Chaval* described his work, and himself through it, in 1965. An exact line, without complacency, a humour often caustic,.... His drawings depict man in the banality of his everyday life. But prostration gives way to well-being when he takes in his hand a glass of Vieux-Temps!

With him the brewery circle gained a new creative impetus. Kris Herteleer chose to design his labels and posters in an extremely original manner. He used, among other things, a calendar where the drawings of his customers' establishments were reproduced. In 1989 he created the beermats for the 10th anniversary of the Hopduvel bar in Ghent.

Julian Key

(Zaventem 1930)

From the age of 15, Julian Key (Julien Keymolen) frequented the studio of the painter Félix Tuyarts, at the same time as following evening courses at Sint-Lukasschool in Schaerbeek. He completed his apprenticeship with the advertising agency Vanypeco who hired him in 1948, and with the Swiss poster designer Donald Brun in 1975. Julian Key is a Belgian graphic artist specialising in large advertising posters. His creations are famous, such as Assubel, Chat Noir, Delhaize the Lion, Batibouw, the motor-rail trains, the Lotto and Ginder-Ale.

Amedee Ernest Lynen

(Saint-Josse-Ten-Noode 1852 - Brussels 1938)

Typographer, lithographer and decorator, founder of the Essor group with A. Dillens and L. Frédéric, he actively

took part in the cultural life of Brussels at the turn of the 20th century.

His posters are often connected with his work for the shadow theatre - he created plays in the style of the Chat-Noir - or his sport presentations in several areas. Poet of the daily and the picturesque, he defended the charm of old Brussels as shown by his posters for the Brussels Universal Exhibition of 1897, and celebrated the life of beer-bars and cafés through post cards.

Auguste Mambour

(Liège 1896- 1968)

Although at the beginning he was the only Walloon expressionist painter, he also made his name in the

Post card by Amédée Lynen, belonging to the series *De-ci, de-là, à Bruxelles et en Brabant* ("Here and there in Brussels and Brabant").

Belgian surrealist movement alongside Magritte and Raoul Ubac.

Winner of the second prize in Rome in 1923, Auguste Mambour made a journey, that same year, to the Congo. It was to mark his art. The Congo period of his work is often considered as the most beautiful. His illustrator's talent was first seen in 1928 with the poster created for the Belgian automobile expedition "Le Raid au Cap", organised by the magazine FN of the National Arms Manufacturer in Herstal, and by Englebert tyre factories. From 1929 to 1931 Mambour contributed to this publication as advertisement artist. His contribution to the beer world was through engraving.

Leo Marfurt

(Aarau, Switzerland, 1894 - Antwerp 1977)

He took up residence in Belgium in 1921 and, in 1927, set up an advertising studio in Brussels, Les Creations Publicitaires, with the Brussels H. Bosinans and the English artist Sterne Stevens. It was this studio which published the major part of his graphic works.

Interior of bistro. Charcoal drawing by Auguste Mambour (1920).

From influences such as Bauhaus, Cubism and Futurism, Leo Marfut developed a personal style which was to play an important part in the evolution of Belgian poster art. He worked for Belgian industrialists, including tobacco industrials, and acquired international notoriety through his posters (for Remington, Minerva, Chrysler, Johnson, etc.). He created advertisements for the Lamot Breweries in Mechelen and Roelants in Brussels.

Kurt Peiser

(Antwerp 1887 - 1962)

A realist painter preoccupied with humanitarian and social matters, he painted landscapes, seascapes and was especially interested in popular character types. The interiors of his cafés are particularly interesting.

Above: engraving by Kurt Peiser (in the Thirties).

Below: the best known brewery work of Marfurt: advertisement for Pick beer from the Roelants Brewery, in Brussels.

Armand Andre-Luis Rassenfosse

(Liège 1862 - 1934)

He was a collaborator of the Liège publisher Auguste Bénard and took over upon the death of the latter. Engraver by heart, he became friendly with Félicien Rops in 1892 and experimented with him on various engraving techniques.

His production of posters mainly took place towards the end of the 19th century and earned him a world-wide reputation, especially in Paris where he worked with the famous Chaix.

His beer advertisements were for: the Bock Champagne of Albert Moussoux in Liège and the Brasserie Moussoux in Falmignoul; the Grande Brasserie Van Velsen in Bornhem and the Brouwerij Mouterij Debie of F. Desmedt Meulestede in Ghent.

Advertisement for the *de Bie Brewery & Maltings*, by Armand André-Louis Rassenfosse.

Georges Redon

(Paris 1869 - ? 1943)

His artistic activity was expressed through engraving, painting, drawing ... and humour.

Around a drawing by Georges Redon...

Above left, an illustration on a calendar printed for Ponselet beers in Anderlues.

Above right, matchbox case for the Wilfrid Methot Inn, in Montreal, Canada.

Below: two beermats; left, Saverne Brewery(France), and, right, The Gay Dog, in Lower Quenton (Great Britain).

Bottom: advertisement in sheet metal for the brewery Cerveceria Nacional, in Potosi, Bolivia.

Other versions have been made: Georges Leduc Brewery (France), Warsteiner Brewery (Germany).

Marius Renard

(Hornu, Mons, 1869 - Anderlecht 1948)

Apart from his industrial activity, he followed a career of writing with novels and short stories of a social character, and a political career, being appointed Permanent Deputy of Brabant, and then Senator.

But art was also his great preoccupation. He himself was a painter and an illustrator. Director of the École Provinciale des Arts et Métiers of Hainaut, he founded, in 1918, the École Marius Renard (technical institute) in Brussels. In 1920, he founded the periodical *Savoir et Beauté*, devoted to Walloon art. He contributed to several newspapers such as *Le Petit Bleu* and to art periodicals such as *La Libre Critique*.

He created his posters towards the end of the 19th century. These were of the Art Nouveau style and were often printed by Dufrane-Friart in Frameries. As far as beer is concerned, Marius Renard created the poster Spéciale Double, for Saint-Joseph (E. Peltier-Levecq), in Pommeroeul.

Raymond Savignac

Paris, France, 1907)

After having studied technical drawing, he learned the advertising profession and worked for various agencies and, amongst others, with the great poster artist Cassandre, between 1935 and 1938.

Renown came at the end of the Forties with the success of his poster for Monsavon and his infamous cow. At that time, he worked in Belgium for the Belgian

The *Special Double* poster by Marius Renard.

advertising agency Vanypeco founded by Adrien Van Ypersele de Strihou and who gathered together the most famous names in poster art.

Savignac produced several hundred posters which were printed in France and abroad. He created, for example, the advertisement for Scotch Ale for the Lootvoet Brewery in Overijse.

Louis Thevenet

(Bruges 1874-1930)

Apprentice baker at first, he chose, at the age of twenty-two, to concentrate on painting and took up residence in Anseremme where he frequented the Café des Artistes.

Louis Thévenet was a fan of Brussels beer. At home, the tobacco jar was next to the faro jug and the lambic pitcher. In 1906, the painter Charles Dehoy introduced him to the gueuze brewer François Van Haelen who, with his brother Dominique, took him under his wing.

Edgar Tytgat

(Brussels 1879 - Woluwe-Saint-Lambert, 1957)

Student of Constant Montald at the Brussels Academy, he asserted himself as a painter and took part, during the 1920's, in the Belgian expressionist movement.

He was a friend of the Van Haelen family and created *Histoire du Faro et du Lambic à travers les âges*, a sort of picture fairy tale which could be seen as a precursor to the comic strips dedicated to beer.

Raymond Van Doren

(Brussels 1907 - 1991)

His work is of a traditional style where pastels have a predominant place. His major work is the 350 square metre fresco which he carried out in Wieze and which represents the peace born from fraternisation between nations, after a poem by Schiller.

From 1956 to 1987 he decorated earthenware beer-mugs used during the Wieze Oktoberfeesten, using the subjects of manufacturing and consuming beer in his illustrations. He also created the logo for Van Roy in Wieze and the logo of the Safir beer for the De Gheest brewery, as well as blotting-pads and menus for Whitbread (Brussels), Moortgat (Breendonk) and Artois (Leuven).

Alfred Van Neste

(Brugge 1874 - Rhode-Saint-Genèse 1969)

Student at the Bruges and Antwerp Academies, he himself taught at the Antwerp Academy.

He illustrated several books and was particularly interested in poster art. As a poster artist he was inspired by the city of Antwerp and by official events which took place there, often staging characters of neo-gothic Flanders.

He created an advertisement for the De Meulemeester Brewery in Bruges.

Contemporary art is to be found in the labels designed by comic strip artists. Here is a label for the Vapeur Brewery, made by Claude Renard in 1989.

Poster by M. Thygat for the City of Brussels Fair in 1928. Gueuze, waffles, mussels and chips are the joy of those taking part.

BEER PLACES

Fairs, village weddings, country meals, ... a thousand and one characters, dressed in the Campine fashion, live in the universe of Pieter Bruegel the Elder. Barrels, tankards, glasses. Cervisia is present at all these rejoicings, even to excess as shown by the famous drawing entitled *Gula - la Gourmandise* (1557), where Gula, represented as an old matron, drinks greedily from a jug, under the eyes of a monster none the less eager to share the drink.

Fairs were an important time of the year for the peasants and were not to be missed. There were processions, dances, games, feasting and drinking, as shown in the *Saint George's Fair* painted by Pieter Bruegel the Younger, eldest son of Pieter Bruegel the Elder. The excessive atmosphere connected with these festivities is probably due to the fact that, at the time, during the outdoor processions of the Blessed Sacrement, profane games were prohibited and drinking establishments were closed.

Some drinking establishments were called *auberges* (inns). Next to the door of the *Auberge Saint-Michel* (Pieter Bruegel the Younger, 1634), at the foot of the facade painted in German style, two men drink from a jug, settled next to a barrel being used as a table. This is a familiar scene, particular to Flemish painting of the 17th century and can be found, for example, in the *Riverside Inn* (David Teniers the Younger, c. 1646).

From the inn to the *cabaret* or to the *estaminet*, the difference is slight. The flag of the drinking establishment floats in the wind. Villagers relax outside with, as a backdrop, a green and serene landscape. They rush into a possessed dance; this is shown in the picture by David Teniers, *Peasant dancing in front of a tavern* (1649). They play various games such as dice, whilst holding a tankard, as in *The Cabaret* (David Teniers). The animation which seems to be permanently prevalent outside the cabaret is even more joyful during village celebrations (*The Villagers*, *Peasant Wedding*, *Flemish Fair*, by David Teniers).

These scenes of rustic life are numerous. Beer is never forgotten. It belongs to every day life as it belongs to festivities.

From one place to another

• **Auberge.** (Inn) This is a place, mostly in the country, where one can drink, eat, and sleep, in exchange for payment.

• **Bistrot or bistro.** This is, in popular language, a wine merchant who has a café or a small restaurant. By extension, the word has developed to indicate a café (where one can also drink beer) or a modest restaurant. The latter prevails today.

The origin of the word dates back to the period when Tsar Alexander III was allied with France (1891-1894). His soldiers asked to drink using the word "bistro" at the end of the sentence. This means "quick".

• **Buvette.** (Bar) This is generally a simple counter where drinks are served and where the customer remains standing. By extension, the word is applied to a drinking establishment which is small and modest. All popular festivities have buvettes.

• **Cabaret.** This word, little used today, comes from the Dutch *cabret*, which in turn comes from the old Picardy word *camberette*, "little room". This is what a small drinking establishment was called. Its owner was called a *cabaretier*. As for the *pilier de cabaret* (cabaret pillar), this was a drinker who spent a lot of time there.

• **Café.** Here coffee is served, but now all other kinds of drinks as well, with or without alcohol. The keeper is called a *cafetier*; he also used to be called a *limonadier*.

• **Débit.** (Drinks outlet). This is a place were drinks are sold retail. In a *débit de bière*, beer is sold retail for takeaway. In Brussels, the taverns had, next to the counter, a window opening onto a corridor where beer was sold to take away.

• **Estaminet.** (Tavern). This word comes from the eastern Walloon word *stamine*, with the meaning of "pillar room" and which, at the end of the 17th century, indica-

Series of enamel plaques, signs at drinks outlets.
Silly Brewery collection.

ted a bad cabaret. Tradition wants that in Spanish times the estaminet was a place were young girls served drinks *(Aqui estan menatas!)*.

However, it was mostly a café where one could smoke. But it was also a small village or town café. As in the case of the cabaret*, there were *tavern pillars*. As for *tavern jokes*, these were stamped as of bad taste.

Lastly, the Flemish word *baes* was used to indicate the manager of an estaminet.

• **Guinguette.** (out of town tavern). This is where one eats, drinks and dances. La guinguette (meaning literally "house of little importance") is a popular cabaret located outside the town.

• **Mastroquet.** (wine shop). This word of popular language, which is hardly ever used today, indicates either a drink retailer or a drinks outlet. Its etymology goes back to the Flemish *maesterke* ("small manager"). *Troquet* ("small café", "bistrot") is the abbreviated form of the word.

• **Taverne** (tavern). This used to be a retail drink shop where one could also eat. The word has often had a disparaging connotation, indicating a cabaret where one went "to drink to excess and surrender to debauchery" (Littré). Also, did one not speak of "bandit taverns"? Today, the tavern is a refined place where one can often eat and drink English and Danish beer.

Glasses and tankards

Indispensable to the beer ritual, glasses and tankards are not the fruit of human fantasy. Every beer has its container. Shapes and materials are there to help the drink express the maximum of its flavour and to be better enjoyed. The receptacles are therefore innumerable, adapted to each kind of beer and its character.

Evidence of past times, the tankard is seen in paintings and engravings. Seated at a barrel, a couple drinks and eats in the *Meal in the barn*, by David Téniers the Younger (17th century). In addition to these domestic moments, there is no Flemish inn scene which does not show characters holding a tankard of Cervoise, drinkers and smokers; beer is often associated with a pipe during the convivial moments, as shown by other paintings by David Téniers (*The Smokers, Village Fair*, for example), as well as the paintings of Adriaen Brouwer in the 17th century.

Wood was the first material used in the manufacture of beer containers. The jug was first encircled with wicker. Then wood was combined with pewter and, later on, with stoneware, and then earthenware. The handle, the stand and the lid, which was used to maintain the temperature, were made of pewter. Pewter was also used for the entire tankard. Indeed, Kings, Princes and Lords had more refined goblets, in silver or silver-gilt, even sometimes in coconut or ivory.

Today, the tankard has lost its luxurious aspect and the taste of the beer has won over appearance. In rustic stoneware, purists find that beer loses quality. In earthenware, the tankard fulfils a certain folklore and is mostly the reproduction of old specimens of which it copies the ornamentation. In glass or crystal, it allows the colour and transparency of the drink to be appreciated, thereby satisfying the enlightened connoisseur.

During past centuries, the utility side of the object did not prevent artists from taking interest in it. Tankards of the 16th century have been found of which the extremely luxurious decoration is a work of art. These tankards are mostly made of pewter. Landscapes, hunting scenes, children playing, people, arabesques... The extremely refined work makes these jugs masterpieces of Renaissance goldsmith craftsmanship.

Metal was more suitable for engraving and glass for painting, hence jugs and tankards decorated with various designs. These luxurious jugs were, in Belgium as in Germany, mainly used in trade guild banquets. Unfortunately, due to their fragility, there are only a few samples left today. Tankards in china or earthenware are more common. They were covered in paintings during the 19th century. These "miniatures" are collectors' items today.

If one cannot purchase these wonderful tankards, one can at least search for the more recent stoneware or glass tankards. Shapes vary, tall or less tall, as does the engraved design (lines, squares, etc.) depending on its origin. The 20th century has often brought them out of anonymity for advertising means.

WHAT DOES ONE MEAN BY...?

- **Chope.** (Tankard). Its capacity is between 25 cl and 5 litres, depending on its size and its country of origin. Today, there are mostly 3 tankards per litre.
- **Chopine.** (Mug). This old capacity measure held approximately 50 cl.
- **Pint.** The Paris "pinte" equalled 0.931 litres. Today this measure is only used in Anglo-Saxon countries (0.568 litres in Great Britain and 0.473 in the United States).
- **Pot.** (Jug). This old container, in terracotta, contained two litres. When musicians or clowns came into the cabaret, a jug was poured and served in small glasses.
- **Ramassis.** (Dregs). The keeper "collects" all the beer which remains at the bottom of the glasses. This is called in Flemish *stort bier*, which can be used as animal feed.

In 1861, petitions were collected to end a cabaret practice which was to use these dregs in the making of beer. However, towards 1875, this practice was still taking place! Thankfully, it did however end.

Left: "coachman's glass", on a wooden stand. The Bosteels Brewery, in Buggenhout, perpetuated the tradition for its *Kwak* beer. (Photo ADS)

Above: glass mug of the Confrérie des Chevaliers du Fourquet.

AN ADAPTED GLASS

The glass plays a major role in the savouring of beer. For a Pils, it is recommended to chose a tall and slim glass so as to retain the carbon gas. A top-fermented beer requires a wider glass, which allows full enjoyment of its taste and aroma. A white beer requires a facet glass from which its cloudiness can be better seen.

In Belgium, the manufacture of beer glasses takes place mostly in the centre of the country, around the two centres of Solignies and Manage.

INFORMATION ON BEER

THE FIGURES

BELGIAN BREWING FROM 1900 TO 1994

	Production (in 1 000 hectolitres)	Number of active breweries	Average gravity	Exports (in 1 000 hectolitres)	Imports (in 1 000 hectolitres)	Consumption (litres per inhabitant)
1900	14,617	3,223	3.29°	5	149	220
1910	16,019	3,349	3.20°	9	272	219
1920	10,408	2,013	2.23°	47	201	143
1930	16,099	1,546	3.36°	10	228	203
1939	12,488	1,120	3.40°	7	65	149
1946	10,802	755	2.67°	—	83	128
1947	12,595	761	2.59°	10	48	148
1948	11,340	722	2.89°	6	97	132
1949	10,494	689	3.19°	3	93	122
1950	10,140	663	3.43°	5	97	118
1951	9,929	640	3.61°	15	121	115
1952	10,171	587	3.68°	31	146	117
1953	10,210	569	3.63°	42	164	117
1954	9,667	554	3.89°	47	187	110
1955	9,998	534	3.92°	110	200	113
1956	9,769	500	3.99°	146	221	109
1957	10,185	476	4.02°	195	265	113
1958	10,148	446	3.99°	137	338	115
1959	10,600	432	4.01°	144	349	—
1960	10,110	414	4.17°	204	377	112
1961	10,514	394	4.14°	296	429	—
1962	10,309	368	4.20°	406	501	—
1963	10,734	343	4.23°	497	622	—
1964	11,330	324	4.28°	621	676	—
1965	11,092	305	4.33°	713	720	117
1966	11,278	284	4.42°	837	717	117
1967	11,723	268	4.37°	838	733	121
1968	11,894	256	4.40°	867	709	122
1969	12,478	242	4.36°	931	672	126
1970	13,015	232	4.45°	976	741	132
1971	12,876	206	4.54°	1,078	778	130
1972	13,495	192	4.38°	1,395	888	134
1973	14,691	190	4.33°	1,789	1,008	143
1974	14,004	185	4.51°	2,127	1,117	133
1975	13,797	174	4.55°	2,210	1,201	130
1976	14,543	165	4.54°	2,281	1,262	138
1977	13,818	159	4.62°	2,042	1,027	130
1978	13,394	151	4.62°	2,054	1,006	125
1979	13,680	147	4.64°	2,308	1,017	126
1980	14,291	143	4.56°	2,315	969	131
1981	13,811	134	4.73°	2,431	870	125
1982	14,628	130	4.66°	2,369	818	133
1983	14,224	134	4.74°	2,389	771	128
1984	14,311	131	4.71°	2,585	715	126
1985	13,930	132	4.69°	2,632	623	121
1986	13,715	125	4.79°	2,462	568	120
1987	13,987	126	4.80°	2,635	565	122
1988	13,792	143	4.78°	2,636	554	118
1989	13,164	128	4.83°	2,394	642	115
1990	14,141	126	4.72°	2,752	648	121
1991	13,799	121	4.82°	3,145	459	112
1992	14,259	126	4.83°	3,458	467	112
1993	* 14,182	* 106	***	* 3,776	* 454	108
1994	14,742	**** 115	***	4,592	570	106

* Estimate made by the CBB statistics working group

** Following the modification of the excise regime, several administrative brewhouses have gone; however, the number of operative breweries remains practically unchanged

*** These figures are no longer available since the modification of the excise regime

**** Customs and Excise (breweries and agreed bonds)

Sources: INS; Customs and Excise; CBB

THE CONSUMPTION OF BEER IN BELGIUM

(in hectolitres)

Type of beer	1993	1994	DEVELOPMENT (percentage)
Pils	7,300,603	7,273,797	- 0.37
Amber beers	731,585	725,698	- 0.80
White beers	653,338	595,851	- 8.80
Abbey beers (including Trappist beers)	505,749	577,484	+ 14.18
Table beers	382,231	358,894	- 6.11
Gueuze, kriek, etc.	246,612	250,276	+ 1.49
British beers	239,319	220,793	- 7.74
Pils de luxe	223,502	195,150	- 12.69
Low-alcohol beers/alcohol-free beers	182,789	158,745	- 13.15
Strong blond beers	166,247	165,733	- 0.31
Regional beers	151,511	115,930	- 23.48
Acid beers	76,816	81,661	+ 6.31
TOTAL	**10,860,302**	**10,720,012**	**- 1.29**

(Source : C.B.B.)

SALES IN BELGIUM BY TYPE OF PACKAGING

(in per centage of total)

	1990	1991	1992
Barrels	42.57	43.26	39.97
Bottles	54.91		
• returnable		46.34	53.00
• disposable		7.44	4.43
Boxes	2.52	2.96	2.59

THE CONSUMPTION OF BEER IN EUROPE IN 1992

(in litres per inhabitant)

Germany	138.5
Denmark	128.2
Ireland	124.0
Austria	121.0
Czech Republic	121.0
Belgium	112.0
Luxembourg	112.0
Great Britain	102.3
Netherlands	90.2
Finland	88.4
Spain	70.5
Portugal	65.4
Sweden	63.3
Norway	50.8
France	40.9
Greece	40.0
Italy	25.9

ACTIVE BREWERIES IN EUROPE IN 1992

Germany	1,290
Belgium	126
Denmark	18
France	29
Great Britain	96
Greece	7
Ireland	7
Italy	20
Luxembourg	5
Netherlands	28
Portugal	8

TRADE IN EUROPE IN 1992

(in thousands of hectolitres)

	Exports	Imports
Germany	6,485	2,969
Belgium	3,458	467
Denmark	2,739	21
Spain	314	1,806
France	1,028	2,754
Great Britain	2,084	5,534
Greece	130	230
Ireland	2,851	771
Italy	136	2,747
Netherlands	7,349	529
Portugal	484	117

EXPORTS OF BELGIAN BEERS (U.E.B.L.)

(in hectolitres)

	1985	1991	1992	1993	1994
Germany	99,655	264,420	270,862	267,179	246,395
Austria	43	380	126	134	117
Canada	865	2,855	2,680	2,654	3,484
C.I.S.	2,410	59,494	31,918	99,877	120,631
Denmark	8,499	1,056	710	609	338
Spain	2,859	42,839	135,172	132,923	90,863
United-States	13,344	7,283	8,757	9,918	15,026
France	1,717,090	1,664,058	1,728,061	1,692,260	2,297,371
Great-Britain	299,525	51,076	91,335	102,728	177,888
Greece	5,024	11,839	18,310	22,398	15,414
Ireland	519	1,120	214	2,091	1,154
Italy	233,905	271,198	312,804	292,766	206,115
Netherlands	319,699	615,466	692,151	798,291	969,002
Poland	899	36,176	565	920	492
Portugal	19	458	981	310	428
Romania	——	24,638	14,656	3,545	1,173
Sweden	4,830	1,668	1,097	1,684	2,220
Switzerland	8,256	10,470	9,209	8,200	10,598
Other European countries * than those indicated above	1,437	6,650	8,107	3,732	——
Other countries outside Europe than those indicated above	25,238	68,012	126,818	170,935	——
Shape	1,621	3,790	3,414	696	——

* Geographical Europe

(U.E.B.L. : Belgian and Luxembourg Economic Union)

IMPORTS OF FOREIGN BEERS (U.E.B.L.)

(in hectolitres)

	1985	1991	1992	1993	1994
Germany	63,789	112,955	107,498	92,816	105,426
Austria	128	97	80	88	98
Denmark	234,422	148,536	145,604	3,096	128,731
Spain	72	177	237	172	705
France	59,290	49,380	46,776	31,476	49,239
Great-Britain	220,427	73,746	67,681	71,693	100,838
Greece	——	——	——	78	——
Ireland	31,903	24,934	26,892	25,161	28,204
Italy	235	391	464	1,066	24,158
Netherlands	14,125	41,013	59,494	64,715	72,798
Portugal	749	1,767	2,913	4,646	6,251
Czech Republic	365	619	1,195	2,260	2,021
Sweden	4	125	106	84	113
Switzerland	11	43	——	65	10
Other european countries * than those indicated above	63	——	41	101	——
Other countries outside Europe	86	4,999	8,117	39,936	——

* Geographical Europe.

(U.E.B.L. : Belgian and Luxembourg Economic Union)

EXCISE ON BEER

As in other countries, the fiscal regime applicable to the brewing industry expresses itself, in Belgium, in an *excise duty*, which has existed for a long time, since it found its origins, in the Middle Ages, in the right of the feudal lord to his tithe. From 1822, under Dutch rule, this tax varied according to the capacity of the mash-tun. Then, from 1885, the brewer had a choice between this method of calculation or a new formula which established the amount of excise on the basis of the quantities of raw materials used (malt, grain, sugar). This second assessment, linked to dosage, was declared the only method in force in 1902. But, after the economic crisis of 1930, with the sole aim of protecting small breweries, the tax on output was introduced, with a progressive rate according to production. It was applied from 1938.

As from 1st January 1969, excise was calculated on the total quantity of wort resulting from the brewing process, in hectolitres degree, which was more fair. One distinguished: normal excise and special excise, both linked by a progressive tariff. Finally, on 1st January 1993, there was an amendment. Henceforward it is the finished product (in degrees Plato), that is to say at the moment of leaving the depot to be sold, which is taken into consideration. It follows that the losses incurred at different stages of manufacture (racking etc.) are not taxed. This is an advantage for brewers, who register an effective loss varying between 7 and 15 per cent.

Excise, which also applies to other consumer products (lemonade, tobacco, etc.) represents 8 per cent of the receipts of the Belgian state. As for the time in which excise duty must be paid, it is fixed at the fifteenth day of the second month which follows the shipment for consumption. Thus for a sale in January, the payment becomes due effectively on 15th March.

CALCULATION OF EXCISE DUTY, ESTABLISHED IN 1993

Brewery production	Excise normal	Excise special	Total
• Less or equal to:			
12,500 hl	16 F	34 F	50 F
25,000 hl	16 F	36 F	52 F
50,000 hl	16 F	38 F	54 F
75,000 hl	18 F	38 F	56 F
200,000 hl	18 F	40 F	58 F
• More then :			
200,000 hl	18 F	41 F	59 F

DEVELOPMENT OF EXCISE DUTY FROM 1882 TO 1969

(per kg of material declared)

From 1882 to 1914	0.10 F
From 1914 (german occupation) to 1926	0.20 F
January 1926	0.40 F
June 1926	1.20 F
August 1931	1.50 F
August 1932 :	
• less than 200,000 kg	1.60 F
• more than 200,000 kg	1.85 F
July 1938 (introduction of progressive rate)	
• from 0 to 40,000 kg	2.00 F
• from 40,000 to 200,000 kg	2.30 F
• from 200,000 to 500,000 kg	2.40 F
• from 500,000 to 10,000,000 kg	2.90 F
• more than 10,000,000 kg	3.00 F
15th November 1939	increase of 1 centime
6th August 1940	increase of 5 centimes
20th January 1941	increase of 5 centimes
January 1962	
• from 0 to 40,000 kg	6.20 F
• from 40,000 to 200,000 kg	7.10 F
• from 200,000 to 500,000 kg	7.50 F
• from 500,000 to 10,000,000 kg	8.00 F
• more than 10,000,000 kg	9.00 F

RECEIPTS OF EXCISE ON BEER

(in millions of Francs)

Year	Receipts
1970	1,722,162
1975	3,608,236
1980	3,754,482
1985	5,540,947
1986	5,535,413
1987	5,674,792
1988	5,453,802
1989	5,350,369
1990	6,860,489
1991	7,583,614
1992	7,974,000
1993 *	6,880,000
1994	7,488,000

* In 1993, the true receipt of excise rose to 8,000,000 BEF. But the administration duly reimbursed 1,200,000,000 BEF of excise following detaxation of stocks.

Collections R. Desmecht, C. Fontaine et P. Pirotte.

AIDE-MEMOIRE OF INDUSTRIAL ARCHAEOLOGY

The information given below concerns brewery suppliers. Some have disappeared today, others still carry on their activities. The authors have preferred here to give them in the language of their registered office.

HOP MERCHANTS

Aalst

De Blieck L. & Cie (1899). [Brand LDB & Cie.]
De Coninck Gustave.
De Coninck C. De Windt (1877).
De Coninck Drowart Jan (Brand DCDW).
De Smedt Blondieu.
De Wolf Cosyns & Fils.
Eeman Camille-Callebaut (1840). [Brand EMC.]
Fache A. & M., formerly maison M. Fache.
Meert J. Eeckhoudt.
Meirschmann Joseph.
Neukermans R. (brand RN).
Samijn.
Vandersmissen Aimé.
Van Mossevelde E., Oudegem near Aalst.

Ieper - Poperinge

Fache Maurice, Poperinge (brand MFP), formerly maison Fache Michel, which had a shop in France, at Boeschaje.
Gekiere Gabriel, Ieper.
Vermeulen P. et Soeur, Ieper.

Asse - Ternat

Les Planteurs Réunis Anckaert-Huygens, Whembeek-Ternat.
Van Mollem, Opwijk.

Others

Bivort De Blieck G., Brussels (brand DBD).
De Coninck Van Noyen (1704), Brussels. The business established in Aalst in 1929, then in Uccle 3 (Brussels) in 1933.
Steyart A., Brussels.
Vermeulen C. & L. Frères (around 1929), Brussels.
Vermeulen Ch. & Cie (around 1942), Brussels.
Dramois Louis (brand DL), **Flamme Léon** (1923), **Gosselin Émile** (death in 1910), **Veuve Gosselin Émile et Gosselin Lucien** (1913), Stambruges.
Lievens & Cie, Liedekerke.
Lievens Adolf -Vande Gucht, Liedekerke.
Mauroy H. Lefranc, Soignies.
Pechoux A., Gigot.
Van der Aa, Antwerp.

MAIZE GROWERS

Distillerie et Malterie de l'Ancre (1898), Antwerp.
Maïserie Anglo-Belge (1930), Zulte. This business changed names in 1934 : Maïserie Flandria.
Maïserie A. Borremans Forest, Brussels. It was taken over by Maïserie De Stordeur.
Maïserie Callebaut, Aalst. It was taken over by Paul Dumont, of Bruges, and became the Maïserie des Brasseurs Réunis.
Maïserie De Stordeur (1835), Tubize. It took over the Maïserie de la Dyle in Leuven and set up in that place. Around 1975, the firm ceased to operate.
Maïserie de la Dyle, Leuven. It was taken over by Maïserie De Stordeur.
Maïserie Europa, Antwerp.
Maïserie Keulemans et Windelinkx, Mechelen. This firm was the first, in 1912, to degerm maize in Belgium.
Maïserie Maselis Frères, Roeselare.
Maïserie Rijpens, Boom. This business was the first to manufacture maize grits in Belgium, in 1893.

YEAST PRODUCERS

Benoît Gustave (1902), Brussels.
Laboratoire Brassicole Liégeois (1908), Liège. Its Director was Y. Denamur, chemist and Professor at the Instut Supérieur des Fermentations de Gent.
Levure Hillaert (1862), Ghent. This firm was taken over, in 1940, by Fr. De Clercq et Fils of Ghent.
Huysentruit A., Kortrijk. (Levure Mère des Flandres, for top-fermentation.)
Société des Levains Purs (end of 19th century), Ghent. This firm had offices in France (Anzin), in Great Britain (Burton-upon-Trent), and in the Netherlands (Maastricht). In 1901 its registered office was in Ghent, but its marketing was established in Brussels.
Veuve Timmerman, Brussels.
S.U.L.B.B. (Société pour l'Utilisation des Levures Belges), Aalst. (Use of yeast).

PRODUCERS OF SUGAR FOR BREWERIES

Devolder S.A., Brussels. The business, founded in 1879, by Victor Devolder, sugar merchant, began modestly. Sales consisted initially in candy sugar for the manufacture of faro. In 1908, the second generation undertook the manufacture of inverted crystalisable sugar, with a sweetening power slightly above that of crystallised sugar. From 1913, Devolder put on the market a non-inverted liquid sugar (crystalisable), which was very successful after the First World War. Today, top or spontaneous fermentation breweries, as well as breweries making lemonade, remain the principal clients of the company.
Lebbe, Poperinge. In 1910, Charles Lebbe, owner of hop fields, traded in hops and sugar in Poperinge. His son Georges then set up in Sint-Andries. His grandson, Paul, decided to restrict himself to sugars for breweries and caramelised sugars. In 1966, the Oostkamp plant was opened. Four years later, the Tirlemont Refinery took a share-holding in the business.
Olbrechts E. et Cie, Antwerp.
Ronneberg G. et Cie, Laeken. Around 1950, the firm was taken over by Devolder.

BREWERY DESIGNERS

De Coninck J. (1946), Ixelles.
Van Cauwenberghe P., Brussels. This fermentation engineer specialised in both manufacture and installation.
Verhelle Ch., architect, Brussels.
Van der Veken J. et F. (1930), Leuven. Plans, estimates, direction of works.

BUILDERS OF MASH-TUNS

Boucgniaux, Boussu. And an address in France, in Fourmies. This workshop, founded in 1860, was bought by Meura after the Great War (1918).
Carlier, Boussu (Belgium), and Anciens Etablissements Éd. Van Hœgaarden in Blanc Misseron Crespin, in the North of France. Created in 1918, this firm succeeded Dincq-Gilbert, in Cuesmes. His MASH-TUN operated with the system from F. W. Hellwig-Dincq-Gilbert.

Chaurobel (Chaudronnerie et Robinetterie Belge), Huyzingen and Forest. This business was born of the merger of the Relecom workshops. First of all set up in Halle, then from 1901 in Brussels; Verbeek Léon et Paul, Brussels; and De Wever and Ver Wilghen. In 1925, Chaurobel represented the maturation tanks of Geertruidenberg tank factory (Netherlands). In 1930, Paul Relecom represented the firm of F. Wegel, Mittelneuland-Neisse (Germany), specialists in brewhouses, in Belgium and the Congo.

De Coster Joseph (1867), Tielt. The enterprise was taken over by De Coster Henri, De Coster Van de Velde, then De Vinten in 1912. It constructed the "Ideal" mash-tun, invented by a brewer, Coomans, of Tunize.

Deligne L., Leuze

Ateliers François d'Hondt, Nivelles (Brussels). Founded in 1890 by François d'Hondt, this company at first made equipment for various agro-alimentary sectors, and, among others, the brewing industry (brewhouses). In 1920, Henri and Gustave d'Hondt followed their father and centred their activity on brewing equipment. This orientation was abandoned in 1958, the development of air coolants opening interesting foreign markets for the company, especially in the Middle East. In 1986, the workshops joined the Hemon Sobelco group, specialising in power station equipment. One can still see, in Belgium, brewhouses installed by this company: at the Orval Brewery and the Gouden Boom Brewery, for instance.

Dincq-Gilbert. The builder Dincq-Gilbert, established in Cuesmes, exploited, in Belgium the grinder perfected by F.W.Hellwig, in 1906. An additional patent joined it "for cross cut in cast iron and blade cut in bronze injecting water sprays into the layers of draff which they cut" (*Le Petit Journal du Brasseur*, 3rd September 1926) The company Dincq-Gilbert was taken over by Carlier, in Cuesmes.

Dincq-Jordan Édouard and Son (1856), Jemappes, Pont Canal. This boiler-maker later became Dincq-Gilbert, in Cuesmes.

Donnay Ed., Braine-le-Comte. (mash-tuns)

Dubois Désiré (1807), Brussels. This business succeeded the firms Bouchaert and Raeckelboon and Cuvelle Frères. A mash-tun made by it is to be found in the De Troch Brewery, Wambeek.

Duez Frères (1899), Qauregnon.

Dufour, Elouges. Its mash-tun operated with the system of E. Willemart, a boiler-maker at Slagmuylder in Ninove.

Freyhoefer, Braine L'Alleud. In 1905 the company set up in Brussels.

Gillain, Aartselaar.

Gillain J.J., Tienen. The brewery section was created in 1912. The consultant engineer Lambert Dacier, who worked there, invented the wort filter without pressure and variable feed. Gillain built a mash-tun according to the system of L. Van den Hulle, Professor at Ghent.

Herman Gaston, Ghent.

Lievans J. (1849), Bevere (Oudenaarde). A mash-tun of his manufacture is to be found in the Boon Brewery.

Mennig Édouard, Brussels.

Meura, Tournai.

Monsville, Quaregnon. This business, founded in 1888, very soon played a leading role in matters of boiler-making for breweries. In 1911 its company name was Société Anonyme Ateliers de Monsville. It specialised in brewhouses, and in equipment for the recovery of carbon dioxide emitted on fermentation. The company was absorbed by Meura in 1990. It added to its activities the installation of micro-breweries.

Naves V. and G. Frères, Lobbes.

Parfait, Tournai. The founder of this firm was a foreman at Meura. His son Charles took over the business.

Struyf E.J. Coppens, Antwerp.

Van de Wyer Gustave, Hoboken.

Vve Éd. Verbeek and Son, Brussels. This enterprise specialised in mash-tuns for raw grain, mashes, clear musts.

Vervoort Auguste (1885), Hautrage-État. Its creator had taken over the workshop of Francois-Joseph Besin. The Vervoort house produced a mash-tun ("La Rénovatrice"), which, equipped with a special domed grooved bottom, led the water to the centre without need for a pipe.

Willemart Édouard (1914), Lens.

Wilms (1912), Tournai. The firm was taken over by Meura in 1990.

SOME MAJOR STEPS IN THE 19TH CENTURY

1834: a steam machine operating with the Watt system was installed in the brewery of La Vignette, in Leuven.

1836: La Cambre perfected the *macerator*, or closed flour boiler.

1836-37: La Cambre and Persac erected a steam brewery in Leuven, equipped with a *double-envelope boiler*. Some boilers were heated by naked flame, outside, while others were heated by steam, inside the double envelope.

1857: J. Vintær, a Ghent builder, took out a patent for a *mash tun system* having a bottom and false bottom in cast iron in twelve sections. It should be noted that it was around 1850 that the first cast iron mash-tuns were constructed. Previously they were of wood, then sheet metal or steel.

1859: Hyacinthe and Henri Gourmont frères, brewers in Dinant, took out the first patent for a *vertical cylindrical double-envelope mash-tun*. From their association with Heyndrickx-Percy, a brewer in Sint-Niklaas-Waas, was born the Heyndrickx-Gourmont tank.

1860: a cast iron and bolted panel mash-tun was constructed for the brewery of Rigaux and Delire fils, Marchienne-au-Pont.

1860: a Liège foundryman, Poncelet, cast an iron mash-tun, in one piece 2.5 metres in diameter.

1863: E. Cousin-Duchateau, of Jemappes, who had already designed a cooler, a *triple-envelope mash-tun*, like a bain-marie.

1865: J.P.Jonard, a mechanic in Gilly, perfected a "system of cast iron mash-tun where two pipes only forming one piece with the bottom are horizontally placed, one crossing the diameter of the vessel and other circular. These two pipes distribute water by drains in the direction of the length of the pipes. This system was so good that the water having so many outlets it picked up the flour more quickly, considerably advanced the work, at the same time that its solidity left nothing to be desired." This invention inaugurated the drained vessel.

1865: Ch. Delnest, builder-mechanic in Mons, and Édouard Dinc-Jordan took out a patent for a *balanced mash-tun cover*.

1866: the same Ch. Delnest registered a patent for a *rotating serpentine* which heated "the material by steam coming from the generator or by discharge from the machine. It makes use of a device preventing any escape of steam as well as any loss of materials to be saccharified. This apparatus can also serve for heating the must." (August Vervoort, 1926)

1866: J.B.Charlier, of Ghent, perfected a vertical mash-tun in cast iron, of which the panels contain eighteen conduits deploying the steam.

1868: a *saccharificator* was put into operation, with multiple taps, by J. Puvrez-Bourgeois. This machine recalled the apparatus invented by La Cambre in 1836.

1869: the same Ch. Delnest invented a system of *rational water distribution* in mash-tuns.

1893: M. Van den Hulle advocated the use of his patented vessel which had been inspired by the macerator with false bottom and drains perfected by Billings at the beginning of the 1880's. In his invention "the agitator of the drain, making forty to sixty revolutions per minute, holds the farinaceous deposit in suspension, which is saccharified thanks to the heat of the double envelope; these materials are then racked and repumped into the tank for clarification." (Auguste Vervoort, 1926)

Last quarter of the 19th century: Albert Heyndrickx invented a double-envelope mash-tun, heated by steam.

1907: Nicolas Coomans, a brewer in Tunize, perfected a false-bottomed mash-tun, equipped with a device for retaining the materials in suspension and accelerating the outflow of the must, This vessel was manufactured by the building workshops of De Coster Van de Velde, in Tielt, and Gustave Bossuyt, in Bergères, in Northern France.

MANUFACTURERS OF STEAM BOILERS

Fumière, Forchies.

Germeau, Jumet.

Meura, Tournai.

Piedbœuf, Jupille. Jacques Pascal Piedbœuf (1783-1839) firstly carried on his trade of blacksmith in the workshops of Cockerill. Then, in 1812, he created in Jupille a forge destined to become a famous boiler-maker. Many breweries were to acquire their steam boilers - today the brewery of Slagmuylder in Ninove possesses one, in operational condition. The activity of boiler-making went beyond the borders, extending especially, from 1833, to Aachen. In fact the young brother of the founder, Jean Pascal, went on to develop a veritable empire in Germany around various sectors of activity (tune manufacture, steelworks, rolling mills, etc.) All the enterprises still exist within the Babcock and Wilcox SA group.

As for steam boilers, they were sold to Russia and even to South America. In 1947 the Piedbœuf Brewery bought the land of the boiler-makers, on which it built garages and a racking line.

MANUFACTURERS OF BREWERY EQUIPMENT

Baele, Brussels. The company was founded around 1932 by Guillaume Baele, workshop chief at Vandergheeten. Its growth was rapid. In the Sixties it took over the Gangloff workshops in Lyon, France. This latter company ceased activity in 1991. In 1974 the Baele company became part of the Crown Cork Company, taking the name of Crown Baele and moving in 1984 to Londerzeel. It is today called Crown Machinery. It makes Fillers and bottle-washers. It is also involved with maintaining the European capsule presses of the Crown Cork Company.

Bollinckx. In 1883 mention was already made of this firm in large British periodicals. It was in 1902 that the "gas motors" division was created, and in 1911 the first extraction machine for collieries was made. In 1921 all the sectors of the business were concentrated at Buizingen. Bollinckx put many of its machines with brewers. It was taken over by the lorry manufacturer Miesse in 1931.

Boucqui Ch. Ateliers de Construction, Ghent. (Fillers)

Braeckman-Herman Fr., Aalst. (Fillers)

Ateliers J. Beusson Dethiers S.A., Liège. (Automatic bottle-rinsing machines)

Dechaîneux, Brussels. Founded in 1888, by the old firm Julien Ponty of Lille. This company closed its doors in 1985.

Établissements R. Demarets, Brussels.

Ateliers Construction M. De Wilde, Brussels. (Washers)

Dubru, Nivelles. Founded by a former mechanic from Baele, in Brussels, the firm closed down in 1984.

Duray, Écausinnes. Created in 1875 by Émile Duray, the boiler-maker specialised in boilers and tanks for breweries. One can still see a boiler of its manufacture in the Vapeur Brewery in Pipaix. The business enlarged into a brewery in 1898, but this was closed in 1925. Ernest Duray took over the business in 1955, then it was the turn of Paul Duray to succeed him in 1981. The same year, the business was in difficulty. The brand and the personnel were "absorbed" by the Usines de Braines-le-Comte.

Ateliers Gilloteaux, Wasmes.

Gimmy et Vermeulen, Brussels.

Hernotte Achille, Brussels.

Mertens, Willebroeck.

Établissement Veuve Louis Oudenot (1930), Brussels, then Ateliers Oudenot, owned by Max Eha, 1934 (Fillers and bottle-cleaning equipment).

Pierret et Stapper, Brussels. This firm still existed in 1942 (Fillers, filters)

Rademaker Jos, Brussels.

Roegist, Antwerp. (Fillers)

Ruben, Brussels. (Fillers)

Simonis, Jupille. The firm later became LMS Jupille. (Malting equipment, crushers, millers)

Vandergeeten Arthur, Brussels. This firm, created in 1909, was taken over by the British company Vickers in 1972, then by Paribas in 1985, and lastly by Établissements Legendre in 1991 (Fillers - cleaners)

Établissements Van Genechten Frères S.A. (1918), Molenbeek-Saint-Jean.

Compagnie Victoria, Brussels. Founded in 1914, Industrie Scientifique de l'Alimentation became a company in 1933 and acquired its new company name.

Vuylsteke Henri (1889), Tournai. (raw grain cookers, mash-tuns, bottling equipment). When it began, it traded in coolers and fermentation tanks. It worked in particular with Great Britain. Then it sold a mash filter of German origin, before working for a Belgian firm and, in 1914, selling British glucose in Paris. Its founder, Henri Vuylsteke, died in 1922.

Société Belge de Matériel de Brasserie, Brussels.

Établissements M. Joseph et Fils, Brussels. (Fillers and bottle-cleaning equipment) In 1920 "Bascours et Lenois". In 1923 "Établissements Franco-Belge".

Lambrechs, Puurs. (Cleaning drums)

Legendre, Asse. (Bottling equipment)

SPECIALIST IN INSULATION

Magniette, Brussels.

Moulin Aristide, Forchies.

Quercine, Brussels.

Van Duyse Frères, Lokeren.

Wanner, Brussels.

MANUFACTURERS OF COOLING EQUIPMENT

Ateliers B. Lebrun (1868), Nimy-lez-Mons. This firm had a factory at Ferrières-la-Petite in France, and offices in Paris and Lille. In 1960 it merged with ACEC. Then in 1970 there was a merger with Westinghouse, and its production was reduced by a half. In 1980 Lebrun Nimy SA limited its activities to the installation and maintenance of cooling apparatus.

Phœnix, Ghent. From 1910, the small cooling machine "Phœnix nouveau" was well-known.

MANUFACTURERS OF TANKS

Ateliers de la Dyle. Formerly : S.A. de Travaux, Dyle et Bacalan.

Boël Marlier, Rocourt.

Compagnie Belge d'Aluminium S.A. L'Hoir Ingénieur, Angleur. In 1930 the firm built the basket for the Picard balloon.

La Ferronnerie Bouillonaise, Bouillon. Founded in 1895, this firm won the Grand Prix at the exhibitions in Antwerp and Liège in 1930

Holvrieka (1973), Menin.

Meura, Tournai.

MANUFACTURERS OF BREWERY ARTICLES

Anciens Établissements G. Breeckman, Brussels.

Anciens Établissements Raquez et De Drijver, Ghent.

Bivort G. - De Blieck, Brussels. In 1940, this firm passed into the hands of Albert Steyart.

Bogaert Robert - De Clerck, Pamel.

Bossuyt, Roeselaere.

A FAMOUS COMPANY

Created in Tournai in 1845, the family company **Meura** had to move to Warchin around 1918. From 1900 its invention of a wort filter brought it fame. The use of this filter was in fact to be extremely widespread in the brewing field for several decades. Beyond this particular sector, the equipment manufactured by Meura was for the most part involved in manufacture processes.

The phenomenon of the restructuring of breweries in the second half of the 20th century gravely affected the firm, which ended by merging in 1986 with Ateliers Louis Carton (ALC) and the Krupp-Polysius group. The latter, majority holder, disengaged itself and it was the French Boccard group, specialists in agro-alimentary equipment, which in 1990 took the holding, with Monsville and Schlumpf-Wilms.

The following year, Meura became an independent company, centring its activity on brewhouses, tanks, and of course the 2001 filter (which is used by breweries such as Suntory in Japan, Zin Tianf in China, and Polar in Venezuela).

Brouckxon, Ostend. This firm later became A. Tiberghien-Brouckxon.
Burghgraeve Franz, Brussels.
Capette Louis, Mons.
Coene, Brussels.
Cognioul Victor, Charleroi.
Comptoir Brassicole Max Havaux, Etterbeek.
Croes Jacques, Brussels. In 1924 he transferred the firm to the company Soxhlet, to which he became technical consultant.
De Clercq René, Aalst.
De Lata Herman, Deinze.
Delbaere Billiau, Dunkirk
Delobe Paul, Brussels.
De Quinnemar Louis, Menin.
De Witte Hilaine, Brussels and Tournai.
Dubois Jules, Nivelles.
Demailly Jacques, Brussels.
Établissement Brassicole Soxhlet, Brussels. It belongs to Bernheim & Cie.
Établissement Brassicole du Hainaut F. Glineux Roland, Mons.
Établissements E. Buisset, Brussels.
Établissements Albert Meyer, Brussels.
Étabissements Martens Bourgeois, Brussels.
Établissements Ernest Deltenre, Brussels.
Esnouf et Cie, Mons.
Gekiere Gabriel, Ieper. The firm established in 1946 in Koksijde.
Générale Brassicole Belge, Brussels.
Heiderich H., Brussels.
Koentjes A., Bruges.
Knudsen Frères, Brussels.
Laton Arsène, Ieper.
Lemaire Émile, Bon Secours.
Lheureux Robert, Gilly and Montignies.
Ligue Nationale des Brasseurs Belges, Brussels. This firm, founded in 1907, passed into the hands of J. Bourgeois.
Lonche Robberecht, Ingelmunster and Ostend.
Maison Paul Carez, Brussels.
Maison Haager-Nihoul, Brussels.
Maison Jules Morraye, Ghent.
Megoeul Charles, Saint-Ghislain.
Meirschman Joseph, Aalst.
Merten César, Antwerp.
Minnaert Jules, Ledeberg.
Snicolers P. J., Antwerp.
Tondeur Arthur, Brussels.
Van Autenboer Victor, Anderlecht.
Vanden Balcke, Roeselaere.
Vandenhaute Dermont Alexander, Saint-Ghislain
Van Marsenille Raymond, Liège.
Veuve Hélène et E. Cavenaille, Brussels.

MANUFACTURERS OF CASKS

Each village used to have its own cooper. However some firms stood out.
Ateliers Comet, Mechelen. (Metal casks)
Ateliers Germain, Marchienne-au-Pont. (Metal casks, covered in wood)
De Ronet, Flawinne. Founded by Lieutenant Colonel Dujardin, aide-de-camp of King Albert I, this workshop was taken over around 1946 by TMT. The first known metal casks were made there in 1910.
Grande Tonnelerie Vve. Aug. Seghers-Pyrins, Temse. (Wooden casks)
TMT (Sheet-work), Forest. (Metal casks)
Tonnellerie Kramer (1875), Laeken. (Wooden casks)
Tonnellerie Émile de Palmenaer (1893), Lokeren. (Wooden casks)
Tonnellerie Persenaire (1824), Antwerp. It was transferred to Merksem in 1913. (Wooden casks)

MANUFACTURERS OF COOPERAGE EQUIPMENT

Atelier Colsoul, Orp-le-Grand. (Cask cleaners)
Brosserie d'Izegem. (Brushes for casks and breweries)
Buyssens. Technical director of the Brasserie et Vinaigrerie de Lembeek, he perfected automatic metal spiles.
Corchelet, brewer in Gourdinne. (Metal bungs). Traces are to be found in 1889.
Dens G., brewer in Floreffe. (Metal bungs). Traces are to be found in 1889.
Établissements Nestor Rosiers, André Rosiers Successeur, Izegem. (Brushes for casks and breweries)
Gantois Ernest, Marchienne-au-Pont. (Metal bungs)
Gennart A., Montignies-sur-Sambre. (Paraffined material for bungs)
Laurent Louis, Fleurus. (Identification plates, intended to carry the name and number of the brewery)
Misonne Auguste, brewer in Lodelinsart. Its metal bungs were the most used in Belgian breweries.
Regnac, Charleroi. (Metal bungs)
Rousseaux Arthur, brewer in Soignies. He perfected automatic metal bungs.
Thonnart (1862), Liège. The company moved to Grâce-Hollogne in 1976 and closed down in 1984. The Thonnart cask-tarrer (by steam jet and pitch) was famous for its being able to cover beer barrels with pitch. Production began with eight pieces of apparatus in 1902. By 9th August 1911 some one thousand had been sold, of which five hundred in the last three years. The pitch which protected from any penetration through the wood and therefore minimised the risk of infection, was made either of resin or of a vegetable fat material (coco butter and flax oil mixed), or with resin lacquer with paraffin added. At the end, the firm produced equipment for automatically cleaning barrels.

BOTTLERS

Bouteilleries de Lommel S.A., Brussels
Cogever S.A. (Comptoir Général du Verre), Brussels.
Comptoirs des Bouteilleries Belges, Brussels.
Verreries Bennert Bivort et Courcelles Réunies, Jumet.
Verreries Cam. Fromont Erlin, Lodelinsart.
Verreries Gobeleteries Havrenne Frères, Jumet.
Verreries J.-B. Gaasch, Antwerp.
Verreries de Jumet S. A., Jumet. This firm became Verlipack.
Verreries de la Réunion F. Dambremez André, Jumet.

LES GROISILS (glass waste)

Odilon Van de Walle, Jumet.

MAKERS OF POINT OF SALE EQUIPMENT

Antoine, Brussels.
Debita, Jette.
Mino Ph., Molenbeek.
Molinet, Tienen.
Jules Ons, Leuven. (Pumps and sale equipment)
Van de Meert P. et H., Mechelen.
Louis Van den Brande, Brussels.
Vervenne et Van Belle, Brussels.

CORK MANUFACTURERS

Amédée Girbal, Brussels.
Gaston Beguin, Marchienne-au-Pont.
Ch. Beyens et Fr. Crols, Brussels.

MANUFACTURERS OF CAFÉ FURNITURE

Bars were often made in Mechelen and the Malinois style made its mark. Few traces of makers exist. Generally small craftsmen, they sold to large brewery suppliers.

As for chairs and tables, their production was concentrated in Western Hainaut. In **Ath**, Cambier (1835), Delmée (1901), Carton. In **Leuze**, Leleng and Guersem.

Bouchons Leclercq, Fleurus.
Bouchonneries Regnier Fooz, Nismes.
Bouchonneries Réunies, Brussels.
Emile Equenne et Cie, Braine L'Alleud. (Mechanical stoppers)
Gérardy Frères, Genval. (Mechanical stoppers)
Goffart et Gonnissen (1919), Wavre. (Mechanical stoppers)
Les Manufactures de Liège Ventura S.A., Brussels. Factory in Lokeren.
Seghers, Anderlecht. This firm was the only maker of mechanical stoppers to survive the Second World War. It sold its machines in Italy. Today Seghers makes formers for washing machines.
Société Anonyme Belge pour la Fabrication des Bouchons Mécaniques, Brussels. (Bouchons mécaniques.)
Van Daele R. Devriendt, Liedekerke.
Zoppé A. Monier, Marchienne-au-Pont.

MANUFACTURERS OF CROWN CORKS

Antwerp Crown Cork, Kontich.
Belcrown, Antwerp.
Crown Cork Company, Deurne.
Société Alphonse Delleur et Cie, Grivegnie. Founded in 1903, it became O.J.Caley et Cie.

CASE MAKERS

Caisserie Gantoise, Ghent.
Caisserie Havrenne Frères S. C., Jumet.
Caisserie Tilkin, Glons.
Caisserie Van Campenhout, Kœkelberg.
Caisserie Émile Vanderputten, Bever-Biévène.
Camille Fremont, Marcinelle.
Carrières Frères, Bressoux.
Désiré Samain, Ghlin.

GLASS MAKERS

Compagnie Internationale de Gobeleterie Inébréchable S. A., Soignies. This firm became Durobor in 1928
Verreries de Braine-le-Comte, Braine-le-Comte.
Verreries L. et A. Dubreuil Frères, Wasmuel. This firm became Verrerie Saint-Antoine S.A.
Verreries et Gobeleteries Nouvelles, Manage. This firm was created in 1910. In 1954 it became the Verrerie Castelain and in 1969 it merged with other glass makers (Doyen Havré, Verrerie de Boussu, Rupel Boom) to found the company Manubelver, which in 1974 at the time of its closure was only involved in decor.
Verreries du Hainaut, Manage. This firm was born of a merger, in 1974 of the glass makers Michotte, Scailment, and the Cristallerie de Manage and the Verrerie de Boussu.
Verrerie Mécanique du Centre, Jumet.

MANUFACTURERS OF BEERMATS

Belgian Beermat, Boechout.
Euromat, Dour.
L'Idéal, Brussels.
Imprimerie Api, Brussels. In 1974, it moved to Beersel.
L. Scory-Moliteur, Montignies-sur-Sambre.
Omer Lebbe. This firm was successively established in Jette (1925), Kœkelberg (1930), and Ganshoren (1938). In 1961 the business was taken over by Rob Otten, Brussels.
Waterlomat. This company, which began in 1955, was initially set up in Waterloo. Today it is in Drogenbos. It provided 20 per cent of the world production of beermats and two thirds of its production is for export. A brewery such as Stella Artois buys 200 milion beermats a year!

ENAMELERS

This concerns makers of enamel publicity material
Artémail, Brussels.
Émaillerie Belge S.A., Molenbeek-Saint-Jean.
Émaillerie Graphique, Brussels.
Émaillerie de Kœkelberg S.A., Brussels (1929). Born of the merger of l'Émaillerie de Kœkelberg, des Anciens Établissements D. et G. Cherton et Cie et Ioxyde, the firm ceased its activity in 1955. In 1965 a new works was set up, specialising in signs.
Émailleries et Tôleries Réunies S.A., Gosselies. Originally this was établissements Aubecq et Cie (1899).
Forbelemail, Jumet.
Foremail ou Émailleries de Forest, Brussels.
Howoco, Brussels.

MANUFACTURERS OF PUBLICITY PANELS

Rob Otten, Brussels.
A. Lambert F. Renotte et Cie, Brussels. This firm made Glassoid panels, very well known in the Thirties. Synthetic mica, of which the panels were made, allowed very beautiful impressions.

MANUFACTURERS OF LUMINOUS SIGNS

Rob Otten, Brussels.
Marmonéon Paul Dessilly, Cuesmes.

MARMORITE
(publicity plates in glass painted on the obverse)

La Marmographie, Brussels.

PRINTERS OF LABELS AND POSTERS

L'Art Graphique du Hainaut, Paturages.
Baudry Cocu et Mairesse, Quaregnon.
Brian Hill, Brussels.
Marcel Collart, Deux Acren.
N. Collier, Sint Denijs Westrem.
Delacre F. & Fils, Charleroi.
Établissements Lithographiques, Gosselies.
Jean Godart, Mons.

THE ART OF THE LABEL

Among the many printers who produce beer labels, one name emerges: Illochroma. Founded in 1898 in Saint Gilles, the company Strickaert-Deschamps printed labels, posters, and publicity panels by the lithographic process. In 1921, it came to be renamed Lithochroma. It was this company which used the first offset "one colour" printing machine in Belgium, 60 x 100 cm.

In 1954, a brewer complained of not being able to label more than 2,250 bottles an hour. In 1958 Lithochroma resolved the problem by using a special paper. From then, the business concentrated on printing bottle labels.

Following merger with the German company Illert from Frankfurt, Lithochroma became Illochroma, in 1968, and moved to Uccle, where the first gravure press was installed. It was in 1975 that Illochroma created its own aluminised paper, which promoted its growth. A second Belgian press was set up at Genk. A subsidiary, Illco (International Label Co.), was created, in association with Anhauser-Busch, the largest brewer in the world. This subsidiary was taken over in 1994 by the American giant.

Today Illochroma employs more than five hundred people in Brussels and Genk. The number of labels printed daily varies between 100 and 120 million, corresponding to some 20 billion each year. 80 per cent of these labels are exported, principally in Europe. The logo of the enterprise - an eye which appears at the bottom of the label - was designed by the famous Belgian graphic artist Jacques Richez, in the Fifties.

Respecting the environment, the company perfected, from 1991, new non-pollutant labels, Illo-Lux and Illo-Gold. And with the same concern an Illo-Recycling department was created in 1993, charged with recovering label waste from clients.

Goddaer, Kortrijk.
Lithographie Laline, Jemappes.
P. Mallund, Liège.
Mynche Frères, Brussels.
Ern. Roose, Hasselt.
Strickaert-Deschamps, Brussels.
Wolf Herman, Liège.

MANUFACTURERS OF ADVERTISING PLAYING CARDS

This type of promotional product began around 1890.
There are three firms in Tournai – **Brepols et Dierickx** (1826), **Glenisson et Vangenechten** (1833) et **Léonard Biermans** (1875) – merged in 1970 to give Carta Mundi.
Wellens-Delhuvenne, Turnhout.
Gebrœders Mesmæckers, Turnhout.
La Turnhoutoise, Turnhout.

"HORSE-DRAWN VEHICLE" ENTERPRISES

Norbert Dassy (Fils), Erquelinnes. This firm was founded in 1861. There were still signs in 1917.
Alfred Goddeliere, Brussels.
Désiré Mathieu, Thuin.
X. Michel et Fils, Brussels. In 1907 this firm became Jos Michel Successeur, then Detry successor to Michel et fils.
Tenret, Erquelinnes. This firm made way for firm Levacq S.A., in 1930.

COLD TEMPERATURES IN BREWING

The success of *pils* type beer was furthered, on one hand, by the development of transport, which permitted rapid delivery of the beer, and on the other, by the progress in industrial cooling equipment, which facilitated the storage of this beverage, and therefore its regular production throughout the year.

Cooling came about around 1860 with machines using ammonia, but it was not until 1864 that the Frenchman Carré installed the first cooling machine at the premises of the brewer Veltem in Marseille. Before this equipment, ice was used from artificial or natural ponds in winter. It was necessary to wait for a compressed ammonia machine, invented by Linde around 1874, before the regularity of manufacture opened larger markets for brewers.

The different services provided by refrigeration to the brewery are: refrigeration of the wort before its being put in the fermentation tank, refrigeration of the fermentation cellars and of the wort in fermentation, refrigeration of the beer during slow fermentation and in the cellar, refrigeration of yeast, and refrigeration of the reserves of hops.

In Belgium, two companies fought over the market: établissements Lebrun of Nimy, and Phœnix of Ghent. The company Lebrun was the more important. In 1887, it produced the first refrigeration machine. Great difficulty remained, at this time, in the realisation of water-proof filling through the shaft of the piston. The problem was significant since the liquids then used, ammonia and sulphur dioxide, were toxic. Furthermore the cylinder of the compressor was subject to the effects of expansion and contraction resulting from strong variations in temperature. The technique of the time did not know the precision which later would permit the construction of metal fillers. The Lebrun company designed its machine with a closed casing and a rotating filler, and this was a success. In 1902 it had already placed 107 pieces of apparatus. In 1923, 1,288 Lebrun installations operated around the world, two thirds of Belgian breweries being equipped with Lebrun equipment.

In 1935 the small refrigerator appeared, for sales outlets, which did away with searching for blocks of ice and the disposal of the water which came on melting.

BOTH BREWERS AND INVENTORS

Maurice Hanquet, at Thorembais-Saint-Trond: fermentation tank in closed vessel with automatic recovery of yeast (1922).
Coveliers, at Geel: fermentation tank in closed vessel.
J.J.De Kersmaecker et Fils, at Wolvertem: "Auto" tank, closed fermentation tank.
Brogniez and Planquart, At La Louvière: "Optima" tank, automatic fermentation tank.
Éd. Willemart-Mignolet, at Lens: intensive circulation boiler. This boiler was constructed by the Dufour workshops in Elouges.
Alfred Lebbe, Director of the Dujardin Brewery in Liège: electric fermentation system. "The quantity of electricity eaten by beer in fermentation converts for the most part into ozone. It is as a consequence a constant and continual food of an antiseptic gas which revives the yeast, purifies the substance, contributes to the oxygenation of the must and the precipitation, thanks to ionisation, of the unstable nitrogenous materials which, in the absence of this elimination, will be liable to provoke clouding".
Decroes in Enghien: automatic water reheater using exhaust steam and apparatus for cooking the beer by steam and for heating water (1903). The two apparatus were constructed by the firm Dincq-Gilbert, of Cuesmes.

THE LARGE BUILDERS OF MALTINGS

Julien Budts, Brussels.
Lafeuillade. Set up in Brussels from 1912, this enterprise made way after 1918 for the firm Mombel Bossaert et Fils, founded in 1860 and H. Lafeuillade became its technical consultant.
De Ruytter et Orval, Brussels.
Jules Pagny (1894), Zaventem.
Van Caspel. Set up in Brussels from 1911, the firm was dissolved in 1966. The new company was then created in Tournai of S.A. Van Caspel. The firm ceased all activity in 1975.

Achille De Baenst a brewing engineer from Mons, and Henri Debeil, a brewer from Obourg, invented the mash-tun "La Rationelle", and sold more than forty three examples. But where were they made? No on ever knew.

FOREIGN SUPPLIERS

The companies indicated below have worked a lot for Belgian breweries.
Otto Barth, of Erfurth (Germany), represented in Brussels. (Drying kilns for maltings)
Bühler, in Switzerland, represented in Brussels. (Crushers and malting equipment)
Seck Frères, in Dresden (Germany, represented in Brussels. (Malting equipment, crushers and degermers)
Wiegelwerk AG., in Neisse Neuland (Germany) (Brewhouses)
A. Ziemann Feuerbach, in Stuttgart (Germany). (Brewhouses). This firm installed brewhouses in the Léopold and Wielemans Breweries in Brussels.
S.A.Gallodona, in Noisy-le-Sec (France). (Fermentation tanks and reinforced concrete vats)
Société de Cuves et Foudres en Acier Emaillé, in Agen (France). (Tanks and vats)
Fruhinsholz, in Nancy (France). (Tanks and vats)

BREWERY SCHOOLS

• **École Supérieure de Brasserie**, Faculty of Science, Catholic University of Leuven.

This school was created out of the École Supérieure d'Agriculture in 1887, by Jules Vuylsteke, with support from the Minister of State Pierre Tack and several brewers, among them Modeste van den Bogært, of Willebroeck. Taking into account the linguistic problems, the school was split into two in 1968: the Fermentation Section in Leuven, and the Brewery Section in Leuven-la-Neuve. Since 1984 the Brewery Section has had the name of "Laboratory of Brewery Sciences and Technologies".

• **Institut Supérieur de Brasserie,** Ghent.

Founded in 1887, by Professor Van den Hulle. In the Thirties, following linguistic problems, the French-speaking section was transferred to Brussels (1935) and took the name of "National Institute of Fermentation Industries". The Flemish section today has the name of "C.T.L.".

• **Institut des Industries de Fermentation**, Anderlecht.

This French-speaking section of the Ghent Institute *(see above)* was established in Brussels until 1955, the year when it was transferred to CERIA, in Anderlecht. Among a large range of studies concerning the food and fermentation industries, training covers various aspects of the brewing industry (Malting, yeast, hops, brewing proper).

• **Hoger Technisch Institut Sint-Lieven**, Ghent.

Created in 1892 by the Bishop of Ghent as an answer to the liberal and French-speaking Institute of Van den Hulle. Today it is called the "K.I.H.O.".

• **École Practique de Brasserie**, Collège Saint Joseph, La Louvière.

This school, founded in 1895, included an experimental brewery, with a 50 hectolitre capacity. It operated until around 1940.

• **École de Brasserie**, École des Industries Chimiques, Saint Ghislain.

This school, founded in 1913, closed after the Great War. It counted Édouard Willemart among its Professors.

• **Institut Supérieur Industriel**, Huy.

Brewery school with micro-brewery founded in 1995.

BOTH COLLEGES AND BREWERIES

Formerly, several colleges, above all in Wallonia, possessed a brewery and made table beer for their own consumption. Often even, these college breweries taught apprentice brewers.

It was thus, for instance, with the Saint Augustin College in Enghien, whose brewery closed in 1919, the Saint Berthuin Institute in Malonne, whose brewery closed in 1944, the Carlsbourg Seminary, whose brewery closed in 1944, and the Établissement Enfant-Jesus in Brugelette, whose brewery also closed in 1944.

THE GREAT MASTERS OF LEUVEN

The son of a brewer, born in Menen, *Jules Vuylsteke* studied as an engineer in art and manufacture, civil engineering, and mining at Leuven, then by stages in the principal brewing centres of Europe, he learnt the various methods of brewing. From 1889 he became Director of the École Supérieure de Brasserie at the Catholic University of Leuven, teaching Zymology (the manufacture of beer), as a full Professor.

After studies as an engineer-brewer, *Léon Verhelst*, the son of a brewer from Dixmuide, became a collaborator of Jules Vuylsteke, his uncle, in 1897. He was promoted to the position of Professor the following year, and succeeded him in 1900 as Head of the School. In 1908, Jules Vuylsteke was on his own wish discharged from the "Chair". Léon Verhelst himself provided the course on "raw materials and the manufacture of beer". He entrusted "brewing and malting equipment" to Alfred Mertens. In parallel to the teaching of future brewers, he was Technical Director of the Brasserie d'Alger *(see page 151)*, then, later, he occupied higher positions in the industry, notably as Chairman of the Artois Brewery.

The personality of Léon Verhelst went hand in hand with the life of the establishment until 1937, the year when Professor *Jean De Clerck (see below)* succeeded him. The latter led the school with the hand of a master until 1973, and largely contributed to its international renown. The school saw its education rethought and reorganised. Moreover, picking up the idea of Jules Vuylsteke, who at the beginning of the 20th century did not achieve the success expected, De Clerck created a test station at the service of members of the industry, who wished to submit their manufacture to scientific examination.

In 1968, when linguistic problems brought about the fall of the Government, and the new Governement decided to split the Catholic University of Leuven, Jean De Clerck, who was bilingual, was called upon to make a choice, on the request of the Rector of the University. And his answer was, "Sir, you appointed me to teach in two languages, it is up to you to chose!"

As Professor, Jean De Clerck was replaced by *André Devreux*, consultant engineer to various enterprises (Unibra, Brasserie Cardinal in Fribourg, Switzerland, Unicer in Portugal etc.).

A PIONEER IN TEACHING

The Belgian brewing industry owes a great deal to Louis Van den Hulle who, at the end of the 19th century, bestowed upon it a professionally structured system of training. This son of a brewer was himself a brewer, with his brother, in Oudenaarde. Perceiving the lack of brewery teaching material, at forty five years of age, he did not hesitate to take up training in chemistry and technology at the École Industriel in Ghent, to be able in 1880 to create a private course in brewing, in his own apartment. His aim was to build a grand school of brewing, which would give methodical and regular training to those who would be supported officially.

In 1884 he was one of the founders of the Association Chimique in Ghent. In 1886 he created the Belgian Brewers' Society, later renamed "The Society of Brewers for professional training", and he arranged for this Ghent society to take his school under its aegis. Thus, on 3rd July 1887, was founded the Institut Supérieur de Brasserie of Ghent. Louis van den Hulle directed it until his death in 1903 in Romerée (Province of Namur).

The success of this man rests of course on his knowledge of brewing, his perception of the needs of the profession, and his desire to lead his project well, but also on the fact that he knew how to surround himself with scientists of the highest level (chemists, physicists, etc.). The Institute operated with exception Professors, such as Henri Van Laer who from 1887 taught chemistry and bacteriology there, and who took over the Directorship of the school after the disappearance of its founder.

A GRAND FIGURE IN THE WORLD OF BREWING

Born in 1902 in Brussels, into a family of grocers, Jean De Clerck was orphaned very young - his father died in 1903 and his mother in 1912. Beginning his studies in 1920 in Leuven, where he had Léon Verhelst as his Professor, his agronomic studies ended four years later in a double diploma as an agricultural chemical engineer and as a brewer engineer. He then married the daughter of the brewer De Becker, of Woluwé-Saint-Pierre, who gave him eleven children.

In 1939 he was appointed to the École Supérieure de Brasserie in Leuven and took over a part of the teaching of Léon Verhelst. His title of Ordinary Professor (1942) became Emeritus Professor in 1972. He was the last Professor at the school before its split into Leuven and Louvain-la-Neuve.

In parallel with teaching, his role as a consultant was also very important. At the beginning of the Sixties he acted in the construction of a new Algerian brewery, the first brewery designed on one level, allowing total surveillance. He was likewise the consulting engineer for several breweries, among them Artois, Van Roy in Weize (he was responsible for the perfection of direct outflow of the maturation tanks in the brewhouses at Wieze) and the Trappist brewery at Chimay. He was also President of the European Brewery Convention from 1963 to 1971.

His immense intellectual curiosity and his taste for reading naturally led him to writing. He published a number of books of which *Cours de brasserie* (Brewery Course) (2 volumes 1948), a huge work of reference recognised throughout the entire world. It was translated into German by Professor Kolbach, of the VLB (Berlin 1949) and then into English in 1958.

Jean De Clerck died in Leuven in 1978. His son Étienne works at Interbrew, in the malting division, and is President of the Association Royals des anciens Étudiants de l'École Supérieure de Brasserie de Leuven, founded in 1985. As for Étienne's son, he similarly works at Interbrew, in the Jupille laboratories.

BEER JOURNALS AND MAGAZINES

• *Le Moniteur de la Brasserie* (1859), weekly. Founder : A. Laurent. Head office : Bruxelles. An office in France, à Blangy-lez-Arras (Pas-de-Calais).

• *Le Brasseur* (1865). Editor : inconnu. Head office : Namur. An office in France, à Sedan.

• *Revue Universelle de la Brasserie et de la Malterie* (1873), weekly. Proprietor : Jean-Paul Roux. Head office : Bruxelles. An office in France, à Paris.

• *La Gazette du Brasseur* (1886), weekly. Editor: Adolphe Frentz. Head office : Bruxelles.

• *Le Progrès de la Brasserie* (1893), monthly. Editor : L. H. Roisard. Head office : Gand.

• *Le Petit Journal du Brasseur* (1893), monthly. a supplement, *Le Bulletin weekly des Cours*, appears every Thursday. Editor : George Maw Johnson.

In 1899, *Le Petit Journal du Brasseur* took over *La Gazette* du Brasseur*, then, in 1906, le *Journal des Brasseurs*, owned by M. Puvrez, of Lille, France.

• *La Brasserie - De Brouwerij* (1901), monthly. Editor : Émile Soxhlet. Head office : Bruxelles.

DIMANCHE, 8 JANVIER 1893.

VOL. I. — N° 1.

LE

Petit Journal du Brasseur

PARAISSANT LE PREMIER DIMANCHE DU MOIS

FONDATEUR-DIRECTEUR : GEORGE M. JOHNSON

RÉDACTION : **Rue du Congrès, 2** ADMINISTRATION ET ANNONCES : *42, Rue des Chartreux, 42, Bruxelles*	ABONNEMENT : Belgique . . . . 1 an. fr. **6,00** Union postale . . » » **6,75**	Notre supplément « *Le Bulletin hebdomadaire des cours* » parait **tous les jeudis**. ABONNEMENT : Pour tous pays : 1 an, fr. **4,00**.

MALTS PELLICULÉS BREVETÉS

DE MAÏS & DE RIZ

Concessionnaires pour la Belgique :

KEULEMANS & Co, Malteurs, MALINES

AVANTAGES & ÉCONOMIE :

1° — **Mode d'emploi le plus rationnel du maïs et du riz** ; aucun cuiseur ou vaisseau spécial n'est nécessaire, les *malts pelliculés brevetés* **se mélangent, sans mouture ni cuisson préalables** à la farine du malt d'orge, dans la cuve-matière du brasseur.

2° — **Economie notable** : on emploie de 20 à 33 p. c. de *malts pelliculés brevetés* de maïs et de riz, lesquels tout en coûtant beaucoup moins cher que les malts d'orges, donnent un **rendement bien plus élevé**.

3° — **Aucun goût particulier**, même de maïs, **n'est communiqué aux bières**, et celles-ci, grâce à des procédés spéciaux auxquels notre agent général initie les acheteurs, sont corsées et moëlleuses, de toute finesse et tenant une mousse persistante. Elles sont aussi très conservables.

4° — *Les malts pelliculés brevetés* sont les seuls produits qui permettent au brasseur d'obtenir **le rendement théorique du malt et du riz.**

5° — Grâce à leur forme spéciale, les *malts pelliculés brevetés* **favorisent la filtration du moût ainsi que l'épuisement complet de la drêche.** Ils permettent la suppression radicale de l'emploi de courte paille ou d'autre matière filtrante.

6° — L'extrait donné par ces malts étant de qualité supérieure à l'extrait que l'on retire des malts ordinaires, **les bières se clarifient et se conservent mieux.**

Agent Général pour la Vente : GEORGE M. JOHNSON, 2, Rue du Congrès, BRUXELLES

à qui on peut s'adresser pour tous renseignements techniques relatifs aux avantages et à l'emploi de ces produits. Sur la demande des clients, M. JOHNSON se met à leur disposition pour confectionner chez eux un brassin avec ces produits.

Echantillons, Prix et Mode d'emploi gratuitement sur demande.

• *Le Fournisseur du Brasseur* (1908), monthly. This journal was sent to all those brewers who did not subscribe to *Petit Journal du Brasseur*. Editor : George Maw Johnson. Head office : Bruxelles.

• *L'Indicateur du Brasseur-Malteur* (v. 1908), monthly (free). Published by Charles Gruell, master-brewer with diploma. Head office : Uccle.

• *La Petite Gazette du Brasseur* (1919-1940), weekly. Editor : Victor Allard (a director of the St. Joseph brewery in Couvin, he also owned a hop-growing business). Head office: Bruxelles.

• *Bières et Boissons* (1941-1944), monthly. Journal of the Groupement des Industries de la Boisson during war. Head office : Bruxelles.

• *Le Brasseur Belge* (1941-1948), weekly. Editor: Paul Mosselmans. Head office : Ledeberg.

• *L'Echo de la Brasserie* (1945-1973), monthly. Editor: Herman Smeets. Head office : Louvain.

• *Bière Magazine* (1986-1989), quarterly. Editor : Charles Fontaine de Ghélin. Head office : Bruxelles.

The magazine was bought by the Capsule Group in 1989. Editor : Marc Vandermuir. Head office : Bruxelles. It ceased publication in 1991.

The Wielemans Brewery was one of the first to possess its own printing works and published an information sheet, intended for its clients, from the beginning of the 20th century.

AN ILLUSTRIOUS FIGURE IN THE WORLD OF BREWING – GEORGE MAW JOHNSON

The Johnson family first of all settled in London. George, the father (1837-1905), of French Huguenot descent, soon distinguished himself in the family tradition as a goldsmith. In 1866 the family moved to Canterbury, where George acquired the Northgate Brewery, which then took the name of Johnson & Co. Ltd. Very quickly the quality of the beers made there became well known, and won medals, in London (1873), Paris (1875), and Hannover (1881). Among the beers brewed were a *Table Ale* (3.5°), a *Porter* (5°), a *Canterbury Pale Ale* (6.3°), and a *Stout* (8°). Their market extended to Poland, Egypt, Central America, and even the Far East. Besides, the brewery became a veritable school where continental brewers came to be initiated in the art of brewing. It was sold in 1900, when George Johnson retired. At the present time, one can still see the buildings, which now serve as garage and warehouse for a builders' merchant.

On 3rd November 1883, the *Canterbury Pale Ale* was registered with the Registrar of the Court in Brussels. For Johnson this was the occasion for a trip to Belgium - the Pêtre family, in Halle, offered him their hospitality.

The eldest of twelve children, George Maw Johnson learnt his trade in the paternal brewery, from 1887. He quit to set up in Brussels in 1890, and followed a career of consultancy to breweries, then as laboratory chief. Thus, on the creation of the *Le Petit Journal du Brasseur*, he was directing the laboratory of the Léopold Brewery in Brussels. Similarly, in 1893 he became general agent, for France and Belgium, of Ateliers Devis, specialists in brewing equipment established in Lodelinsart, and the consultant brewer for the "Cercle Intime des Brasseurs".

His taste for writing, which expressed itself in a *Treatise on English Brewing and Malting* (1887) and in the *Essays on the Practical Science of Brewing*, soon brought fame in brewing circles. This *Treatise* was invaluable to Belgian brewers, at a time when the tax connected with the capacity of the mash-tun was done away with. It contributed to the production of quality beers. George Maw Johnson also wrote a book on the saisons in Wallonia, in which he shows how to obtain *saisons* of quality.

Moreover, George Maw Johnson made his debut in journalism in collaborating with *La Gazette du Brasseur*, from its foundation in 1886, as well as the *Brewers' Journal* in London. In 1890 he edited the *Brasseur-Conseil*, a free journal, which he published for almost a year and which led him to create, three years later, *Le Petit Journal du Brasseur*, which was at first a monthly. The first issue appeared on Sunday 8th January 1893. This periodical, rich in practical advice, deep studies and brewery news, soon became an inestimable source of information for the profession. Johnson included among his collaborators his brother Grove (1868-1947), Technical Director of the City Brewery Co. Ltd., of Lichfield, his brother Harold (1867-1941), Doctor of Science at the University of Brussels, Henri Van Laer, Professor at the École de Brasserie in Ghent, who came to attain the rank of scientific adviser to the journal in 1895, and numerous famous brewers, technicians, and scientists. Of course, the two wars broke the rhythm of publication from August 1914 to May 1919, and then from May 1940 to 1946. In July 1919 the publication became the official journal of the General Federation of Belgian Brewers (see page 82).

George Maw Johnson died in July 1928. He left behind a patented invention for the manufacture of ferruginous beers, registered on 29th March 1882. His journal is today considered as the most certain and the most complete evidence on the evolution of Belgian brewing. Renamed in 1975 under the title *Le Journal du Brasseur*, it is the official organ of the Belgian Confederation of Brewers. It is published quarterly in French and Dutch.

BIBLIOGRAPHY

• *Instructions sur l'art de faire la bière*, M. le Pileur d'Appligny, Paris, 1783.
• *Den Volmaekten Bier-Brouwer*, anon., Brussel, 1793.
• *Dissertation sur la manière de faire l'Uytzet et sur sa salubrité*, P. E. Wauters, Gand, 1798.
• *Traité Théorique et Pratique de la fabrication de la Bière*, F. Rohart, Paris, 1848.
• *Traité complet de la Fabrication des Bières et de la Distillation des Grains,* G. La Cambre, Bruxelles, 1856.
• *Règne de Jean Ier, duc de Brabant*, Philippe De Bruyne, Namur, 1855.
• *Dictionnaire de la Brasserie*, A. Laurent, Bruxelles, 1875.
• *Recueils officiels des marques de Fabrique et de Commerce*, Bruxelles, 1880.
• *Traité pratique de la Brasserie et du Maltage anglais et fabrication des bières anglaises y compris leur adaptation aux systèmes belges et français*, G. M. Johnson, Canterbury, 1887.
• *Moyen simple et pratique de faire des bières très claires en été*, Titeux-Masson, Bruxelles, 1888.
• *Les Bières Belges*, Garnblum, Bruxelles, 1889.
• *Le Livre d'Or du brasseur*, A. Laurent, Bruxelles, 1890.
• *Cours de Brasserie à l'usage des brasseurs*, L. Van den Hulle, Gand, 1890-91.
• *Annuaire de la Brasserie Belge*, 1896 (première année).
• *Rapport sur les travaux de l'Association des Brasseurs du Hainaut*, exercice 1904-5, Paturages.
• *La Brasserie de fermentation haute*, G. Vanderstichele, Turnhout, 1905.
• *Développement et progrès de la fabrication du malt pendant les quarante dernières années*, E. Eckentein, Paris, 1907.
• *Praktisch Handboek der Gistingsindustrie,* H. Verlinden, Brecht, 1916.
• *L'Industrie en France occupée*, ouvrage établi par le grand quatier général allemand en 1916, Imprimerie Nationale, Paris, 1923.
• *La Bière*, H. Van Laer, Paris, 1937.
• *De Mechelse Bierhandel*, J. Van Balberghe, Antwerpen, 1945.
• *Cours de Brasserie*, J. De Clerck, Louvain, 1948.
• *Formulaire Technique et Technologique du Brasseur-Malteur*, Marcel Gocar, Bruxelles, 1949.
• *Les Brasseurs*, *in* « Règlements et Privilèges des XXXII métiers de la cité de Liège », textes édités par René Van Santbergen, Liège, 1952.
• *Études sur la consommation des bières étrangères en Belgique*, brasserie Léopold, Bruxelles, 1959.
• *L'Industrie Brassicole Belge*, Société Générale de Banque, 1966.
• *Recherches sur les Brasseries de la région mosane au Moyen Age*, Joseph Deckers, mémoire de licence, Université de Liège, 1968-69.
• *Histoire de l'Économie Mondiale*, Frédéric Mauro, Paris, 1971.
• *Guide pratique de malterie et de brasserie*, J. Vermeylen, Bruxelles, 1973.
• *L'Évolution de la concentration dans l'industrie de la Brasserie et des Boissons en Belgique*, Commission des Communautés Européennes, Bruxelles, 1976.
• *Urbanisme en Kapitalisme te Antwerpen in de 16de eeuw*, Hugo Soly, Historische Uitgaven Pro Civitate, n° 47, 1977.
• *Bier,* Patroons, Antwerpen-Bussum, 1979.
• *Fabrication de la bière et fiscalité paroissiale. Le droit de « signage » en Hainaut au Moyen Age*, Daniel Van Overstræren, *in* « Annales du Cercle d'histoire et d'archéologie de Saint-Ghislain et de la région », T. 3, Saint-Ghislain, 1982.
• *Les Wallons pionniers de l'industrie allemande*, Hans Seeling, Liège, 1983.
• *La Maison des Brasseurs*, Frans Smekens, Ville d'Anvers, 1983.
• *Mouterij en Brouwerij technologie,* G. Baetslé, Gent, 1984.
• *The Book of Guinness Advertising,* Brian Sibley, Guinness Superlatives Ltd, London, 1985.
• *Statistiques communes CBMC/EBIC*, Bruxelles, 1985.
• *Optimo Bruno Grimbergensis*, Marie-Anne Wilssens, Bruxelles, 1986.
• *Belgische Biergids*, J. Tulfer, Antwerpen, 1986.
• *Guide de l'Architecture des années 25 à Bruxelles*, Bruxelles, 1988.
• *Les Brasseries en Belgique*, André Pierre et Agnès Vertbrugghen, BBL, Département Études Analyse Financière, 1989.
• *Name Your Poison !, A Guide to Additives in Drinks*, Ted Parratt, London, 1990.
• *Les Cahiers de la Fonderie*, n° 8, juin 1990. Numéro spécial consacré à la brasserie Wielemans et aux brasseries constituant un patrimoine industriel.
• *Terminologie du Maltage et du Brassage*, Laurent Verrellen, mémoire, Institut d'Enseignement Supérieur Lucien Cooremans, Bruxelles, 1889-90.
• *Histoire de la Belgique*, Marie-Thérèse Bitsch, Paris, 1992.
• *La Naissance de la Révolution Industrielle Belge*, Léon Dubois, 1994.
• *L'Influence de l'Industrie Brassicole sur les finances communales à Hasselt aux XVIe et XVIIe siècles,* Jos Martens, s. d.

Various publications, old and recent, among which are the following **:**
• *Le Petit Journal du Brasseur*,
• *La Petite Gazette du Brasseur*,
• *Le Moniteur de la Brasserie*,
• *Le Brasseur Belge*,
• *Annales de la Brasserie et de la Distillerie*,
• *Annales des Industries de la Boisson*,
• *Brasserie et Malterie de Belgique*,
• *Bière Magazine*,
• *La Boisson*,
• *L'HORECA Officiel*,
• *Brasserie Malterie Europe* ,
• bulletin d'information de la F.N.N.B.E.B.(Fédération Nationale des Négociants en Bières et Eaux de Boison),
• *Café Revue*,
• *Bulletin Hebdomadaire*, Kredietbank.

BROUWERIJ VAN WINTAM
H.R.M. 32.971
SINDS 1753
SPECIALE
Brabo
HOGE GISTING - FERMENTATION HAUTE

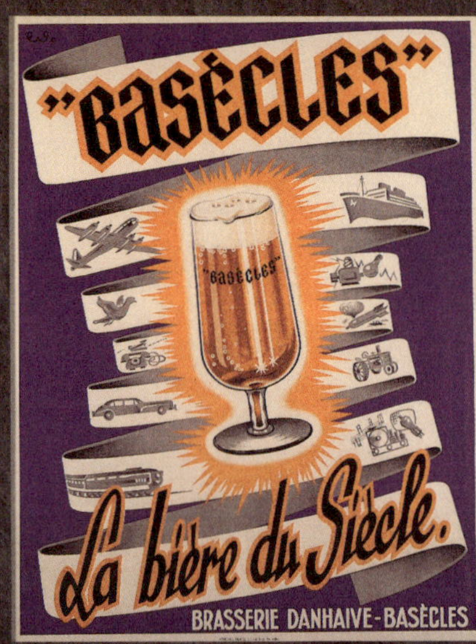

"BASÈCLES"
La bière du Siècle.
BRASSERIE DANHAIVE-BASÈCLES

BELGIË - BELGIQUE
MADE IN BELGIUM

BIERE DE TABLE AVEC EDULCORANT ARTIFICIEL
TAFELBIER BEVAT KUNSTMATIGE ZOETSTOF
Régionale
BRASSERIE ALLIÈS BROUWERIJ
BIERE CAT. III
70 CL. BIER
MARCHIENNE
BELGIQUE
BELGIE

Liège
Pils
une exclusivité
Brasserie de
Liège

MILLENEIR
BAARLE - NASSAU
Baarle-Hertog

FARO
Cette bière étant brassée avec froment, malt et houblon et préparée au sucre de canne pur, est sans conteste la plus FORTE et la plus NUTRITIVE des bières.
BRASSERIE-MALTERIE
A. DEGREEF
RHODE-ST GENÈSE

Saxo
"La Caracole"
Bière belge artisanale refermentée en bouteille
Ambachtelijk belgisch bier met hergisting op fles

Stropken
UNIEK BIER
BIERE UNIQUE

LA
CHOUFFE
Blonde d'Ardenne
Ardense Blonde
e 0,75L
ALC. 8% VOL.
Brie D'ACHOUFFE - 6666 ACHOUFFE - TEL. 061/28.81.47 - BELGIQUE

CAROLO
PILS
BRASSERIE
LES OUVRIERS RÉUNIS
CHARLEROI

La
BRUXELLOISE
BIÈRE DÉLICIEUSE
BIB

14-18 MAY 1995
EBC
BRUSSELS
EUROPEAN BREWERY CONVENTION